Zondervan Minister's Tax & Financial Guide

For 2017 Tax Returns

2018 EDITION

Dan Busby
Vonna Laue
Michael Martin
John Van Drunen

ZONDERVAN

Appreciation
The authors express their sincere appreciation to Mr. Michael Batts, CPA and managing partner, Batts Morrison Wales & Lee, P.A., Orlando, FL and the staff of the firm for their valued assistance in reviewing the two sample tax returns included in this guide.

ZONDERVAN
Zondervan 2018 Minister's Tax and Financial Guide
Copyright © 2018 by ECFA (Evangelical Council for Financial Accountability)

This title is also available as a Zondervan ebook.

Requests for information should be addressed to:
Zondervan, *3900 Sparks Dr. SE, Grand Rapids, Michigan 49546*

ISBN 978-0-310-58875-7

Publisher's note: This guide is published in recognition of the need for clarification of the income tax laws for ministers. Every effort has been made to publish a timely, accurate, and authoritative guide. The publisher, author, and reviewers do not assume any legal responsibility for the accuracy of the text or any other contents.

Taxpayers are cautioned that this book is sold with the understanding that the publisher is not engaged in rendering legal, accounting, or other professional service. You should seek the professional advice of a tax accountant, lawyer, or preparer for specific tax questions.

References to IRS forms and tax rates are derived from preliminary proofs of the 2016 forms or 2015 forms and some adaptation for changes may be necessary. These materials should be used solely as a guide in filling out your 2016 tax return. To obtain the final forms, schedules, and tables for filing your return, contact the IRS or a public library.

Any Internet addresses (websites, blogs, etc.) and telephone numbers in this book are offered as a resource. They are not intended in any way to be or imply an endorsement by Zondervan, nor does Zondervan vouch for the content of these sites and numbers for the life of this book.

All rights reserved. No part of this publication may be reproduced, stored in a retrieval system, or transmitted in any form or by any means—electronic, mechanical, photocopy, recording, or any other—except for brief quotations in printed reviews, without the prior permission of the publisher.

Printed in the United States of America

17 18 19 20 21 22 23 24 25 /DHV/ 20 19 18 17 16 15 14 13 12 11 10 9 8 7 6 5 4 3 2 1

Contents...

■ **Introduction** vi

■ **1 Taxes for Ministers** 1
- Ministers ordained, licensed, or commissioned 3
- Performing ministerial services 5
- Individuals not qualifying for ministerial tax treatment .. 9
- Income tax status of ministers 9
- Importance of the employee vs. self-employed decision on income taxes 11
- Recommended filing status for income taxes 13
- Social security tax status of ministers 13

■ **2 Compensation Planning** 15
- Determine the current compensation 15
- Plan the compensation package 19
- Routinely evaluate compensation 22
- Use fringe benefits wisely 22
- Use accountable expense reimbursements 24
- Checklist for churches demonstrating integrity in compensation-setting 26

■ **3 The Pay Package** 29
- Avoiding the nondiscrimination rules 29
- Tax treatment of compensation elements 30
- Reporting compensation, fringe benefits, and reimbursements 50

4 Housing Exclusion ... 53
- Types of housing arrangements ... 56
- Establishing and modifying the housing designation ... 57
- Reporting the housing allowance to the minister ... 60
- Accounting for the housing exclusion ... 61
- Other housing exclusion issues ... 62
- Housing exclusion worksheets ... 66

5 Business Expenses ... 69
- Accountable and nonaccountable expense reimbursement plans ... 70
- Substantiating and reporting business expenses ... 73
- Travel and transportation expenses ... 74
- Auto expense deductions ... 79
- Home-office rules ... 85
- Other business expenses ... 87
- Allocation of business expenses ... 91

6 Retirement and Social Security ... 95
- Preparing for retirement ... 96
- The fundamentals of social security ... 99
- Taking out retirement money ... 100
- The two social security tax systems ... 101
- Computing the self-employment tax ... 102
- Both spouses are ministers ... 105
- Self-employment tax deductions ... 105
- Use of income tax withholding to pay social security taxes ... 106

- Opting out of social security 106
- Working after retirement 110
- Canada Pension Plan 111

7 Paying Taxes 113
- Tax withholding 113
- Estimated tax 115
- Excess social security withheld (FICA) 115
- Earned income credit 118
- Extension of time to file 119
- Extension of time to pay 121
- Offers in compromise 122
- Filing an amended tax return 124

Form 1040 – Line by Line 127

Sample Returns 146
- Example No. 1

  Minister-employee for income tax purposes (accountable plan) 146
- Example No. 2

  Minister-employee for income tax purposes (nonaccountable plan) 156

Citations 175
Index 181
Projected 2018 Filing Dates 184

How You Can Keep Up with Changes Impacting Minister's Taxes and Finances

When each of the 27 annual editions of the *Zondervan Minister's Tax & Financial Guide* has gone to press, as authors, we have done our best to be sure the latest changes coming from Capitol Hill, the courts, and beyond, are included in the book.

Still, the tax and finance changes keep coming at a relentless pace between book editions. In this era, tax reform is in the wind, challenges to the minister's housing allowance constitutionality persist, and changes to the Affordable Care Act seem inevitable—and that is just to name three issues.

So, how can you keep up with the developments between book editions? Let us suggest two important ways:

- Check the "In the News" link at www.ECFA.org/News for breaking news that affects ministers and churches.

- Join the ChurchExcel community at www.ECFA.church/ChurchExcel to receive FREE monthly digital updates, including podcasts, ebooks, and much more.

We are committed to simplify the most complex minister's tax and financial issues, freeing you to more clearly focus on fulfilling the Great Commission.

Dan Busby

Vonna Laue

Michael Martin

John Van Drunen

CHAPTER 1
Taxes for Ministers

In This Chapter

- Ministers ordained, licensed, or commissioned
- Performing ministerial services
- Individuals not qualifying for ministerial tax treatment
- Income tax status of ministers
- Importance of the employee vs. self-employed decision on income taxes
- Recommended filing status for income taxes
- Social security tax status of ministers

Ministers' compensation may seem like a maze at first, but it does not have to be overwhelming! With practical pointers and easy-to-understand explanations, this guide is here to help ministers each step of the way.

It all begins with a proper understanding of the special tax provisions available to ministers and who qualifies as a "minister" for tax purposes, which is the focus of this first chapter.

Here are six special tax provisions for ministers:

➤ Exclusion (for income tax purposes) of the housing allowance and the fair rental value of a church-owned parsonage provided rent-free to clergy

➤ For social security tax purposes, treatment of all ministers as self-employed

➤ Exemption of ministers from self-employment social security tax under very limited circumstances

➤ Exemption of ministerial compensation from mandatory income tax withholding

Remember
There is some flexibility in applying certain ministerial tax provisions. For example, a minister is exempt from mandatory income tax withholding but can enter into a voluntary income tax withholding arrangement. However, if a minister qualifies for the housing allowance, he or she is subject to self-employment social security tax (using Schedule SE), not FICA—this is not optional.

➤ Eligibility for a voluntary income tax withholding arrangement between the minister-employee and the church

➤ Potential "double benefit" of mortgage interest and real estate taxes as itemized deductions *and* as excludable housing expenses for housing allowance purposes for ministers living in minister-provided housing

Determining Ministerial Tax Status

STEP 1 (see pages 3-5)
Is the worker duly ordained, licensed, or commissioned by a church or denomination?

— NO → The worker generally does not qualify for ministerial tax status.

↓ YES

STEP 2 (see pages 5-9)
Does the worker perform some of the following ministerial duties?

- administer sacerdotal functions (weddings, baptisms, etc.)
- conduct religious worship
- management responsibility in the control, conduct, or maintenance of a church or denomination
- considered a religious leader by a church or denomination

— NO → The worker generally does not qualify for ministerial tax status.

↓ YES

The worker generally qualifies for ministerial tax status.

CHAPTER 1 ➤ TAXES FOR MINISTERS

The six special tax provisions apply only to individuals who, under federal tax rules,

➤ qualify as ministers of the gospel, and

➤ are performing services that qualify in the exercise of ministry.

When it comes to who should be considered a minister for tax purposes, the opinion of the IRS (based on tax law) is the only one that counts. The opinion of the worker or employer is not important. But unfortunately even the IRS does not seem to consistently apply the same rules in determining who is a minister.

Classification as a minister for tax purposes is very important. It determines how a minister prepares the tax return for income and social security tax purposes. For example, a qualified minister is eligible for the housing allowance. This alone can exclude thousands of dollars from income taxation. Also, ministers calculate self-employment social security tax on Schedule SE and pay the tax with Form 1040. Nonministers have one-half of their social security (FICA) tax withheld from salary payments, and the employer pays the other half.

According to tax law, there is a two-step process for determining whether the special tax provisions available to ministers apply to a particular worker. The first is whether the individual qualifies as a minister. The second is whether the minister is performing ministerial services.

Related to the first step, whether an individual qualifies as a minister generally begins with determining whether he or she has been ordained, licensed, or commissioned.

Ministers Ordained, Licensed, or Commissioned

Denominations and churches generally have a process for ordaining, licensing, or commissioning ministers. While the IRS has not directly addressed the process of ordination, licensing, and commissioning, the following steps are recommended (ordination, licensing, and commissioning by parachurch organizations are generally not recognized by the IRS):

➤ **Appropriate bylaw provisions.** The denomination's or church's (if the church is incorporated) bylaws should provide specific authority to ordain, license, or commission individuals as ministers of the gospel. This is essential to develop the proper chain of authority for ordination, licensure, or commissioning. The bylaw provision could be a general or summary description of ordination or licensure such as the following:

> *An individual may be ordained, licensed, or commissioned as a minister of the gospel by ABC church after the candidate has met the qualifications for ordination, licensure, or commissioning. These qualifications may include, but are not limited to, education, experience, and training. The qualifications will be determined by the governing board of the church.*

The bylaw language should not reference the tax benefits or provisions afforded to those who qualify for ordination, licensure, or commissioning. That could be an indication to the IRS that the church is only ordaining, licensing, or commissioning individuals for the tax benefits.

➤ **Development of ordination, licensure, or commissioning guidelines and procedures.** If the church wishes to ordain, license, or commission individuals as ministers of the gospel, the church governing board should adopt written guidelines and procedures for ordination, licensure, or commissioning.

➤ **Revocation of ordination, licensure, or commissioning status.** Ordination, licensure, or commissioning guidelines should give authority to the governing board to revoke the status, absent termination of employment (e.g., in a "revocation for cause" provision). Otherwise, lifetime ordination, licensure, or commissioning status might be implied.

➤ **Privileges granted by ordination, licensure, or commissioning.** The procedures and guidelines should stipulate what privileges are conveyed to an individual upon ordination, licensure, or commissioning (i.e., duties that changed after the individual is ordained, licensed, or commissioned, such as conducting weddings and funerals). Additional duties and responsibilities generally come with ordination, licensure, or commissioning. Detailed job descriptions could supplement the general description of the additional privileges granted.

While the process of ordination, licensing, or commissioning varies depending on church belief and tradition, the major point to remember is that, under the tax law, individuals cannot be self-appointed as ministers in order to qualify for special tax treatment.

What about licensed or commissioned ministers?

Some religious groups ordain, license, and commission ministers. Other groups only ordain, only commission, or only license and ordain ministers or provide some other combination of the three types of special recognition of ministers.

Will a worker be treated as a minister by the IRS if only licensed or commissioned? Perhaps. Ministerial status with the IRS will depend on all the facts and circumstances, e.g., the validity of the licensing or commissioning process and the extent to which the worker administers the sacraments, is considered to be a religious leader by the church, conducts worship services, and has management responsibility in the control, conduct, and maintenance of the church.

Example: Rev. Smith is an ordained minister who serves as a minister of counseling at his church. He does not preach or conduct worship services and never administers sacraments. He has management responsibility for the operation of a counseling center in the local church. He occasionally makes hospital visits. While he qualifies under the "control, conduct, and maintenance of the church" test, he does not administer sacraments or conduct worship services. With professional advice, the church must decide whether he qualifies as a minister for tax purposes.

Performing Ministerial Services

The second step in determining whether an individual is subject to the special tax provisions available to ministers is analyzing whether the minister is performing ministerial services.

Ministers may perform ministerial services in various settings, including within a local church, as evangelists and missionaries, or in denominational or other service.

Ministers serving local churches

If a worker is employed by a local church and is an ordained, commissioned, or licensed minister, four factors are generally applied by the IRS to determine whether ministerial status applies under the tax law. The worker must perform some or all of the following

> **Warning**
> Individuals serving local churches must meet certain factors to qualify as a minister in the eyes of the IRS. The individual should generally be ordained, licensed, or commissioned.

- administer sacerdotal functions (such as performing marriage and funeral services, dedicating infants, baptizing, and serving communion)
- are considered to be a religious leader by your church or parent denomination
- conduct religious worship
- have management responsibility in the control, conduct, or maintenance of your local church or religious denomination

The IRS and the courts generally use a balancing approach to the four factors; i.e., some, but not necessarily all, must be met in determining ministerial status. This flexible approach is beneficial to many ministers because some ministers of music, education, youth, or administration will not meet all four factors.

Some individuals who are ordained, licensed, or commissioned still may not qualify for ministerial tax status. The duties performed by the individual are also important to the determination of whether he or she is a duly ordained, commissioned, or licensed minister. Because religious disciplines vary in their formal procedures for these designations, whether an individual is duly ordained, licensed, or commissioned depends on a number of factors.

There is no requirement that one must be qualified to perform and actually perform every sacrament or rite of his or her religion. If one is qualified to perform certain sacraments and actually performs or could perform some of the sacraments on occasion, he or she will generally meet this test. A similar test applies to conducting religious worship and providing management services. If one currently conducts religious worship and provides management services, has done it in the past, or could do it in the future, the test will generally be met.

Job titles have little significance for tax purposes. A licensed, commissioned, or ordained minister may have a job title that implies a ministry function. However, the actual responsibilities of the position will determine if the four-factor test is met. Ministers performing services of a routine nature, such as those performed by secretaries, clerks, and janitors, generally do not qualify as ministers for tax purposes.

> **Caution**
> Determination of ministerial status is far from a precise matter. There has been considerable inconsistency in the position of the IRS and Tax Court on this issue across the years. Only a review of all the pertinent facts and circumstances for a particular minister will assist in determining whether an individual qualifies for ministerial tax status.

If a local church or parachurch organization ordains, licenses, or commissions ministers, it is very important that certain guidelines are followed. These issues are addressed in the 2018 edition of the *Zondervan Church and Nonprofit Tax & Financial Guide*.

Evangelists and missionaries

The qualifications for itinerant evangelists for the special ministerial tax provisions are generally the same as for ministers serving local churches.

Most evangelists are self-employed both for income tax and self-employment social security tax purposes. An exception is an evangelist who has formed a corporation and is an employee of the corporation. In this instance, the evangelist is an employee for income tax purposes but remains self-employed for social security tax purposes (as is true for all ministers).

Missionaries are also subject to the same rules to qualify for ministerial status for tax purposes. Qualifying for benefits such as a housing allowance is often not so important for a minister-missionary because of the foreign-earned income exclusion. However, the issue of ministerial tax status is vitally important to determine if the minister is subject to social security as an employee or as a self-employed person.

A missionary may qualify for the foreign-earned income exclusion (Form 2555) whether or not the missionary qualifies for ministerial tax treatment. The foreign-earned income exclusion affects income tax but not social security tax.

Ministers in denominational service, on church assignment, and in other service

Ordained, commissioned, or licensed ministers not serving local churches may qualify as "ministers" for federal tax purposes in the following situations:

Denominational service

This category encompasses the administration of religious denominations and their integral agencies, including teaching or administration in parochial schools, colleges, or universities that are under the authority of a church or denomination.

The IRS uses the following criteria to determine if an institution is an integral agency of a church:

- Did the church incorporate the institution?
- Does the corporate name of the institution suggest a church relationship?
- Does the church continuously control, manage, and maintain the institution?
- If dissolved, will the assets be turned over to the church?
- Are the trustees or directors of the institution appointed by, or must they be approved by, the church and may they be removed by the church?
- Does the church require annual reports of finances and general operations?
- Does the church contribute to the support of the institution?

Assignment by a church to another parachurch ministry

Services performed by a minister for a parachurch organization based upon a substantive assignment or designation by a church may provide the basis for ministerial tax treatment. The housing allowance should be designated by the employing organization, not the assigning church.

The following characteristics must be present for an effective assignment:

- A sufficient relationship must exist between the minister and the assigning church to justify the assignment of the minister.

- An adequate relationship must exist between the assigning church and the parachurch organization to which the minister is assigned to justify the assignment.

> **Caution**
> Too often, a denomination lists a minister as being assigned to a parachurch ministry, for example, in an annual directory, and the minister believes he or she has been assigned for tax purposes. But effective assignments are generally based on the substantive relationship and ongoing documentation of the assignment that are needed.

To substantiate the relationship between the minister and the church, the church must determine "if there is sufficient authority, power, or legitimacy for the church to assign this particular minister." Such matters as being the ordaining church, providing ongoing supervision, denominational affiliation, contributing significant financial support, or being the long-term "home church" would all appear to support this relationship.

In addressing the relationship between the church and the parachurch organization, the church must answer the question "why the church should assign a minister to this particular ministry." Essentially, the assignment of the minister must accomplish the ministry purposes of the church.

In considering an assignment, it is important to distinguish between the process of assigning and the documentation of the assignment. The process of assigning expresses the church's theology, philosophy, and policy of operation—its way of doing ministry. The documentation of the assignment provides evidence that the church is providing ministry through the particular individual assigned.

The following are keys to a proper assignment:

➤ A written policy describing the specific requirements for the relationship of the church both to the minister being assigned and to the parachurch organization to which the minister is assigned. This would include the church's theological and policy goals for the assignment.

➤ A formal review to confirm the qualifications of the minister and the proposed ministry with a parachurch organization.

➤ A written assignment coupled with guidelines explaining how the church should supervise the minister and how the parachurch organization should report to the church.

➤ A periodic (at least annual) formal review of the minister's activities to confirm that the assignment continues to comply with the policy.

A sample assignment resolution is included in the 2018 edition of the *Zondervan Church and Nonprofit Tax & Financial Guide*.

Other service

If a minister is not engaged in service performed in the exercise of the ministry of a local church or an integral agency of a church, or if a church does not assign their services, then the definition of a qualifying minister becomes much narrower. Tax law and regulations provide little guidance for ministers in this category.

Tax Court cases and IRS rulings suggest that an individual will qualify for the special tax treatment of a minister only if the individual's services for the employer *substantially involve conducting religious worship or performing sacerdotal functions*. This definition might include preaching, conducting Bible studies, spiritual and pastoral counseling, conducting crusades, producing religious television and radio broadcasts, and publishing religious literature.

> **Caution**
> Many ministers are serving organizations other than local churches or integral agencies of churches and do not have an effective assignment by a church. The employer may be a rescue mission, a youth ministry, Christian radio or TV station, or a missionary-sending organization. Qualifying for ministerial status is based on the degree to which the individual is performing sacerdotal functions or conducting religious worship.

How much time constitutes substantial involvement in conducting worship or administering the sacraments? This is difficult to say. However, in two IRS letter rulings, the IRS determined that 5% of the minister's working hours were not sufficient to qualify for tax treatment as a minister.

Based on IRS rulings, it is clear that ministers serving as chaplains in government-owned-and-operated hospitals or in state prisons fall in a special category. They are employees for social security (FICA) purposes and qualify for the housing allowance exclusion. If they have opted out of social security by filing Form 4361, the exemption does not apply to this employment.

Individuals Not Qualifying for Ministerial Tax Treatment

One does not qualify as a "minister" if he or she is

- a theological student but does not otherwise qualify as a minister
- an unordained, uncommissioned, or unlicensed individual not performing sacerdotal functions or conducting religious worship
- an ordained, commissioned, or licensed minister working as an administrator or on the faculty of a nonchurch-related college or seminary
- an ordained, commissioned, or licensed minister working as an executive of a non-religious, nonchurch-related organization
- a civilian chaplain at a Veteran's Administration hospital (the tax treatment of ministers who are chaplains in the armed forces is the same as for other members of the armed forces)
- an ordained, licensed, or commissioned minister employed by a parachurch organization but does not perform sacerdotal functions or conduct religious worship

Income Tax Status of Ministers

Are ministers employees or self-employed (independent contractors) for income tax purposes? The IRS considers virtually all ministers to be employees for income tax purposes. The income tax filing status has many ramifications for what and how a church and the minister report to the IRS.

Employees report compensation on Form 1040, line 7, not on Schedule C or C-EZ (used by self-employed individuals). Employees receive Form W-2 each year from their employer, while Form 1099-MISC is used to report compensation received by a self-employed individual.

Employees deduct unreimbursed business expenses and expenses reimbursed under a nonaccountable plan on Form 2106 (2106-EZ) with the amount carried forward to

Schedule A as itemized deductions. The expenses are subject to a 2% of adjusted gross income limitation, and only 50% of business meals and entertainment expenses are deductible.

Self-employed individuals deduct expenses on Schedule C or C-EZ whether or not they are eligible to itemize deductions. Expenses are not subject to the 2% of adjusted gross income limitation, but the 50% of business meals and entertainment limit still applies. Whether expenses are deducted on Schedule A, Schedule C, or C-EZ, they are subject to the allocation rules explained on pages 91-93.

> **Key Issue**
> The defining court case on the topic of income tax status for ministers was a 1994 case in which a Methodist minister took the position he was self-employed for income tax purposes. The Tax Court held that he was an employee for income tax purposes. A federal appeals court upheld the decision.

The IRS often applies a common-law test to individuals, including ministers, to determine whether they are employees or self-employed for income tax purposes. Ministers are generally considered employees for income tax purposes if they meet the criteria reflected under these three categories:

Behavioral control:

- follow the church's work instructions
- receive on-the-job training
- provide services that are integral to the church
- hire, supervise, and pay assistants for the church
- follow set hours of work
- work full-time for the church
- do their work in a church-determined sequence
- submit regular or written reports to the church

Financial control:

- receive business expense reimbursements
- receive routine payments of regular amounts
- need the church to furnish tools and materials
- do not have a major investment in job facilities
- cannot suffer a loss from their services
- work for one church at a time
- do not offer their services to the general public

Relationship of the parties:
- have an ongoing work relationship with the church
- provide services that must be rendered personally
- work on the church's premises
- can be fired by the church
- may quit work at any time without penalty

Some of the above factors are often given greater weight than others. *Generally a minister is an employee if the church has the legal right to control both what and how work is done, even if the minister has considerable discretion and freedom of action.* The threshold level of control necessary to find employee status is generally lower when applied to professional services than when applied to nonprofessional services.

Importance of the Employee vs. Self-Employed Decision on Income Taxes

Documenting a minister's employee status for income tax purposes is important both for the church and the minister. This issue has a direct impact on several tax-related issues:

- Minister-employees must be given Form W-2 and report their compensation on page 1 of Form 1040. They are eligible to claim unreimbursed business expenses and expenses reimbursed under a nonaccountable plan on Schedule A (nonaccountable plan reimbursements must be included in compensation on Form W-2). If a minister itemizes deductions, business and professional expenses are deductible only to the extent that such expenses exceed 2% of adjusted gross income. Deductible business meals and entertainment expenses are limited to 50%.

> **Key Issue**
> It is vital for churches and other employers to treat ministers as employees (Form W-2) for income tax purposes in nearly every instance. If the minister is not considered an employee for income tax purposes, it jeopardizes the tax-free treatment of many fringe benefits.

- Accident, long-term care insurance, and qualified group health insurance premiums paid directly by an employer or reimbursed by an employer after the minister provides substantiation are not reportable as income to the minister-employee but must be reported as taxable income to the self-employed minister.

Minister-employees may deduct accident and long-term care insurance and qualified group health insurance premiums paid personally, and not reimbursed by the church, on Schedule A as a medical and dental expense, generally subject to a 10% limitation of adjusted gross income.

The impact of a minister being considered self-employed for income tax purposes is generally very significant even if only health insurance is considered. With health insurance premiums often running thousands of dollars per year, reporting these premiums as taxable (self-employed minister for income purposes) versus tax-free (minister-employee) can impact the minister's tax bill by thousands of dollars. If health insurance premiums are included in taxable income, a low-income minister might also have his or her earned income tax credit reduced or eliminated.

> **Warning**
> Employers should consult professional tax advisors before reimbursing medical expenses for employees. Under changes brought by the Affordable Care Act, non-compliant reimbursements may result in penalties of $100 per employee per day.

Example: The church has a qualified group health insurance plan and pays health insurance premiums of $12,000 for the minister (and his or her dependents). Since the church considers the minister an employee for income tax purposes, the payment of the group health insurance premiums are tax-free for income and social security tax purposes and are not reported on Form W-2. The minister's marginal federal and state income tax rates are 25% and 5%, respectively. For social security tax purposes, the minister's rate is 15.3% (all ministers are self-employed for social security tax purposes).

Therefore, the tax-free reimbursement of the health insurance premiums saves the minister over 45%, or almost $5,500 (45.3% x $12,000). Conversely, if a church pays health insurance premiums for a minister who is self-employed for income tax purposes, the total amount is taxable for income and social security tax purposes.

➤ Health savings accounts, health reimbursement arrangements, or flexible spending arrangements are only available to employees or ministers who are treated as employees. See chapter 3 for a more detailed discussion.

➤ Group-term life insurance, provided by an employer, of $50,000 or less is tax-free to employees but represents taxable income for the self-employed.

➤ A voluntary arrangement to withhold income tax may be used by a minister-employee but may not be used by the self-employed.

CHAPTER 1 ▸ TAXES FOR MINISTERS

Recommended Filing Status for Income Taxes

Nearly every local church minister qualifies as an employee for income tax purposes and should receive Form W-2. Few ministers can adequately substantiate filing as self-employed for income tax purposes.

Even though the minister might take exception to this reporting by the church, the church still has a responsibility under the law to determine the proper filing method and proceed accordingly.

Social Security Tax Status of Ministers

Ministers engaged in the exercise of ministry are *always* treated as self-employed for social security tax purposes. Self-employed individuals pay social security tax under the Self-Employment Contributions Act (SECA) instead of under the Federal Insurance Contributions Act (FICA).

The application of the correct method of contributing social security tax for ministers is often confusing. A church should *never* deduct FICA-type social security tax from the pay of a qualified minister. If the individual is a qualifying minister, SECA coverage is then applied. The type of social security coverage is not optional for a minister. It is the responsibility of the church to determine the appropriate type of social security based on whether the individual qualifies as a minister in the eyes of the IRS.

> **Caution**
>
> Social security tax is one of the most confusing issues for many ministers. FICA-type social security never applies to an individual who qualifies as a minister for tax purposes. Stated another way, if a housing allowance has been designated for a minister, FICA tax should not be deducted from pay—the minister is responsible to determine social security tax by completing Schedule SE each year.

If a church withholds and matches FICA-type social security tax for a qualified minister, the minister is incorrectly being treated as a lay employee. The FICA matched by the church is improperly treated as tax-free when it is taxable for both income and social security purposes.

It is possible for a minister to be exempt from SECA in only a few situations. To claim a SECA exemption, a minister must be conscientiously opposed to receiving public insurance (including an opposition to receiving social security benefits) because of the minister's religious beliefs or because of the position of the minister's religious denomination regarding social security (see pages 106-10).

A minister's earnings that are not from the exercise of ministry are generally subject to social security tax under FICA for nonministerial employment or SECA for nonministerial independent contractor earnings.

Integrity Points

- **Ministers who do not qualify for tax treatment as a minister in a local church.** While most ordained ministers employed by a local congregation qualify for special ministerial tax treatment, some do not. While a congregation may be able to "get away" with designating a housing allowance for an individual who does not qualify for ministerial tax treatment, the law and integrity requires more.

- **Assignment of ministers to a parachurch organization.** Many ministers request an assignment from a local congregation in relation to their employment with a parachurch organization. Why are these requests made by ministers? It's very simple! If a minister has an effective assignment, he or she has a much lower threshold to meet to qualify as a minister for tax purposes with the parachurch organization.

    What should a local congregation do when a request for assignment is received? It should determine if an assignment of the minister can be done with integrity. An effective assignment is more than the congregation simply sending a letter of assignment to the parachurch organization. For example, does the church have a written policy which outlines the criteria for assignment of ministers? Does the assignment accomplish the ministry purposes of the church?

- **Ministers employed by a parachurch organization.** Unless a minister has a valid assignment from a church to a parachurch organization (other than a denomination or one of its agencies), qualifying for ministerial tax status with the parachurch organization is much more difficult than with a local church.

    In the non-assignment, nondenominational setting, a minister is left to rely on performing substantial sacerdotal functions with respect to his or her employment with the parachurch organization to qualify for special ministerial tax treatment.

- **Proper social security treatment of ministers.** When an individual qualifies as a minister in the eyes of the IRS, he or she automatically becomes subject to social security under the self-employment (SECA) rules and is ineligible for FICA-type social security treatment. In other words, a church or other employer of a qualified minister should never deduct FICA social security tax from a minister's pay.

CHAPTER 2
Compensation Planning

In This Chapter

- Determine the current compensation
- Plan the compensation package
- Use fringe benefits wisely
- Use accountable expense reimbursements
- Checklist for churches demonstrating integrity in compensation-setting

Even church board members often do not know their pastor's true compensation. When a church financial report is prepared, the data may be presented in such a way that there is not a clear reflection of salary as contrasted with fringe benefits and expense reimbursements. Too often, all of these expense elements are added together, leaving the appearance that the pastor is making much more than he or she really is.

It is often helpful to review compensation data for other ministers who serve churches of similar size in the same geographic area. While precise data based on all of these factors is difficult to determine, the most detailed annual surveys available of church staff compensation are the Large Church Salary Report by Leadership Network (www.leadnet.org/salary), MinistryPay.com by The Church Network (www.nacba.net), and the Compensation Handbook for Church Staff by Christianity Today (www.churchlawandtax.com). These surveys include data for various ministerial levels, church business administrators, and many other staff positions.

> **Key Issue**
> If a church does not increase the pastor's pay each year, it has in effect reduced the pay. Inflation is very low today, but it still exists, even at a few percentage points. It does cost more each year to live. Just as laypersons expect their employers to provide them with a cost-of-living pay increase each year, a pastor should expect the same.

Determine the Current Compensation

Ask a pastor how much he or she is paid and the response will often be "My check from the church is $1,000 a week." But that tells us very little. Let's look at a few examples:

Example 1: Pastor A receives cash salary of $75,000, but the church does not directly pay or reimburse his group health insurance premiums of $10,000. Pastor B receives cash salary of $65,000, but the church directly pays his $10,000 group health insurance premiums. Which pastor has the better compensation plan based on just these factors?

The church pays the same dollars either way, but Pastor B has the better compensation plan in nearly every instance. Why? Health insurance premiums paid by a pastor out-of-pocket have absolutely no tax value if the minister uses the standard deduction (as does nearly every pastor who lives in church-provided housing). And even ministers who itemize their deductions on Schedule A only receive tax benefits from the premiums they pay when their medical expenses, including health insurance, are greater than 10% of their adjusted gross income.

> **Key Issue**
> In trying to determine which has the best pay plan, one pastor may compare notes with another pastor by asking, "How much does your church pay you per week?" But this data doesn't begin to tell which pay plan is better. Determining what a minister is really paid is a challenging task but worth the effort.

Example 2: Is it better stewardship for a church to pay its pastor a cash salary of $40,000 and provide a professional expense allowance (nonaccountable plan) of $8,000 or pay its pastor cash salary of $40,000 and reimburse up to $8,000 of professional expenses under an accountable plan?

The church is going to spend the same amount of money either way: $48,000. But the pastor will almost always have less money in his or her pocket at the end of the year with the nonaccountable plan. Why? Because the $8,000 of professional expense allowance under a nonaccountable plan must be added to the pastor's Form W-2 as taxable compensation (see chapter 5 for more information on accountable and nonaccountable plans). Then, the pastor must deduct the expenses not reimbursed under an accountable plan. If the pastor could not itemize his deductions before considering this $8,000 of unreimbursed expenses, there will be deductions lost just to get up to the itemized deduction level. Even if the minister was already beyond the itemizing threshold for the year, only 50% of meals and entertainment expenses are deductible (versus 100% eligible for reimbursement), and the first 2% times adjusted gross income of miscellaneous expenses are not deductible.

> **Key Issue**
> Document the minister's pay using the worksheet on page 18. This exercise will reveal how well your church has provided for fringe benefits. It will also show the gross pay (including housing allowance or parsonage value) that can be evaluated for adequacy.

Reporting Ministerial Compensation to the Church

Common reporting practice to avoid

	Church-Provided Housing	Minister-Provided Housing
Pastor's cash salary	$ 40,000	$ 50,000
Parsonage utilities	3,000	
Pension	1,000	1,000
Social security reimbursement	4,000	4,000
Disability and group health/life insurance	8,000	8,000
	$ 56,000	$ 63,000

Better reporting approach

Salary and equivalent compensation		
Cash salary	$ 40,000	$ 50,000
Fair rental value of parsonage provided (including utilities)	9,000	
Social security reimbursement (in excess of 50% of total social security)	2,000	2,000
	$ 51,000	$ 52,000
Fringe benefits		
Pension	1,000	1,000
Social security reimbursement (up to 50% of total social security)	2,000	2,000
Disability and group health/life insurance	8,000	8,000
	$ 11,000	$ 11,000

Confusion over how much the pastor is paid all starts with the church's financial reporting approach. In reporting to the congregation, many churches include the pastor's expense reimbursements and fringe benefits in the same section of the report with cash salary. In these examples, the common reporting practice makes it appear the pastor is being paid $56,000 or $63,000, depending on church-provided or minister-provided housing. Actually, the compensation is only $51,000 or $52,000 respectively. Use the worksheet on the following page to determine what and how the minister is paid.

Minister's Compensation Worksheet

	This Year	Next Year

Salary and Equivalent Compensation:

A. Cash salary, less designated housing/furnishings allowance $_____ $_____

B. If parsonage owned by church, fair rental value including utilities and any housing/furnishings allowance _____ _____

C. If parsonage not owned by church, cash housing allowance provided (plus utilities, maintenance, or any other housing expenses paid directly by church) _____ _____

D. Cash bonus _____ _____

E. Social security reimbursement _____ _____

F. Other _____ _____

Total Salary $_____ $_____

Fringe Benefits:

A. Denominational pension fund $_____ $_____

B. Tax-deferred employer payments (TSA/403[b], 401[k], IRA) _____ _____

C. Health reimbursement arrangement _____ _____

D. Insurance premiums paid by church

   1. Group health _____ _____

   2. Disability _____ _____

   3. Long-term care _____ _____

   4. Group-term life _____ _____

   5. Dental/vision _____ _____

   6. Professional liability _____ _____

   7. Malpractice _____ _____

E. Other _____ _____

Total Fringe Benefits $_____ $_____

CHAPTER 2 > COMPENSATION PLANNING

Plan the Compensation Package

The participation of the pastor with an individual or a small group for compensation discussions is crucial. The entire congregation may ultimately approve the annual budget that includes pastoral pay and benefits. But the pay package needs to be carefully developed before it reaches the congregational approval stage. Even the entire church board is too large of a forum for the initial compensation discussions.

An annual review of a pastor's pay is vital. The pastor should know exactly what to expect from the congregation during the coming year. It is inexcusable to wait until the new church year begins or later to decide the new pay plan for the pastor.

Late in 2017 is a good time for the committee responsible for recommending compensation matters to put a plan together for the new church year that might begin in early to mid-2018. A representative or a small committee from the church board should meet with the pastor,

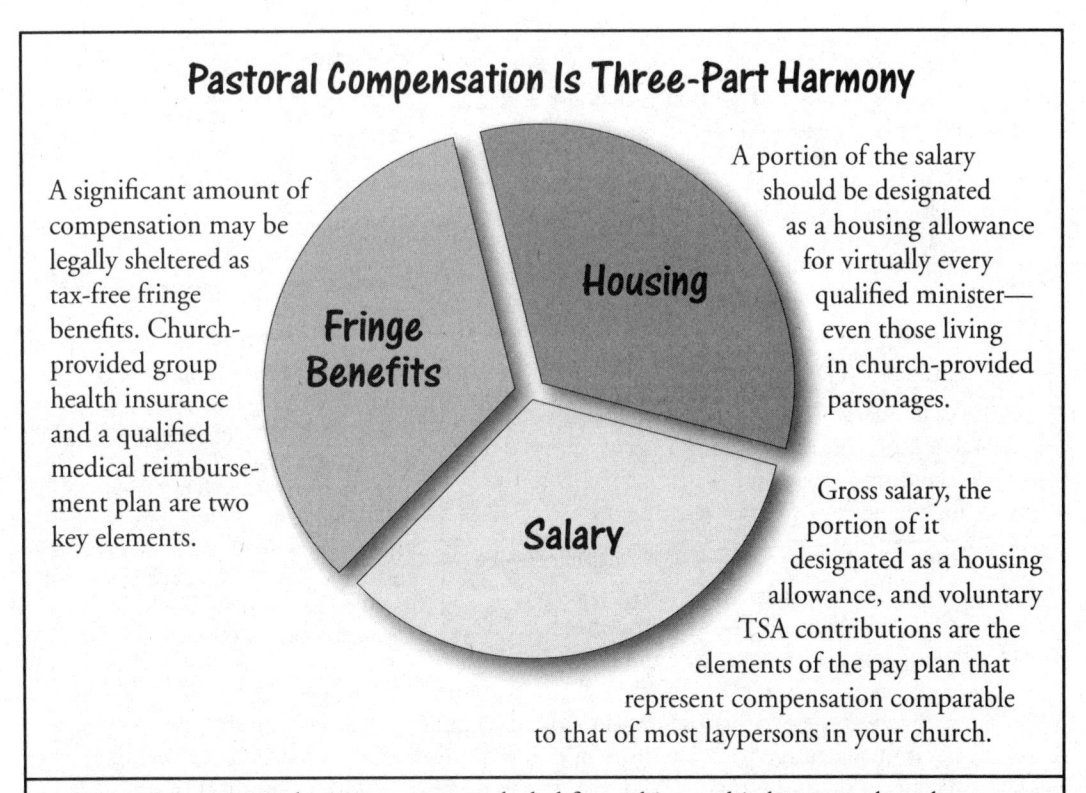

Pastoral Compensation Is Three-Part Harmony

A significant amount of compensation may be legally sheltered as tax-free fringe benefits. Church-provided group health insurance and a qualified medical reimbursement plan are two key elements.

Fringe Benefits

Housing

A portion of the salary should be designated as a housing allowance for virtually every qualified minister—even those living in church-provided parsonages.

Salary

Gross salary, the portion of it designated as a housing allowance, and voluntary TSA contributions are the elements of the pay plan that represent compensation comparable to that of most laypersons in your church.

Note: Expense reimbursements are excluded from this graphic because when they are processed with an accountable reimbursement plan, they are not part of compensation.

talk about pay expectations, review past pay patterns, discuss the tax consequences of compensation components, then make recommendations to the appropriate body.

The church board should act on the recommendations by March for a fiscal year beginning in mid-2018. Then the compensation package may be included in the congregational budget for the next year. The detailed elements of the pay plan, while fully disclosed to the church board, are often summarized for presentation to the congregation.

Consider goals and objectives

Does your church have goals and objectives? Perhaps goals include a percentage increase of Sunday school and worship attendance, growth in giving to missions, paying down or paying off the mortgage, or raising money for a building expansion.

Have you stated the specific objectives of your pastoral compensation policy? Here are a few examples:

> **Remember**
> All of the elements of a minister's compensation plan should be annually evaluated. A thorough evaluation is much more than just tacking on an inflationary increase to gross pay. If the gross pay was inadequate before the increase, it is still too low after the inflationary increase.

➤ **Attraction.** Our goal is to attract a pastor who has a record of leading spiritually and numerically growing churches.

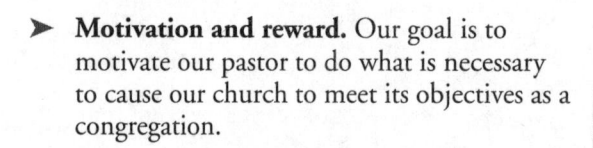

➤ **Retention.** Our goal is to increase the average time a pastor stays at our church to more than ten years.

➤ **Motivation and reward.** Our goal is to motivate our pastor to do what is necessary to cause our church to meet its objectives as a congregation.

Taking your overall church goals and objectives and pastoral compensation objectives into account, it may be helpful to establish a written compensation policy for the pastor or pastoral staff.

> **Remember**
> Ministers who live in church-provided housing are penalized when residential real estate values are increasing. Even if real estate is modestly increasing, it is important for a church to provide an equity allowance. This annual payment in lieu of home ownership permits the pastor to invest the amount that might have been received through growth in the real estate market.

Example: Based on our goals to develop three satellite congregations in the next five years and expand our international missions outreach, our compensation policy will attract, retain, reward, and motivate a pastor in a fair and equitable manner, when considering the compensation of other pastors in our denomination but particularly pastors in our local community, the compensation of citizens of our community, and the members of this congregation.

Compare the job description to benchmarks of other jobs

The pastor's job description should be compared to other jobs based on the following requirements: knowledge base, problem-solving ability, and the personal accountability for results. How much are other well-educated professionals paid in the community or the area? A possible comparison may be to pay the minister similar to an elementary school principal, middle school principal, or high school principal in your area. This data is public information and can be readily obtained.

Recognize the motivational factors and job description

It is important to recognize factors that commonly motivate pastors. These include extrinsic factors (God's call to preach the Word), intrinsic factors (the pastoral role and relationships with church attendees and those in the community), and external factors (salary and benefits).

But the job description for most pastors is astounding! Typically, the job includes preaching the Word; equipping the saints for the work of ministry; administering the sacraments; visiting the sick and the needy; comforting those who mourn; correcting, rebuking, and encouraging; caring for the departments of the church; giving leadership to evangelism and education programs of the church; supervising the preparation of statistical reports; and so much more.

> **Key Issue**
> Compensation paid to the minister should be fair and a reasonable indication of the congregation's evaluation of the minister's worth. Above all, compensation should reflect the congregation's assessment of how well the minister handles a multitude of challenges and effectively serves a diverse congregation. Pay should relate to the responsibilities, the size of the congregation, the economic level of the locale, and the experience of the pastor.

Elements of the package to review

In too many congregations, the church leadership may say, "We can pay you $75,000. How do you want the money divided among salary, housing allowance, fringe benefits, and expense reimbursements?" The salary may be considered as $75,000 when it is really considerably less. Salary is just one component of compensation. And this approach lacks good stewardship as it almost always results in the minister paying more taxes than necessary.

In another church, the church leadership may set the salary at $70,000, professional reimbursements at $4,000, and pension contributions at $2,000. Thus, the salary may be viewed as $76,000, not what it really is: $70,000.

Some congregations may choose to boost the minister's salary 4% this year, leaving other elements

> **Key Issue**
> Few churches in America compensate ministers adequately. First, consider the minister's job description. Then, compare the job description to benchmarks of other jobs in the community based on the knowledge base, problem-solving ability, and personal accountability required for the minister.

of the pay package as they are. This practice presumes that the base salary for the previous year was adequate. This may or may not have been true.

For compensation planning, churches should consider salary ranges rather than fixed amounts. Show the pastor that based on experience, longevity, and education, he or she will start at a higher rate and receive better periodic increases.

An accountable expense reimbursement plan should be provided to every minister. An ideal policy provides for full reimbursement of all professional expenses. Alternately, the plan should provide for reimbursements up to a specified annual limit. It is generally counterproductive to set expense plan limits by segments of expense like automobile, meals and entertainment, dues, and so on. If an expense limit is set, use one limit for all business and professional expenses (see chapter 5).

After the reimbursement policy and the fringe benefit items are decided, housing and salary should be reviewed. Housing and salary are the true "compensation" items of the pay plan. Accountable reimbursements are not a part of salary. Accountable reimbursements are simply a form of church operating expenses. Fringe benefits are not salary even if they are taxable. They are simply benefits.

Just as laypersons do not include the payments made by their employers to pension or group health plans as part of their salary, a congregation should not add those costs as part of the pastor's salary. True, they are a real cost for having a pastor, but they are fringe benefits, not salary. Housing, salary, church-funded IRA payments, and voluntary tax-sheltered annuity (403[b]) contributions are generally the only elements that represent compensation comparable to most laypersons in your church.

Routinely Evaluate Compensation

Once the work has been completed to determine a fair and reasonable compensation package, it needs to be considered carefully in the future. While the amounts paid are included in personnel costs, and are part of the budget, the minister's compensation should not receive a flat percentage or cost of living increase without additional thought. The pastor's role may change. The needs of the pastor may be different. The ministry may even find they are in a better financial position and able to do more than previously possible.

Use Fringe Benefits Wisely

Fringe benefit plans should be established by the church separately from housing allowance resolutions, accountable expense reimbursement arrangements, and compensation resolutions. There are different tax rules that apply to gross pay, the housing allowance, and the various fringe benefits. Too often, churches try to wrap too many plans into one resolution. This can result in improperly establishing important elements in the compensation plan.

There are several key fringe benefits that many churches consider for ministers:

- **Tax-deferred accounts.** The minister should contribute as much as he or she can (see chapter 3 for limitations) to tax-deferred accounts such as tax-sheltered annuities (TSAs) or 401(k) plans. Also, the church is encouraged to pay in the maximum to a denominational pension plan if one is available to you. Caution: Do not exceed retirement plan limits.

- **Group health insurance.** This benefit is tax-free to a minister-employee if the church pays the group health insurance policy premiums directly to the insurance carrier.

- **Life insurance.** Church-provided group life insurance coverage for a minister is an excellent fringe benefit. The first $50,000 of coverage under a nondiscriminatory plan is tax-free for the minister. Premiums for coverage over $50,000 are taxable to the minister.

> **Idea**
> A sound fringe benefit package almost always starts with the church or other employer paying for the minister's health insurance. This is vital because payments for coverage under the church's group plan are tax-free. If the minister has to pay the health insurance premiums, they can be claimed on Schedule A but rarely produce a tax benefit.

- **Disability insurance.** The church can provide disability insurance coverage as part of the minister's taxable compensation, and disability insurance benefits are tax-free. Or, the church could pay the premiums as a tax-free fringe benefit. If the premiums are tax-free to the minister, disability insurance benefits are taxable.

- **Social security reimbursement.** All ministers pay self-employment social security tax of 15.3% on the first $127,200 of income in 2017. The Medicare tax of 2.9% is still due for all income above this limit, as well as an additional tax of 0.9% on wages above $200,000 for ministers filing as single and $250,000 for ministers married filing jointly. The only exception from paying self-employment social security tax is for the few ministers who qualify, file, and are approved for social security exemption.

  Churches often provide a reimbursement or allowance to assist the pastor in paying a portion or all of the social security tax. The payments are taxable for income and social security tax purposes whether paid directly to the minister or the IRS, and the payments should be included on the minister's Form W-2 in Box 1 as compensation.

> **Caution**
> An allowance to cover the minister's self-employment social security tax provides absolutely no tax benefit since the amount is fully taxable. However, paying at least one-half of the minister's social security tax is important, so this amount can be properly shown as a fringe benefit for compensation analysis purposes.

- **Sabbaticals.** Some churches and nonprofit organizations choose to provide their ministers a sabbatical either to focus on a project such as writing a book, or as a respite for a certain number of years of service. This usually takes the form of an extended paid leave. A housing allowance is still appropriate if they otherwise qualify. No other benefits would be impacted.

Use Accountable Expense Reimbursements

Since all ministers incur travel expenses while conducting the ministry of the local church, an adequate accountable reimbursement plan is vital. Auto expenses are generally a minister's most significant ministry-related expense. If payments to the minister with respect to these and other ministry expenses are not made subject to the accountable plan rules, the payments simply represent additional taxable compensation. The difference between treating several thousands of dollars of ministry-related expenses as tax-free under an accountable expense reimbursement plan or as fully taxable under a nonaccountable plan can be very significant in terms of dollars saved by the minister.

Ministers also incur other business expenses such as entertainment, professional books and magazines, membership dues, and supplies. Some churches reimburse their ministers in full for these expenses. Other churches reimburse the minister for these expenses up to certain limits.

> **Remember**
> Expense allowances have no tax value to a minister—they simply represent fully taxable compensation, and the minister must try to deduct as many church-related expenses as possible. It is only through an accountable expense reimbursement plan that the reimbursement of expenses can be tax-free.

All churches should establish a fair and equitable reimbursement plan, comparable to most business situations. The reimbursement plan should meet the rules for accountable plans explained in chapter 5. Full reimbursement of reasonable professional expenses should be the goal. If the church does not reimburse for 100% of professional expenses, the unreimbursed expenses will probably not be fully deductible for tax purposes and perhaps not deductible at all. Anything less than 100% reimbursement of church-related expenses is poor stewardship of the money entrusted to a church.

In addition to the adoption of an accountable reimbursement plan by the church, the minister must keep proper records and provide substantiation to the church for the expenditure of funds. The failure to account adequately for the expenses may be very expensive in terms of income taxes.

Avoid recharacterization of income

Some churches pay their employees' business expenses through a salary reduction arrangement. These approaches frequently violate the tax code.

Accountable business expense reimbursement arrangements must meet the business connection, substantiation, and return of excess reimbursement requirements of the income

CHAPTER 2 > COMPENSATION PLANNING

Income Tax Reporting and Expense Reimbursements

[Form W-2 Wage and Tax Statement 2017]

The IRS treats most ministers as employees for income tax purposes. Churches must issue Form W-2 to minister-employees.

Box 1 will be completed for all ministers. Box 2 will reflect any voluntary withholding the minister chose for the ministry to withhold from their pay. Boxes 3 through 11 should be blank. Per IRS Publication 517, the housing allowance amount will be reflected in Box 14.

Every church should adopt an accountable expense reimbursement plan. Expenses paid under an accountable plan are not includible on the minister's Form W-2. The expenses are not reported in any manner on the minister's Form 1040. Therefore, the expenses are not subject to any of the expense deduction limitations for Form 1040 or subject to IRS income tax audit.

Minister-employees without accountable reimbursement plans will generally pay unnecessary income taxes.

tax regulations. There is an additional requirement. If a church agrees to pay a minister (or other staff member) a specified annual income, and also agrees to reimburse the employee's business expenses out of salary reductions, the IRS takes the position that the church has arranged to pay an amount to an employee regardless of whether the employee incurs business expenses.

The following example illustrates the key principles:

> **Example:** A church pays its minister an annual salary of $72,000 ($6,000 each month). Additionally, the church agrees to reimburse the minister's substantiated business expenses through salary reductions. For example, the minister's business expenses for January were $1,000. She substantiates these expenses to the church treasurer during the first week of February. While the minister receives her monthly check of $6,000, only $5,000 of the check issued to the minister for February is considered taxable salary and accumulated for purposes of reporting on the minister's Form W-2 at year-end.
>
> Based on the tax regulations, the entire $72,000 is reportable on the minister's Form W-2 because the minister would receive the entire $72,000 salary whether or not she incurred any business expenses.

While churches can pay for a minister's business expenses through salary reductions, such an arrangement is nonaccountable and, therefore, there are no tax advantages associated with such an arrangement.

Can a church prospectively reduce a minister's salary and increase the amount available for accountable business expense reimbursement? Or, can a church prospectively hold a minister's salary level and increase the amount available for accountable business expense reimbursement, when the minister otherwise would have received a salary increase? The answer to these questions may depend on whether the church has authorized the minister's salary and established the business expense reimbursement arrangement as two separate actions of the governing board or appropriate committee, without any indication that the reimbursements are being funded out of what otherwise would be the minister's salary.

Checklist for Churches Demonstrating Integrity in Compensation-Setting

Follow steps 1-3 for all churches:

1. **Approval for the lead pastor** – The full church board (i.e., entire corporate governing body) or a committee authorized by the board annually approves total compensation of the lead pastor or comparable position.

2. **Notification for family members** – The full church board or a committee authorized by the board is notified annually of the total compensation of any of the lead pastor's family members employed by the church.

3. **Documentation** – Approval (Step 1) and Notification (Step 2, if applicable) are documented in the church's board minutes.

Follow step 4 for churches where the lead pastor's total compensation is $150,000 or more, and *recommended* for all churches regardless of the lead pastor's compensation amount:

4. **Additional due diligence** – In setting the lead pastor's compensation, the board or a committee authorized by the board must:

   - *Exclude* anyone with a conflict of interest from the decision-making process
   - *Obtain* reliable comparability data for similar churches within the past five years
   - *Determine* appropriate compensation considering the comparability data and factors unique to the lead pastor (skills, talents, education, experience, performance, knowledge, etc.)
   - *Document* these additional due diligence steps, its decision regarding total compensation and, if applicable, its rationale for establishing compensation at a level exceeding that which is supported by the comparability data

FAQs

1. *How is "total compensation" defined?*

   Total compensation includes salary, wages, other payments for services, and benefits of all types, whether taxable or non-taxable, and whether paid directly or indirectly by the organization or one or more of its subsidiaries or affiliates.

2. *What if the church's bylaws outline a different compensation-setting process?*

   The church should consider amending its bylaws in consultation with legal counsel.

Integrity*Points*

- **The compensation approval basics.** Although compensation approval is the responsibility of the governing body or congregation, the minister should assist in observing these three fundamental practices:

  - **Independent compensation approval.** While the governing body or congregation may consult with a minister concerning financial needs, the formal approval of a minister's compensation should be done independently of the minister. In other words, a minister should be recused from the meeting in which his or her compensation is approved.

  - **Documenting the compensation package.** A minister's compensation package should be formally documented in the minutes of the approving body. The details of the package may be placed in a document separate from the meeting minutes (see the 2018 edition of the *Zondervan Church and Nonprofit Tax & Financial Guide* for a sample form to record compensation).

  - **Obtaining competitive compensation data.** It may be appropriate to periodically obtain comparability data before approving a minister's compensation package. Rarely is the data necessary to avoid paying excessive compensation to a minister. The comparability data is more often important to demonstrate how much a minister's pay is below that of a similar position in a similar church in the same geographic region.

- **Working with the congregation to optimize the stewardship opportunities.** Stewardship is generally maximized for the congregation and minister by initially focusing on tax-favored or tax-free fringe benefits and accountable expense reimbursements, then the housing allowance, and finally cash compensation.

CHAPTER 3
The Pay Package

In This Chapter
- Avoiding the nondiscrimination rules
- Tax treatment of compensation elements
- Reporting compensation, fringe benefits, and reimbursements

Ask most ministers about their compensation and they will tell you the amount of their weekly check, including a cash housing allowance, but there is more to it than that. Not only is the salary subject to tax, but so are many fringe benefits that may be received.

What are fringe benefits? A fringe benefit is any cash, property, or service that an employee receives from an employer in addition to salary. The term "fringe benefits" is really a misnomer because employees have come to depend on them as a part of their total compensation package. All fringe benefits are taxable income to employees unless specifically exempted by the Internal Revenue Code.

Many fringe benefits can be provided by a church to a minister without any dollar limitation (group health insurance is an example), while other fringe benefits are subject to annual limits (dependent care is an example). The annual limits by fringe benefit type are reflected in this chapter.

Avoiding the Nondiscrimination Rules

To qualify for exclusion from income, many fringe benefits must be provided in a nondiscriminatory manner. In other words, the benefits must be offered to all employees or all employees in certain classes. A fringe benefit subject to the nondiscrimination rules that is offered by a church only to the senior pastor, when other individuals are employed by the church, could trigger the nondiscrimination rules.

Failure to comply with the nondiscrimination rules does not disqualify a fringe benefit plan entirely. Only the tax-free nature of the benefit is lost to the highly compensated employee.

The nondiscrimination rules apply to several types of fringe benefit plans including

- qualified tuition and fee discounts (see page 48),
- eating facilities on or near the employer's premises (see pages 41–42),
- educational assistance benefits (see page 35),
- dependent care assistance plans (see page 33),
- tax-sheltered annuities (TSAs), 401(k) plans, and other deferred compensation plans (see pages 44–45),
- group-term life insurance benefits (see pages 40–41),
- certain group medical insurance plans,
- health reimbursement arrangements (see pages 38–39),
- health savings accounts (see pages 39–40), and
- cafeteria plans (see pages 36–37), including a flexible spending account dependent care plan (see page 37), and a health care flexible spending account (see page 36).

For purposes of the nondiscrimination rules, a "highly compensated employee" for 2017 is someone paid more than $120,000 in the previous year (and in the top 20% of employees when ranked by pay for the preceding year).

Tax Treatment of Compensation Elements

- **Awards.** Ministers rarely receive awards based on performance, but such awards are generally taxable income unless the value is insignificant. If an award is made to the minister in goods or services, such as a vacation trip, the fair market value of the goods or services is includible in income.

- **Bonuses.** A bonus received by a minister is taxable income.

- **Books.** A church may reimburse a minister for ministry-related books with a short life (a current best-selling book) as a tax-free benefit under an accountable plan. To avoid confusion, it is wise for churches to have a policy covering who owns books (and other property with a useful life longer than one year) paid for by the church. Books funded by the church budget or reimbursed under an accountable expense reimbursement plan belong to the church.

- **Business and professional expenses reimbursed with adequate accounting.** If the church reimburses the minister under an accountable plan for employment-related professional or business expenses (for example, auto, other travel, subscriptions, entertainment, and so on), the reimbursement is not taxable compensation and is not reported to the IRS by the church or the minister (see pages 70–73). A minister's tithes and charitable contributions to the church are not reimbursable or deductible as business expenses. Per diem allowances up to IRS-approved limits also qualify as excludable reimbursements (see page 77).

➤ **Business and professional expense payments without adequate accounting.** Many churches pay periodic allowances or reimbursements to ministers for business expenses with no requirement to account adequately for the expenses. These payments do not meet the requirements of an accountable expense reimbursement plan.

Allowances or reimbursements under a non-accountable plan must be included in a minister's taxable income. For an employee, the expenses related to a nonaccountable reimbursement plan are deductible only if the minister itemizes expenses on Schedule A. Even then, the business expenses, combined with other miscellaneous deductions, must exceed 2% of adjusted gross income.

> **Idea**
> To avoid confusion, it is wise for churches to have a policy covering who owns books (and other property with a useful life longer than one year) paid for by the church. Books funded by the church budget or reimbursed under an accountable expense reimbursement plan belong to the church.

A portion of unreimbursed expenses are subject to disallowance when they relate to a housing allowance according to the IRS (see pages 91–93).

➤ **Clothing.** Ordinary clothing worn in the exercise of a minister's duties for the church is a personal expense and is not deductible as a business expense or reimbursable by the church under an accountable plan.

If a minister wears clothing for ministry that is not adaptable to general use, such as vestments, it is deductible or reimbursable as a business expense.

➤ **Club dues and memberships.** Dues for professional organizations (such as ministerial associations) or public service organizations (such as Kiwanis, Rotary, and Lions clubs) are generally deductible or reimbursable. Other club dues are generally not deductible or reimbursable (including any club organized for business, pleasure, recreation, or other social purposes). If the church pays the health, fitness, or athletic facility dues for a minister, the amounts paid are generally fully includible in the minister's income as additional compensation.

> **Idea**
> The goal of every minister should generally be to have all or most employment-related expenses reimbursed by the employer. Covering all of these accountable expenses is often more advantageous to a minister than a general pay raise which is taxable.

➤ **Computers.** The value of the business use of a church-provided computer may be

31

excludable from gross income as a "working condition" fringe benefit (see pages 108–9 for a discussion of personally owned computers). In order for the exclusion to apply, the minister's business use of the computer must

- ☐ relate to the work of the church
- ☐ entitle the minister to a business deduction if purchasing the computer personally, and
- ☐ meet any substantiation requirements that apply to the deduction

A minister must include the value of the benefit of a church-provided computer in income if:

- ☐ the use is nonbusiness (personal)
- ☐ the use does not qualify as a working condition fringe benefit (see the three requirements shown above) or
- ☐ the minister does not keep records to substantiate business use

Even if church-provided computer use qualifies as a "working condition" fringe benefit, the minister must allocate the value of any personal use of the computer and add it to taxable income.

Tax law does not provide for reimbursements of property, other than property with a short life (such as books), under an accountable expense reimbursement plan, when an employee substantiates the cost and business purpose. However, if an employee substantiates the cost and business purpose of property such as a laptop computer and is reimbursed, the laptop generally becomes the property of the church.

➤ **Conventions.** Expenses incurred when a minister attends a ministry-related convention or seminar are generally deductible. (See pages 76–77 for rules for the travel expenses of spouses and children.)

If the convention is held outside North America, expenses are deductible only if attendance is ministry-related and is considered reasonable (see IRS Publication 463 for factors considered as part of the reasonableness test).

When a minister travels away from home to attend a convention and combines personal activities with ministry activities, the deduction for convention expenses may be subject to certain limitations. When a minister attends a convention on a cruise ship, expenses incurred in connection with the convention are deductible only if the convention is ministry-related, the cruise ship is registered in the United States, and the ship does not stop at a port outside the United States or one of its possessions. (See IRS Publication 463 for written statements that must be attached to returns if deducting expenses incurred when attending ministry-related conventions or seminars held on a cruise.) Additionally, there is a $2,000 limit on expenses that may be deducted for a convention of this type.

▶ **Deferred compensation.** A church may maintain a retirement or other deferred compensation plan for employees that is not qualified under the Internal Revenue Code and is not a 403(b) tax-sheltered annuity (see pages 44–45) or a "Rabbi Trust" (see page 43). If the plan is unfunded (the church makes a promise, not represented by a note, to pay at some time in the future), contributions to the plan are generally not taxable currently.

> **Tip**
> Under the current 403(b) plan contribution limits, relatively few ministers will need to look for other retirement plan options. If the church funds an unqualified plan (such as purchasing an annuity contract) that is not a tax-sheltered annuity or a Rabbi Trust, the contributions are generally taxable when made.

Funds placed in an investment account (other than in a tax-sheltered annuity or "Rabbi Trust") under the church's control to provide retirement funds for the minister have no tax consequence to the minister until the funds are paid or available to the minister.

▶ **Dependent care.** If the church pays or reimburses child or dependent care services, the minister can exclude the amount of this benefit from income within certain limits (see also page 37 for a flexible spending account dependent care plan). The dependent must be (1) under 13 years old, (2) physically or mentally incapable of self-care, or (3) a spouse who is physically or mentally incapable of self-care. The amount excludable is limited to the smaller of

☐ the minister's earned income

☐ the spouse's earned income

☐ $5,000 ($2,500 if married filing separately)

The dependent care assistance must be provided under a separate written plan of the employer that does not favor highly compensated employees and that meets other qualifications.

Dependent care assistance payments are excluded from income if the payments cover expenses that would be deductible if the expenses were not reimbursed. If the minister is married, both spouses must be employed. There are special rules if one spouse is a student or incapable of self-care.

▶ **Dependent educational benefits.** The church may provide educational benefits for the minister's children when they attend college or a pre-college private school. When the church makes the payment to the college, the funds are taxable income to the minister. If the church withholds money from pay and forwards the funds to a college for the education of the minister's child, the amount withheld does not reduce taxable compensation. See the 2018 edition of the *Zondervan Church and Nonprofit Tax & Financial Guide* for more information on scholarship funds established by churches.

➤ **Disability insurance.** If the church pays the disability insurance premiums (and the minister is the beneficiary) as a part of the compensation package, the premiums are excluded from income. However, any disability policy proceeds must be included in gross income. This is based on who paid the premiums for the policy covering the year when the disability started. If the premiums are shared between the church and the minister, then the benefits are taxable in the same proportion as the payment of the premiums.

Conversely, if a minister pays the disability insurance premiums or has the church withhold the premiums from salary, the minister receives no current deduction and any disability benefits paid under the policy are not taxable.

> **Idea**
>
> Statistics suggest that a minister is seven times more likely to need disability insurance than life insurance before age 65. When a church provides the maximum disability insurance as a tax-free benefit, it could reduce the awkwardness of a pastoral transition should the minister become disabled while serving the congregation.

A third option is for the church to pay the disability premiums. But instead of treating the premiums as tax-free, the church treats the premiums as additional employee compensation. Benefits received under this option are tax-free.

How do you determine whether disability benefits are taxable if the disability insurance premiums are paid by the church for some years and by the minister for other years? Taxability of the benefits generally depends on who paid the premiums for the policy year in which the disability benefit payments begin.

➤ **Discretionary fund.** Churches often establish a fund to be disbursed upon the discretion of the pastor. If the funds are used for church business or the needs of individuals associated with the church in a benevolent manner and if a proper accounting is made, there is no tax impact on the minister. If there is no accounting to the church and if it is permissible to distribute some of the funds to the minister, money placed in the fund becomes additional taxable income to the minister in the year the money is transferred by the church to the discretionary fund.

> **Caution**
>
> Discretionary funds often serve a useful purpose for the pastoral staff—giving them the flexibility to provide immediate financial assistance, generally in small amounts, to those in need (larger amounts should be handled through a formal benevolence fund). However, an adequate accounting (dates, names, amounts, and need) must be maintained by the church.

➤ **Dues, ministerial.** Ministers often pay an annual renewal fee to maintain their credentials. These and other similar professional expenses may be reimbursed tax-free by the church or deducted by the minister.

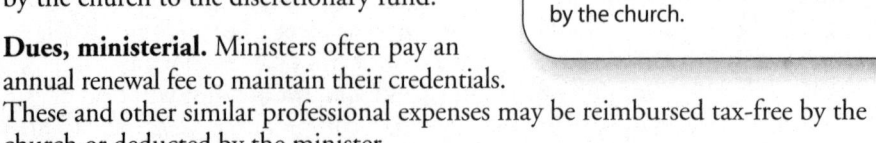

➤ **Educational assistance benefit plans.** An educational assistance program is a separate written plan of a church to provide educational assistance to employees (generally including books, equipment, fees, supplies, and tuition). A program may include courses whether or not they are job-related. Graduate-level courses are covered under the program.

The program must be nondiscriminatory. Other requirements include giving reasonable notice of the program to eligible employees and not allowing employees to choose to receive cash or other benefits that must be included in gross income instead of educational assistance.

No benefits may be provided to the employee's spouse or dependents. The church should exclude from income the first $5,250 of any qualified educational assistance paid for a minister during the year.

➤ **Educational reimbursement plans.** If a church requires the minister to take educational courses or job-related courses, and the church either pays the expenses directly to the educational organization or reimburses the minister for the expenses after a full accounting, the minister may not have to include in income the amount paid by the church. (See page 88 for two types of deductions for education expenses and page 135 for three types of education credits.)

While there are no specific dollar limits on educational expenses paid under a non-qualified reimbursement plan, the general ordinary and necessary business expense rules do apply. These types of payments may be discriminatory.

> **Idea**
> In addition to educational reimbursements, a special $4,000 deduction may be taken for college costs by itemizers and nonitemizers alike. To take this deduction, the education need not be necessary to keep the minister's position. The education can even qualify the minister for a new occupation.

Though the education may lead to a degree, expenses may be deductible or reimbursable if the education:

- ☐ is required by the church to keep the minister's salary, status, or job (and serves a business purpose of the church)
- ☐ maintains or improves skills required in the minister's present employment

Even though the above requirements are met, expenses do not qualify if the education is:

- ☐ required to meet the minimum educational requirements of the minister's present work
- ☐ part of a program of study that will qualify the minister for a new occupation

➤ **Entertainment expenses.** A minister may deduct ministry-related entertainment expenses. Entertainment expenses must be directly related to, or associated with, the work of the church. Documentation of entertainment expenses must reflect the relationship of entertainment to church ministry. Entertainment expenses are not deductible if they are lavish or extravagant.

If business meal and entertainment expenses are not reimbursed under an accountable plan, only 50% of the expenses are deductible. If the church reimburses the expenses, a 100% reimbursement may be made.

➤ **Equity allowance.** If a minister lives in a church-owned parsonage, only the church is building up equity. If the church provides a cash allowance for the minister to purchase a home, the minister may establish some equity.

An equity allowance is an amount paid to the minister living in a church-owned parsonage. This allowance may partially or fully offset the equity that the minister would have accumulated in a personally owned home.

An equity allowance is fully taxable and not excludable as a housing allowance. However, the church could make the equity payments to a tax-sheltered annuity (TSA) or 401(k) plan. This would be consistent with the desire of a congregation to provide funds for housing at retirement. Under current law, the funds received at retirement from church-sponsored TSA or 401(k) plans may be eligible for tax-free treatment as a housing allowance (see pages 63–64).

➤ **Flexible spending account (FSA).** "Cafeteria" or FSAs are plans used to reimburse employees for certain personal expenses. They are provided by employers in conjunction with group health plans to pre-fund dependent care, medical, or dental expenses (often called a health care flexible spending account) in pre-tax dollars (see the 2018 edition of the *Zondervan Church and Nonprofit Tax & Financial Guide* for more information on FSAs).

The only taxable benefit that a cafeteria or FSA can offer is cash. A nontaxable benefit to the participant includes any benefit that is not currently taxable upon receipt. Examples of these benefits are group-term life insurance up to $50,000, coverage under an accident or health plan, and coverage under a dependent care assistance program.

A cafeteria or flexible spending plan cannot discriminate in favor of highly compensated participants for contributions, benefits, or eligibility to participate in the plan. While only larger churches generally offer cafeteria plans because of plan complexity and cost, many churches could feasibly offer an FSA.

There is a $2,600 per person per year FSA contribution limit indexed for inflation for 2017. The money is the account holder's to use during the plan year. Ultimately the employer owns the account and any unused balance at the end of the plan year or any administrative grace period is forfeited to the employer.

An administrative grace period may be adopted as a way to provide relief without running afoul of the prohibition on deferred compensation. Under this provision, employees are permitted a grace period of 2½ months immediately following the end of the plan year. Expenses for qualified benefits incurred during the grace period may be paid or reimbursed from benefits or contributions remaining unused at the end of the plan year. There is also the option of rolling over any unused FSA dollars into the next plan year, but this option is subject to a $500 limit.

➤ **Flexible spending account dependent care plan.** Generally, a dependent care flexible spending account (FSA) is designed to pay for the care of dependent children under age 13 by a babysitter, in a day care center, or in a before-school or after-school program. The maximum amount that may be funded through a dependent care FSA is $5,000 (married, filing jointly), earned income, or spouse's earned income, whichever is lowest.

➤ **Frequent flyer awards.** Free travel awards used personally that were received as frequent flyer miles on business travel paid by the church are not taxable when the awards are used. However, if these awards are converted to cash, they are taxable.

> **Idea**
> The IRS formerly took the position that an individual had tax liability because he or she had received or used frequent flyer miles or other promotional benefits related to the individual's business travel. However, the IRS has reneged, saying these benefits are generally tax-free.

➤ **Gifts/personal.** Money that a minister receives directly from an individual is usually considered a personal gift and may be excluded from income if the payments are intended for the personal benefit of the minister and not in consideration of any services rendered. If the gift is a check, it should be made payable directly to the minister to qualify for tax exclusion for the minister. A personal gift of this nature will not qualify as a charitable contribution by the giver.

➤ **Gifts/special occasion.** Christmas, anniversary, birthday, retirement, and similar gifts paid by a church to its minister are typically taxable compensation. This is true if the gift came from the general fund of the church or from an offering in which tax-deductible contributions were made to the church for the benefit of the minister.

> **Filing Tip**
> Checks payable to the church designated for the benefit of a minister typically represent taxable income when paid to the minister. Such payments may not qualify as charitable contributions because of their possible appearance as conduit/pass-through payments. It is highly preferable for payments of this nature to be made directly to the minister instead of "running them through the church" to try to get a tax deduction.

To qualify as a nontaxable gift, the payment must be based on detached and disinterested generosity, out of affection, respect, admiration, charity, or like impulses.

The transferor's intention is the most critical factor. Also, the gift must be made without consideration of services rendered.

If the church gives the minister a turkey, ham, or other item of nominal value at Christmas or other holidays, the value of the gift is not income. But if the church gives the minister cash or an item that can easily be exchanged for cash, such as a gift card, the gift is extra compensation regardless of the amount involved.

▶ **Health insurance.** If the church pays a minister-employee's qualified group health insurance premiums directly to the insurance carrier, the premiums are tax-free to the minister. However, if similar payments are made for a minister whom the church considers to be self-employed for income tax purposes, the payments represent additional taxable income.

> **Caution**
> Certain non-insurance arrangements (for example, health care sharing ministry plans) are used by some ministers. Since such plans are typically described as non-insurance, the payments by a church to these plans (or to reimburse a minister's payments to these plans) are generally fully taxable.

▶ **Health insurance mandate.** Individuals are now generally required to maintain "minimum essential" health care coverage. If not provided by their employer, ministers must purchase the required coverage from a private insurer or a government-run exchange program. For 2017, the individual tax penalty for not maintaining required coverage equals the greater of (1) $695 per year, up to a maximum of three times that amount per family ($2,085), or (2) 2.5% of household income over the threshold amount of income required for income tax filing.

Among other general exemptions, two specific exemptions from the individual mandate are based on religious belief, one for "religious conscience" and another for "health care sharing ministries." Both exemptions are restrictive, though, in that they require membership or participation in organizations that well pre-date the passage of the health care law (1950 for the religious conscience exemption and 1999 for the health care sharing ministry exception).

For more information on the changes brought by health care reform, see www.healthcare.gov and the 2018 edition of the *Zondervan Church and Nonprofit Tax & Financial Guide*.

▶ **Health reimbursement arrangement (HRA).** A properly designed, written HRA under which the church pays the medical expenses of the minister, spouse, and dependents may be nontaxable to the minister-employee.

> **Caution**
> An HRA may reimburse health care expenses under a plan in which the employer decides how much will be available for each employee. This amount is generally the same for all eligible employees because the nondiscrimination rules apply. Account balances may be carried forward to increase the maximum reimbursement amount in subsequent coverage periods.

HRAs must be integrated with the church's group health insurance plan and only be funded by church-provided funds. Funding by a salary reduction election is not permitted. Excess money in a church-funded HRA can be carried over to a future year without any tax implications to the minister. Because benefits can be carried over indefinitely, the only danger of losing the balance in an HRA account is at retirement or other separation of employment.

Typical expenses covered by such a plan are deductibles, coinsurance, and noncovered amounts paid by the individual.

HRAs may not discriminate in favor of highly compensated employees with regard to either benefits or eligibility. HRAs are only available to employees.

➤ **Health savings account (HSA).** HSAs are individual, portable, tax-free, interest-bearing accounts (typically held by a bank or insurance company) through which individuals with a high-deductible health plan (HDHP) save for medical expenses. The purpose of an HSA is to pay what basic coverage would ordinarily pay.

Within limits, HSA contributions made by employers are excludable from income tax and social security wages and do not affect the computation of the earned income credit. HSA contributions may not be funded through salary reduction. Earnings on amounts in an HSA are not currently taxable, and HSA distributions used to pay for medical expenses are not taxable.

> **Tip**
> HSAs are confidential. Employees are not required to provide medical bills to their employer or to the trustee or custodian of the plan. The employee is responsible to reconcile withdrawals from the HSA with unreimbursed medical expenses.

HSAs can be funded up to $3,400 for individuals and $6,750 for families to cover health care costs (2017 limits). In addition to the maximum contribution amount, catch-up contributions may be made by or on behalf of individuals age 55 or older and younger than 65. Individuals who have reached age 55 by the end of the tax year are allowed to increase their annual contribution limit by $1,000.

Funding of an HSA by the employer may fluctuate from one month to the next. This is unlike a cafeteria or flexible spending account, under which changes in contributions are generally only available on each January 1.

Only employees who are enrolled in qualifying high-deductible plans may participate in an HSA. A HDHP has at least $1,300 annual deductible for self-only coverage and $2,600 deductible for family coverage (2017 limits). Additionally, annual out-of-pocket expenses for HSAs must be limited to $6,550 for individuals and $13,100 (2017 limits) for families. A state high-risk health insurance plan (high-risk pool) qualifies as an HDHP if it does not pay benefits below the minimum annual deductible under the HSA rules.

HSA withdrawals do not qualify to cover over-the-counter medications (other than insulin or doctor-prescribed medicine). Additionally, there is an excise tax for nonqualified HSA withdrawals (withdrawals not used for qualified medical expenses) of 20%.

▶ **Home office.** If their home is their principal place of business, certain taxpayers can deduct a portion of their home expenses (for example, depreciation, utilities, and repairs). However, a home provided by a minister does not generate any home-office deductions if the church designates a housing allowance. With the exclusion of the housing allowance from salary, the housing expenses—including the housing element of home-office expenses—have already been treated as tax-free for income tax purposes.

The status of a home office as a regular or principal place of business may have a direct bearing on the status of commuting vs. business transportation expenses (see pages 105–7).

▶ **Housing allowance.** A properly designated housing allowance may be excluded from income subject to certain limitations (see chapter 4). The fair rental value of a parsonage provided to a minister is not taxable for income tax purposes but is includible for social security tax purposes.

Any housing allowance paid to a minister that is more than the excludable amount is taxable compensation. The excess must be determined by the minister and reported on Form 1040, page 1. The church does not have a reporting requirement to the minister or the IRS regarding any portion of the designated housing allowance that exceeds the amount actually excluded.

▶ **Life insurance/group-term.** If the group life coverage provided under a nondiscriminatory plan does not exceed $50,000 for the minister, the life insurance premiums are generally tax-free to the minister-employee. Premiums for group-term life insurance coverage of more than $50,000 provided to the minister-employee by the church is taxable under somewhat favorable IRS tables. Group-term life insurance is term life insurance protection that:

- ☐ provides a general death benefit that can be excluded from income
- ☐ covers a group of employees (a "group" may consist of only one employee)
- ☐ is provided under a policy carried by the employer
- ☐ provides an amount of insurance for each employee based on a formula that prevents individual selection

> **Caution**
>
> If the church pays the premium on a whole life or universal life policy on the life of the minister and the minister names personal beneficiaries, all the premiums paid are taxable income to the minister.

If a minister pays any part of the cost of insurance, the entire payment reduces, dollar for dollar, the amount the church would otherwise include in income.

CHAPTER 3 ➤ THE PAY PACKAGE

If the minister's group-term life insurance policy includes permanent benefits such as a paid-up or cash surrender value, the minister must include in income the cost of the permanent benefits, reduced by the amount the minister paid for them.

Retired ministers should include in income any payments for group-term life insurance coverage over $50,000 made by a former employing church, unless the minister otherwise qualifies to exclude the payments.

➤ **Loan-grants.** Churches may provide a loan-grant to a minister relating to moving expenses, the purchase of a car, or the purchase of other property. In these instances, compensation is reported on Form W-2 for the minister based on the amount of the loan forgiven in a calendar year. The rules on compensation-related loans (see below) apply to loan-grants over $10,000.

➤ **Loans.** If the church provides a below-market, compensation-related loan to a minister-employee or to a self-employed minister, the employer may be required to include the additional compensation for the foregone interest on the minister's Form W-2 or 1099 (if self-employed).

If the loan proceeds are used for housing, the loan is secured and properly recorded, and the minister itemizes deductions, the minister may be able to deduct the imputed interest as mortgage interest. However, term loan interest must be prorated over the term of the loan. The interest is also eligible for inclusion in housing expenses for housing allowance purposes.

A "compensation-related" loan is any direct or indirect loan of over $10,000 made below market interest rates that relates to the performance of services between a church and a minister. There is an exception for certain employee-relocation loans.

For term loans, additional compensation equal to the foregone interest over the entire term of the loan is considered as received on the date the loan was made. For demand loans, the foregone interest is added to compensation each year that the loan is outstanding.

Loans to minister-employees may be prohibited by state law. Employers should consult with legal counsel before making such a loan.

➤ **Long-term care insurance.** Long-term care or nursing home insurance premiums paid or reimbursed by the church are tax-free. If the premiums are paid by the minister and not reimbursed by the church, they are deductible as medical expenses subject to annual limits based on age.

➤ **Meals.** If meals provided by the church are a means of giving the minister more pay and there is no other business reason for providing them, their value is extra taxable income.

If the meals are furnished by the church for the church's convenience (e.g., having a minister on call) and as a condition of employment, a minister-employee does not include their value in income if the benefits are nondiscriminatory. However, the benefits are taxable for social security purposes.

➤ **Minimal fringe benefits.** If fringe benefits are so small (*de minimis*) in value that it would be unreasonable or impractical to account for them, the minister does not have to include their value in income. If the value of the benefit is not small, its entire value must be included in income.

De minimis fringe benefits for ministers might include traditional holiday gifts with a low fair market value, occasional typing of personal letters by the church secretary, or occasional personal use of the church copy machine.

> **Example:** A minister uses the church copy machine for personal items. The machine is used at least 85% of the time for business purposes since the church restricts personal use of the copy machine. Though the minister uses the machine for personal purposes more than other employees, the use is *de minimis* and not taxable.

➤ **Moving expenses (paid by the church).** Moving expenses paid directly or reimbursed by the church are excludable from gross income (reported on Form W-2, only in Box 12, using Code P to identify them as nontaxable reimbursements) for minister-employees. Amounts are excludable only to the extent that they would be deductible as moving expenses; i.e., only the cost of moving household goods and travel, other than meals, from the old residence to the new residence. Distance and timing tests must also be met.

> **Caution**
> Churches and other employers should review the distance and timing tests to determine if moving expenses paid or reimbursed are includible in, or excludable from, gross pay. For example, the new principal place of work must be at least 50 miles farther from the minister's old residence than the old residence was from the minister's old place of work.

Moving expenses are not deductible in computing self-employment tax on Schedule SE for ministers considered to be self-employed for income tax purposes. For ministers filing as employees for income tax purposes, there is no requirement to add moving expense reimbursements, excluded on Form W-2, to Schedule SE income.

➤ **Parking.** Ministers do not have to include in income the value of free parking facilities provided on or near the church premises if it is $255 or less per month for 2016. This also applies for reimbursements from the church for renting a parking space on or near the church premises. A church can also sell transit passes or tokens to ministers at discounts of up to $255 (2017 limit) per month tax-free or give cash up to $255 for passes and tokens tax-free.

➤ **Pre-employment expense reimbursements.** Prospective ministers may be reimbursed for expenses related to seeking a position with a particular church.

CHAPTER 3 ▸ THE PAY PACKAGE

Substantiated expenses related to interviews (meals, lodging, and travel) are not includible in the prospective employee's gross income whether or not the minister is subsequently employed.

▶ **Property transfers/restricted.** To reward good work, a church may transfer property to a minister subject to certain restrictions. The ultimate transfer of the property will occur only if the restrictions are met at a later date.

Property that is subject to substantial risk of forfeiture and is nontransferable is not substantially vested. No tax liability will occur until title to the property is vested with the minister. This simply represents a deferral of the tax consequences.

> **Caution**
> If property is transferred by the church to a minister at no charge or less than fair market value, the church should report the difference as additional income on the minister's Form W-2.

When restricted property becomes substantially vested, the minister must include in income, for both income and social security tax purposes, an amount equal to the excess of the fair market value of the property at the time it becomes substantially vested, over the amount the minister pays for the property. The church should report the additional income on the minister's Form W-2 or 1099-MISC.

For tax planning purposes, the "vesting" of a restricted property transfer to a minister may be staggered over several years. The reporting of a sizable restricted gift in one year may have significant tax consequences.

Example: A church transfers a house to a minister subject to the completion of 20 years of pastoral service to the church. The minister does not report any taxable income from the gift until the year that includes the twentieth anniversary of the agreement.

▶ **Property transfers/unrestricted.** If a church transfers property (for example, a car, equipment, or other property) to a minister at no charge, this constitutes taxable income to the minister. The amount of income is generally the fair market value of the property transferred as of the date of the transfer.

If a minister buys property from the church at a price below its fair market value, the minister must include in compensation the difference between the property's fair market value and the amount paid for it and liabilities assumed.

▶ **Rabbi Trust.** Rabbi Trusts are used by some churches to "fund" nonqualified 457 deferred compensation plans. Churches make cash contributions to the trust to fund their future obligation to pay deferred compensation benefits. The funds contributed are tax deferred in a similar manner to other tax deferred vehicles such as a 403(b) plan. The name "Rabbi Trust" was established because the first IRS letter ruling with respect to this type of trust involved a rabbi. However, the Rabbi Trust is now widely utilized in commercial enterprises and nonprofit organizations.

In some instances, depending on a participant's includible income (generally, includible income is a participant's salary without including parsonage), churches can make contributions that exceed the IRS maximum annual contribution limits for a 403(b) plan.

A Rabbi Trust is intended to provide a degree of certainty that accumulated deferred compensation benefits will actually be paid. Amounts contributed to an irrevocable Rabbi Trust should not revert to the church until all nonqualified deferred compensation benefits have been paid to eligible participants.

Because trust assets are subject to the claims of the church's creditors in the case of insolvency or bankruptcy, the creation of a Rabbi Trust does not cause the arrangement to be treated as "funded" for income tax purposes.

Distribution rules for Rabbi Trust accounts are not as flexible as for 403(b) accounts. For example, money in a Rabbi Trust is not eligible to be rolled over into qualified retirement plans such as 403(b) plans or IRAs.

➤ **Recreational expenses.** A minister may incur expenses that are primarily recreational, e.g., softball or basketball league fees, greens fees, and so on. Even if there is an element of ministry purpose, the deduction or reimbursement of such fees as business expenses is generally not justified.

➤ **Retirement gifts.** Gifts made to a minister at retirement by the employing church are usually taxable compensation. This is particularly true for minister-employees. Retirement gifts made by an individual directly to a minister may be tax-free to the minister, but they will not qualify as charitable contributions by the donor.

➤ **Retirement plans**

- **401(k) plans.** A church may offer a 401(k) plan to its employees. Under a 401(k) plan, an employee can elect to have the church make tax-deferred contributions, up to $18,000 for 2017 (in addition to catch-up contributions).

- **403(b) plans .** Ministers who are employees for income tax purposes may have a Section 403(b) salary reduction arrangement based on a written plan. Payments to a 403(b) contract by chaplains filing as self-employed for income tax purposes must be deducted on Form 1040, line 36. Such payments are not eligible for pre-tax treatment.

    A minister's housing allowance or the fair rental value of church-provided housing is not included in gross income for income tax reporting purposes. Thus, the definition of computing the limit on 403(b) contributions is generally considered to exclude the portion of a minister's housing allowance excluded

    Caution

    A designated housing allowance generally must be excluded from compensation when calculating TSA contribution limits.

for income tax purposes or the fair rental value of church-provided housing.

Compliance with special nondiscrimination rules may be a condition to a minister benefiting from the Section 403(b) exclusion allowance (see pages 29–30 for more information on these rules). Churches and elementary or secondary schools controlled, operated, or principally supported by a church or convention or association of churches are not subject to the nondiscrimination rules.

Both nonelective (for example, payments by a church into a denominational 403[b] other than funded through a salary reduction agreement) and elective (funded through a salary reduction agreement) contributions for a minister to a 403(b) are excludable for income and social security tax (SECA) purposes. While permissible, after-tax employee contributions are the exception.

There are two separate, yet interrelated limitations on the amount of contributions to a 403(b) plan that are excludable from gross income:

- **Salary reduction limitation.** This limitation is $18,000 for 2017. Employees over age 50 can make a "catch-up" contribution of $6,000 in 2017.

- **Maximum exclusion allowance.** For 2017, the maximum exclusion allowance is $54,000 or 100% of compensation, whichever is less.

A minister can roll funds tax-free from one 403(b) to another 403(b) and from a 403(b) to an IRA. Rollovers are not subject to annual limits.

Withdrawals from a denominationally sponsored 403(b) plan may qualify for designation as a housing allowance and are not subject to social security (SECA) tax (see pages 63–64).

For a comparison between 403(b) and 401(k) plans, see the 2018 edition of the *Zondervan Church and Nonprofit Tax & Financial Guide*.

☐ **Individual retirement accounts.** Amounts contributed by a church for a minister-employee's Individual Retirement Account (IRA) are includible in the employee's compensation on the Form W-2 and are subject to self-employment tax. IRA contributions may fall into one of the following categories:

- **Contributions to a regular IRA.** Each spouse may, in the great majority of cases, make deductible contributions to his or her IRA up to the dollar limitation (e.g., $5,500 reduced by adjusted gross income limits). The adjusted gross income phaseout ranges for 2017 are $99,000 to $119,000 for married taxpayers and $62,000 to $72,000 for singles. (The phaseout amounts are different if the minister-employee is not an active participant but his or her spouse is.) Catch-up contributions of $1,000 may be made by taxpayers age 50 and over.

- **Contributions to a Roth IRA.** Nondeductible contributions may be made to a Roth IRA. The buildup of interest and dividends within the account may be tax-free depending on how and when you withdraw the money from the account.

- ☐ **Keogh plans.** If a minister has self-employment income for income tax purposes, a Keogh plan (also called "qualified retirement plans") may be used. Amounts contributed to a Keogh plan are not taxed until distribution if the contribution limits are observed. If a minister withdraws money from a Keogh plan before reaching the age of 59½, the minister will be subject to a 10% early withdrawal penalty.

➤ **Sabbatical pay.** Unless payments qualify as a tax-free scholarship, sabbatical pay generally represents taxable income. To achieve treatment as a scholarship, the recipient must be a candidate for a degree at an educational institution and the scholarship must be used for tuition.

➤ **Salary.** The cash salary (less the properly designated and excludable housing allowance amount) is taxable income.

➤ **Severance pay.** A lump-sum payment for cancellation of a minister's employment contract is income in the tax year received and must be reported with other compensation.

> **Key Issue**
> The U.S. Supreme Court confirmed in a 2014 case that severance payments constitute taxable wages and are subject to FICA.

➤ **Sick or disability pay.** Amounts ministers receive from their employer while sick or disabled are part of their compensation (sick or disability pay is distinguished from payments for injury provided under Workers' Compensation insurance, which are normally not taxable). A minister must also include in income any payments made by an insurance company if the employer paid the premiums.

If the minister paid the premiums on an accident or health insurance policy, or if the premiums paid by the employer were treated as part of the minister's taxable compensation, the benefits received under the policy are not taxable.

➤ **Simplified employee pension plan (SEP).** Through a SEP, an employer may contribute amounts to a minister's IRA. But there are many nondiscriminatory limitations on SEP contributions that most churches will find insurmountable.

➤ **Social security tax reimbursement.** Churches and other employers commonly reimburse ministers for a portion or all of their self-employment social security (SECA) tax liability. Any social security reimbursement must be reported as taxable income.

Because of the deductibility of the self-employment tax in both the income tax and self-employment tax computations, a full reimbursement is effectively less than the gross 15.3% rate:

Minister's Marginal Tax Rate	Effective SECA Rate
0%	14.13%
10	13.42
15	13.07
27	12.22
30	12.01

It is usually best to reimburse the minister for self-employment tax on a monthly or quarterly basis. An annual reimbursement may leave room for misunderstanding between the church and the minister if the minister moves to another church before the reimbursement is made.

Caution

An allowance to cover the minister's self-employment social security tax provides no tax benefit since the amount is fully taxable. However, paying at least one-half of the minister's social security tax is important so this amount can be properly shown as a fringe benefit for compensation analysis purposes.

For missionaries who are not eligible for the income tax deduction of one-half of the self-employment tax due to the foreign earned income exclusion, the full reimbursement rate is effectively 14.13%.

➤ **Subscriptions.** A church may reimburse a minister for ministry-related magazine subscriptions as a tax-free benefit. Unreimbursed ministry-related subscriptions may be deducted on Schedule A.

➤ **Telephone.** A minister is denied a business deduction or reimbursement for basic local telephone service charges on the first landline in the residence. Additional charges for ministry-related long-distance calls, equipment, optional services, or additional telephone lines may be deductible.

Cell phones and similar devices provided to employees are excludable from an employee's income as a fringe benefit and are not subject to stringent recordkeeping requirements in certain situations. The cell phones must be provided for "substantial reasons relating to the employer's business, other than providing compensation to the employee." Cell phones provided for employee morale or goodwill, or to recruit prospective employees, are not provided for "noncompensatory business purposes." If the organization does not have a substantial noncompensatory business reason for providing a cell phone to an employee, or reimbursing the employee for business use of his or her personal cell phone, the value of the use of the phone or the amount of the reimbursement is includible in gross income, reportable on Forms 941 and W-2, and for lay employees is subject to federal and state employment tax withholding.

➤ **Travel expenses.** Travel expenses of a minister are reimbursable or deductible as business expenses if they are ordinary and necessary and are incurred while traveling away from the minister's tax home for business-related reasons. Expenses that are for personal or vacation purposes, or that are lavish or extravagant, may not be reimbursed or deducted.

Travel expenses incurred outside the United States may be subject to a special business vs. personal travel-expense allocation of the transportation costs to and from the business destination. This allocation can apply even when foreign travel expenses are incurred primarily for business purposes. Expenses incurred for travel as a form of education, such as a tour of the Holy Land, are generally not reimbursable or deductible (see pages 95–96).

If a minister incurs travel expenses for a spouse or child, the minister may deduct or receive a tax-free reimbursement for the spouse's and children's expenses if they qualify for employee treatment and:

> **Caution**
> The travel expenses of an employee's spouse and children often do not qualify for tax-free reimbursement or as a business tax deduction. There must be a bona fide business purpose for the spouse and children to travel, in addition to substantiation of expenses.

☐ the travel is for a bona fide business purpose

☐ the minister-employee substantiates the time, place, amount, and business purpose of the travel under an accountable business expense reimbursement plan

➤ **Tuition and fee discounts.** If a minister is an employee of a church-operated elementary, secondary, or undergraduate institution, certain tuition and fee discounts provided to the minister, spouse, or dependent children are generally tax-free. The discounts must be nondiscriminatory and relate to an educational program.

If the minister is employed by the church and not by the church-related or church-operated private school, any tuition and fee discounts received are taxable income.

> **Tip**
> Tax-free tuition and fee discounts are only available to the dependents of an employee of a school. Discounts provided to church employees are taxable. This is true if the school is operated as part of the church, is a subsidiary corporation under the church, or is separately incorporated.

➤ **Vacation pay.** Payments made by the church to a minister for vacations are taxable income.

➤ **Vehicles/personal use of employer-owned vehicle.** One of the most attractive fringe benefits for a minister is for the church or other employer to own or lease a vehicle for the minister. The church generally makes the lease payments or car loan payments, if any, plus paying for all gas, oil, insurance, repairs, and other related expenses. Unless the vehicle is always parked on the church premises (e.g., where business trips start) and is never used for personal purposes, the minister must maintain a log to document personal use of the vehicle.

The fair market value of the personal use must be included in the minister's gross income unless the minister fully reimburses the value to the church.

Many churches use the annual lease value rule to set a value on the use of a church-provided vehicle. (There are also several other valuation rules that are available.) If the church provides the fuel, 5.5 cents per mile must be added to the annual lease value. See IRS Publication 535 for more information.

> **Example:** The church provides a vehicle for the minister's use for a full year. The vehicle cost was $16,000, and the annual lease value for the year is $4,600 (see table in the 2018 edition of the *Zondervan Church and Nonprofit Tax & Financial Guide*). The minister drives 6,000 miles during the year for the church and 2,000 miles for personal use. The value of the working condition fringe is 6,000 (business miles) divided by 8,000 (total miles) times $4,600 (total value) equals $3,450. The $3,450 value of the working condition fringe is excluded from income. The remaining $1,150 value is for the personal use of the vehicle and must be included in the minister's income. The minister must also add 5.5 cents per mile unless he or she paid for the fuel when the vehicle was used for personal purposes.

➤ **Vehicle use/nonpersonal.** The total value of a qualified nonpersonal-use vehicle is excluded from income as a working condition fringe. The term "qualified nonpersonal-use vehicle" means any vehicle that is not likely to be used more than a small amount for personal purposes because of its nature or design.

> **Example:** A church provides the minister with a vehicle to use for church business. The minister does not qualify for a home office and leaves the car parked at the church when it is not being driven for business purposes. There is a written agreement with the church that prohibits personal use of the vehicle. Only in an emergency is the car driven for personal benefit. This vehicle should qualify under the nonpersonal-use provision, and the entire value of the nonpersonal use of the vehicle would be excluded from income.

➤ **Withholding.** Amounts withheld from pay or put into a minister's bank account under a voluntary withholding agreement for income tax or savings bonds are compensation as though paid directly to the minister. These amounts must be included on Form W-2 in the year they were withheld. The same is generally true of amounts withheld for taxable fringe benefits.

If the church uses wages to pay a minister's debts, or if wages are garnished, the full amount is compensation to the minister.

➤ **Workers' compensation.** A minister who receives workers' compensation benefits due to his job-related injuries or sickness may generally exclude the benefits from gross income. In addition, the minister is not taxed on the value of the insurance premium paid by the church.

Minister-employees are subject to workers' compensation laws in many states. It is often important to cover ministers under workers' compensation insurance even if it is not a state requirement. For work-related injuries of minister-employees, many health benefit plans will not pay medical expenses unless the minister is covered by workers' compensation insurance.

Reporting Compensation, Fringe Benefits, and Reimbursements for Income Tax Purposes*

Compensation, fringe benefit, or reimbursement	Minister-Employee
Bonus or gift from church	Taxable income/Form W-2
Business and professional expenses reimbursed with adequate accounting	Tax-free/excluded
Business and professional expense payments without adequate accounting	Deduction on Schedule A, Miscellaneous Deductions. Subject to 2% of AGI and 50% meals and entertainment limits
Club dues paid by the church	Taxable income/Form W-2 (exception for dues for professional organizations and civic and public service groups)
Compensation reported to minister by church	Form W-2
Dependent care assistance payments	Tax-free
Educational assistance programs	May be eligible to exclude up to $5,250 of qualified assistance
401(k) plan	Eligible for 401(k) (either tax-deferred or taxable with tax-free growth)
403(b) plan	Eligible for 401(k) (either tax-deferred or taxable with tax-free growth)
Gifts/personal (not handled through church)	Tax-free/excluded
Housing allowance	Excludable
Health reimbursement arrangement	Tax-free
Health savings account	Tax-free
Health care flexible spending account	Tax-free
IRA payments by church	Taxable income/Form W-2, may be deducted on Form 1040, line 32
Insurance, disability, paid by church, minister is beneficiary	Premiums are tax-free, but proceeds are taxable
Insurance, disability, paid by minister, minister is beneficiary	Premiums paid after-tax, proceeds are tax-free
Insurance, group-term life, paid by church	Premiums on first $50,000 of coverage is tax-free

*Many of these compensation elements are conditioned on plans being properly established and/or subject to annual limits.

CHAPTER 3 ➤ THE PAY PACKAGE

Compensation, fringe benefit, or reimbursement	Minister-Employee
Insurance, health	Tax-free if directly paid by church as part of a qualifying group plan If paid by minister and not reimbursed by church, deduct on Schedule A subject to 10% floor
Insurance, life, whole or universal, church is beneficiary	Tax-free/excluded
Insurance, life, whole or universal, minister designates beneficiary	Taxable income/Form W-2
Insurance, long-term care	Tax-free if directly paid by church or reimbursed to minister on substantiation. If paid by minister and not reimbursed by church, deduct on Schedule A subject to limitations
Loans, certain low-interest or interest-free to minister over $10,000	Imputed interest (the difference between the IRS-established interest rate and the rate charged) is taxable income/Form W-2
Moving expenses paid by the church (only applies to certain qualified expenses)	Tax-free if directly paid by church or reimbursed to minister on substantiation. Reported on Form W-2, only in Box 12 using Code P
Pension payments to a denominational plan for the minister by the church	Tax-deferred. No reporting required until the funds are withdrawn or pension benefits are paid
Per diem payments for meals, lodging, and incidental expenses	May be used for travel away from home under an accountable reimbursement plan
Professional income (weddings, funerals)	Taxable income/Schedule C (C-EZ)
Property transferred to minister at no cost or less than fair market value	Taxable income/Form W-2
Retirement or farewell gift to minister from church	Generally taxable income/Form W-2
Salary from church	Report salary on Form W-2, Box 1
Social security reimbursed by church to minister	Taxable income/Form W-2
Travel paid for minister's spouse by the church	May be tax-free if there is a business purpose
Tuition and fee discounts	May be tax-free in certain situations
Value of home provided to minister (parsonage)	Tax-free/excluded
Vehicles/personal use of church-owned auto	Taxable income/Form W-2
Voluntary withholding	Eligible for voluntary withholding agreement

Integrity Points

- **Reimbursing out-of-pocket medical expenses.** Sadly, most ministers do not have one of the four plans under which out-of-pocket medical expenses may be reimbursed on a tax-free basis. As explained in this chapter, offering these plans has become more complex under health care reform.

  ○ Cafeteria plan. Generally only very large churches can justify establishing and maintaining a cafeteria plan. These plans can cover much more than medical expenses—for example, dependent care, life insurance, and disability insurance.

  ○ Health Savings Account (HSA). This concept is valid but it has grown very slowly.

  ○ Health reimbursement arrangement (HRA). The same HRA benefit must be provided to all employees. This makes this concept very limiting since out-of-pocket costs significantly vary employee-to-employee.

  ○ Flexible spending account (FSA). The FSA should generally be the plan of choice for many ministers and churches. The FSA is simple to establish and easy to administer by the church.

- **The impact of the nondiscrimination rules on ministers.** While the nondiscrimination rules do not impact many fringe benefits (see pages 49–50), these rules do apply to all of the four plans under which out-of-pocket medical expenses (see above) may be reimbursed.

  Often a congregation will reimburse out-of-pocket medical expenses for the staff at varying levels, e.g., up to $1,000 for the senior pastor, up to $500 for the associate pastor, and up to $300 for a secretary under an HRA. This arrangement fails the nondiscrimination test.

- **Discretionary funds.** If a congregation provides a minister with discretionary funds (funds to provide benevolence assistance as needs are identified by the minister), the accounting to the church for these funds is vital. Unless a minister documents the date the funds were spent, the recipient of the funds, and the benevolent need, discretionary funds are generally taxable to the minister as compensation.

- **Other integrity points.** Appropriate tax reporting of love offerings, gifts, and the personal use of employer-provided vehicles are other areas requiring integrity.

CHAPTER 4
Housing Exclusion

In This Chapter

- Types of housing arrangements
- Establishing and modifying the housing designation
- Reporting the housing allowance to the minister
- Accounting for the housing exclusion
- Other housing exclusion issues
- Housing exclusion worksheets

Qualified ministers (see chapter 1 for who is a qualified minister under tax law) are eligible to receive lodging from a church free of income tax liability by excluding dollars from gross income. Maximizing housing benefits requires careful planning. Used properly, the housing allowance can truly be the minister's best tax friend.

If the church properly designates a portion of the minister's cash salary for expenses of a home they provide, it is commonly referred to as a "housing allowance." If the church properly designates a portion of the minister's cash salary for expenses they incur in relation to church-provided housing, it is often called a "parsonage allowance." In either instance, it is an exclusion from federal income tax, not self-employment social security tax.

It is a tax advantage for nearly every qualified minister to have a portion of salary designated as a housing allowance. For ministers living in church-owned housing, the housing exclusion covering expenses such as furnishings, personal property insurance on contents, and utilities could save several hundred dollars of income taxes annually. For ministers living in their own homes or rental housing, a properly designated housing allowance may be worth thousands of dollars of income tax saved.

The designated housing allowance should be subtracted from compensation before the church completes the data on Form W-2. The housing allowance designation is not entered on Form 1040 or related schedules, except Schedule SE, since it is not a deduction for income tax purposes. However, any unused portion of the housing designation must be reported as income on page 1, Form 1040.

53

Employer-Provided Housing

The fair rental value of the housing plus utilities (if the utilities are paid by employer) is

- Excludable for federal income tax purposes, and
- Includible for social security (SECA) purposes.

A housing allowance may also be provided to a minister living in employer-provided housing. It is a designation of the cash salary. A minister may utilize the housing exclusion to exclude certain housing expenses paid by the minister (see the worksheet on page 66).

Minister-Provided Housing

The housing exclusion is not taxable for federal income tax purposes. The entire housing allowance is taxable for social security tax (SECA) purposes. See the worksheets on pages 67 and 68 for excludable expenses. The housing exclusion (which doesn't exceed reasonable compensation) is the lowest of these three factors:

1. Amount used from current ministerial income to provide the home
2. Amount prospectively and officially designated by the employer
3. Fair rental value of the home including utilities and furnishings

Any excess over the lowest of these factors is reportable as additional income for income tax purposes.

CHAPTER 4 > HOUSING EXCLUSION

Ministers are eligible to exclude the fair rental value of church-provided housing for income tax purposes without any official action by the church. However, a cash housing allowance related to church-provided or minister-provided housing is only excludable under the following rules:

➤ **The allowance must be officially designated by the church.** The designation should be stated in writing, preferably by resolution of the top governing body, in an employment contract, or by a committee of the board. If the only reference to the housing allowance is in the church budget, the budget should be formally approved by the top governing body of the church. See the 2018 edition of the *Zondervan Church and Nonprofit Tax & Financial Guide* for examples of housing allowance resolutions.

Tax law does not specifically say that an oral designation of the housing allowance is unacceptable. In certain instances, the IRS has accepted an oral housing designation. Still, the use of a written designation is preferable and highly recommended. The lack of a written designation significantly weakens the defense for the housing exclusion upon audit.

➤ **The housing allowance must be designated prospectively by the church.** Cash housing allowance payments made prior to a designation of the housing allowance are fully taxable for income tax purposes. Carefully word the resolution so that it will remain in effect until a subsequent resolution is adopted.

➤ **Only actual expenses can be excluded from income.** The source of the funds used to pay for a minister's housing expenses must be compensation earned by the minister in the exercise of ministry in the current year.

➤ **Only an annual comparison of housing expenses to the housing allowance by a minister is required.** For example, if the housing allowance designation is stated in terms of a weekly or monthly amount, only a comparison of actual housing expenses to the annualized housing allowance is required. However, if there is an adjustment during the year in the amount that was designated by the church, the minister must consider how the actual expenses were incurred before and after the amount was changed when determining the amount for exclusion.

➤ **The housing allowance exclusion cannot exceed the fair rental value of the housing, including furnishings, plus utilities.**

Another useful resource is the ECFA eBook *10 Essentials of the Minister's Housing Exclusion*.

> **Key Issue**
> Understanding the distinction between a housing allowance designation and the housing exclusion is fundamental. The designation is officially made by the church or other employer. The exclusion is the amount the minister actually excludes for income tax purposes after applying the limitations outlined in this chapter.

Types of Housing Arrangements

Minister living in church-provided housing

If you live in a church-owned parsonage or housing rented by the church, the fair rental value of the housing is not reported for income tax purposes. The fair rental value is subject only to self-employment tax.

The minister may also request a housing allowance to cover expenses they incur in maintaining the church-owned or church-rented housing. The cash housing allowance that is not more than reasonable pay for services is excludable for income tax purposes, subject to the lowest of (1) actual housing expenses paid from current ministerial income, or (2) the amount prospectively and officially designated. Examples of allowable expenses are utilities, repairs, furnishings, and appliances. If the actual expenses exceed the housing allowance designated by the church, the excess amount cannot be excluded from income. The expenses shown on the worksheet on page 66 qualify as part of the housing allowance for a minister living in housing owned or rented by the church.

> **Tip**
> The designation of a housing allowance for a minister living in church-provided housing is often overlooked. While the largest housing allowance benefits go to ministers with mortgage payments on their own homes, a housing allowance of a few thousand dollars is often beneficial to a pastor in a church-provided home.

It is appropriate for the minister's out-of-pocket expenses for the maintenance of a church-owned parsonage to be reimbursed by the church if a full accounting is made. Such reimbursements do not relate to a housing allowance. If such expenses are not reimbursed, they could be excludable from income under a housing allowance.

If the church owns the parsonage, the church may wish to provide an equity allowance to help compensate the minister for equity not accumulated through home ownership. An equity allowance is taxable for both income and social security tax purposes unless directed to a 403(b) tax-sheltered annuity, 401(k) plan, or certain other retirement programs.

Minister owning or renting own home

If the minister owns or rents their own home, they may exclude, for income tax purposes, a cash housing allowance that is not more than reasonable pay for services and that is the lowest of (1) the amount used to provide a home from current ministerial income, (2) the amount prospectively and officially designated, or (3) the fair rental value of the furnished home, plus utilities.

The expenses shown on the worksheet on page 67 qualify as part of the housing allowance for a minister owning or buying a home. Page 68 shows a similar worksheet for a minister renting a home.

CHAPTER 4 ➤ HOUSING EXCLUSION

Many ministers make the mistake of automatically excluding from income (for income tax purposes) the total designated housing allowance, even though the fair rental value of the furnished home or actual housing expenses are less than the designation. This practice may cause a significant underpayment of income taxes.

The housing expenses related to a minister-owned house should not be reimbursed by the church. These expenses should be covered by the minister under a cash housing allowance paid by the church.

> **Example:** A minister lives in a personally owned home. The church prospectively designates $18,000 of the salary as housing allowance. The minister spends $17,000 for housing-related items. The fair rental value of the home is $19,000.
>
> Since the amount spent for housing expenses is lower than the designated housing allowance or the fair rental value, the excludable portion of the housing allowance is $17,000. Therefore, $1,000 ($18,000 less $17,000) must be added to taxable income on the minister's Form 1040, page 1, line 7. Unless the minister has opted out of social security, the entire $18,000 is reportable for social security purposes on Schedule SE.

Establishing and Modifying the Housing Designation

Before paying compensation

The employer should take the following steps to designate a housing designation before paying compensation:

➤ Verify the qualified tax status of the minister. Does the minister meet the tests found on pages 2–9?

➤ Verify the qualified nature of the minister's services, e.g., administering sacraments, conducting religious worship, performing management responsibilities for a church, a denomination, or an integral agency of a church or denomination, or the services performed for a parachurch or other organization (see pages 2–9).

➤ Determine the extent to which payment of housing expenses will be the responsibility of the minister. For example, will the utilities for a church-owned parsonage be paid by the church or the minister?

➤ Request that the minister estimate the housing-related expenses expected in the coming year which are the minister's responsibility.

Warning

It is the responsibility of the church or other employer—not the minister—to determine if an individual qualifies as a minister in the eyes of the IRS and, therefore, qualifies for a housing designation. Simply being ordained, licensed, or commissioned is not enough to qualify for this status.

57

➤ Adopt a written designation based on the minister's estimate. This designation may be included in minutes or resolutions of the top governing body, an employment contract, annual budget, or another appropriate document if official action on the document is recorded.

During the calendar year

The following actions should be taken during the year (after the housing designation is made):

➤ The minister should keep records of allowable housing expenses incurred.

➤ The minister should make payments to the IRS to cover the self-employment tax (SECA) on the entire housing allowance (and other income subject to SECA) plus federal income tax on any anticipated unexpended portion of the allowance and other taxable income. This may be accomplished by submitting quarterly tax installments with Form 1040-ES, voluntary income tax withholding by the minister's employer, or spousal income tax withholding.

➤ The minister should identify any significant change in housing expenses and estimate the amount by which the total actual expenses may exceed the amount designated as the housing allowance.

➤ When housing expenses are running higher than anticipated or are expected to do so, the minister should ask the church to prospectively increase the housing allowance designation. A retroactive housing allowance increase is ineffective.

➤ The church should prospectively amend the minister's housing allowance as appropriate to reflect the anticipated change in housing expenses (see page 60).

After each calendar year

The following steps should be taken after the close of each calendar year with respect to the housing allowance:

➤ The church should provide the minister with copies of Form W-2. An approved housing allowance paid to the minister may be included on Form W-2 in Box 14 with the explanation: "Housing Allowance." As an option, the church can provide the minister with a separate statement showing the amount of any housing allowance paid to or for the minister and omit the data from Form W-2.

The minister who provides his or her own housing should compare reasonable compensation, the amount designated for housing, actual housing expenses, and the fair rental value. The lowest of these amounts is excluded for income tax purposes.

Ministers living in church-provided housing must compare reasonable compensation, the amount designated, and actual housing expenses, and exclude the lowest of these amounts.

Designation limits

The IRS does not place a limit on how much of a minister's compensation may be designated as a housing allowance by the employer. In a few instances, as much as 100% of the cash compensation may be designated. But practical and reasonable limits apply.

A housing allowance must not represent "unreasonable compensation" to the minister. Unfortunately, neither the IRS nor the courts have provided a clear definition of unreasonable compensation. The IRS considers the total compensation package, including the housing allowance and taxable and nontaxable fringe benefits. This amount is often compared with the church's annual budget and may be compared with other similar-sized churches.

Unless the amount is justified based on anticipated housing expenses within the exclusion limitations, it is generally unwise for the employing church to exclude 100% of compensation.

> **Caution**
> How high is too high? Can even 100% of a minister's cash salary be designated as a housing allowance? Yes, but only in limited situations. The fair rental value and actual housing expense limitations usually make the 100% designation inappropriate.

Example 1: A minister provides her own housing. The fair rental value, furnished plus utilities, is $15,000. She anticipates spending $18,000 on housing. Should the church designate a housing allowance of $15,000 or at least $18,000? A designation of $15,000 should be made since the minister cannot exclude more than this amount.

Example 2: A bi-vocational minister receives a salary of $10,000 per year from the church and provides his home. Actual housing costs are $12,000. If the church sets the housing allowance at 100% of compensation, or $10,000, the minister may exclude $10,000 for federal income tax purposes. If the church had set the housing allowance at 50% of compensation, or $5,000, only $5,000 could be excluded.

Example 3: A minister has a voluntary withholding arrangement with the church, and the church sets the housing allowance at 100% of compensation. Form W-2 would show no salary (ignoring other compensation factors) but would reflect federal income tax and possibly state income tax withheld. While Form W-2 would be correctly stated, its appearance would be most unusual.

> **Remember**
> The housing allowance designation may be prospectively amended at any time during the year, regardless of whether the church or other employer uses a calendar or fiscal year. Changing the designation to cover expenses that have already been paid (almost all ministers use the cash basis for tax purposes) is not advantageous.

It is often best to over-designate your housing allowance by a reasonable amount, subject to the fair rental value limitation, to allow for unexpected housing expenses and increases in utility costs.

Any excess housing allowance designated should be shown as income on line 7 of Form 1040 with the notation "Excess allowance."

More than one housing allowance?

The Tax Court has ruled that a minister may only exclude housing expenses of one home, the principal residence. This ruling is important to many ministers because it is not unusual for a minister to own two homes at the same time. Multiple ownership most often occurs when a minister buys a new home and has not yet sold a former home. Based on the Tax Court ruling there is no basis to exclude housing expenses of two homes owned concurrently.

Amending the housing designation

If a minister's actual housing expenses are or will be higher than initially estimated and designated, the church may prospectively amend the designation during the year.

> **Example:** The church sets the housing allowance at $2,000 per month on January 1. On July 1, the church approves an increase in the housing allowance to $2,400 per month. Therefore, the housing allowance for the year totals $26,400 ($12,000 for the first six months and $14,400 for the last six months). Actual housing costs are $2,100 per month for the first six months and $2,300 per month for the last six months. The fair rental value of the home is $2,500 per month. The minister excludes $25,800 for federal income tax purposes: $12,000 for the first six months (limited by the designation) and $13,800 for the last six months (limited by the actual housing costs).

Housing allowance adopted by denomination

If the local congregation employs and pays a minister, a resolution by a national or area office of their denomination does not constitute a housing allowance designation. The local congregation must officially designate a part of the minister's salary as a housing allowance. A resolution of their denomination can designate their housing allowance if they are employed and paid by a national or area office or if they are a retired minister receiving retirement funds from a denominational retirement plan.

Reporting the Housing Allowance to the Minister

The designated housing allowance may be reflected on Form W-2 in Box 14 with the notation, "Housing Allowance." Though not required, this reporting method is suggested by IRS Publication 517.

Alternatively, a church can report the designated housing allowance to a minister by providing a statement separate from Form W-2. This may be in a memo or letter. The statement need not be attached to your income tax returns.

CHAPTER 4 ➢ HOUSING EXCLUSION

A church might erroneously include the housing allowance on the minister's Form W-2, Box 1. If this happens, the church should prepare a corrected form.

There is no requirement for the minister to account to the church for the actual housing expenses. Many ministers consider this as an intrusion into their personal finances. However, if the church requires this reporting, based on administrative discretion, the church would prepare Form W-2 with the adjusted housing allowance excluded. Under this approach, the excluded housing is always equal to or less than the housing designation.

> **Tip**
> The designated housing allowance should always be excluded from Form W-2, Box 1, as compensation. Including the housing allowance in this box can cause unnecessary communication between the IRS and the minister.

Accounting for the Housing Exclusion

Determining fair rental value

The determination of the fair rental value of church-provided housing for self-employment social security tax purposes is solely the responsibility of the minister. The church is not responsible to set the value. The fair rental value should be based on comparable rental values of other similar residences in the immediate community, comparably furnished.

One of the best methods to establish the fair rental value of the minister's housing is to request a local realtor to estimate the value in writing. They can place the estimate in their tax file and annually adjust the value for inflation and other local real estate valuation factors.

> **Caution**
> Even though the fair rental value test is etched into law, there have been no changes in the sketchy guidance provided by the IRS as to how to determine the fair rental value.

Housing allowance in excess of actual expenses or fair rental value

Some ministers erroneously believe that they may exclude every dollar of the housing designation adopted by the church without limitation. The housing designation is merely the starting point. If reasonable compensation, actual expenses, or the fair rental value is lower, the lowest amount is eligible for exclusion from income.

> **Example:** A minister living in a personally-home owned receives cash compensation from the church of $60,000. The church prospectively designates $20,000 as a housing allowance. The fair rental value is $21,000. Actual housing expenses for the year are $18,000. The amount excludable from income is limited to the actual housing expenses of $18,000.

61

Determining actual expenses

The actual amount expended for housing and furnishings is limited to amounts expended in the current calendar year. Amounts expended in a prior year cannot be carried forward to a following year through depreciation or by carrying forward actual current year expenses that exceeded amounts designated in a prior year. Housing expenses from prior years that are not used to justify a housing allowance exclusion simply have no value in future years.

Home equity loans and second mortgages

Without a home mortgage, a minister has no mortgage principal and interest amounts to exclude under a housing allowance. Also, there would be no "double benefit" of the mortgage interest as an itemized deduction and as a housing expense for purposes of the housing allowance exclusion.

> **Warning**
> Loan payments on home equity loans and second mortgages qualify as housing expenses only in certain instances. The use of the loan proceeds as housing expenses vs. non-housing expenses determines whether the loan payments may be excluded for income tax purposes.

What is the treatment of principal and interest payments on a second mortgage or a mortgage that has been refinanced to increase the indebtedness? This issue has not been addressed by the IRS or a court. However, it appears that an allocation of the loan payments between excludable housing expenses and nonexcludable personal expenses would be required based on the use of the additional loan proceeds.

Do principal and interest payments on a home equity loan qualify as excludable housing expenses? The IRS and the Tax Court have ruled that the loan or mortgage payments are excludable as housing expenses only if the loan proceeds are used for housing expenses. The exclusion is not available if the loan proceeds are used for personal expenses such as the purchase of an auto or for a child's college education. The interest is only deductible on Schedule A if the note is secured.

> **Example:** A home equity loan of $20,000 was obtained by a minister, secured by the residence. The money was used as follows: $10,000 for a new car and $10,000 to add a deck and screened-in porch to the minister's home. The home equity loan payments relating to funds used to purchase the new car are not excludable as housing expenses. Since the other $10,000 was used for housing, the payments relating to this portion of the loan qualify as housing expenses.

Other Housing Exclusion Issues

Payment of the housing allowance to the minister

It is immaterial whether the payment of a properly designated cash housing allowance is a separate payment or is part of a payment that also includes other compensation.

A cash housing allowance is usually included with the minister's salary check.

Cost of the housing allowance to the church

Some churches mistakenly believe that providing a housing allowance to their minister will increase the church budget. This is not true. If a portion of the minister's compensation is designated as a housing allowance, it costs the church nothing and increases the "take home pay" of the minister.

> **Example:** A church pays a minister $75,000 per year but does not presently designate a housing allowance. The minister provides the home. The minister requests that the church designate a housing allowance of $30,000 per year. The church adopts a resolution reflecting compensation of $75,000 per year, of which $30,000 is a designated housing allowance. Before the designation, Form W-2 for the minister would have shown compensation of $75,000. After the designation, Form W-2 would reflect compensation of $45,000. The cash spent by the church is the same before and after the designation, and the minister saves a significant amount in taxes.

"Double benefit" of interest and taxes

Ministers who own their homes and itemize their deductions are eligible to deduct mortgage interest and property taxes on Schedule A even though these items are also excluded from taxable income as part of the housing allowance. This is also referred to as a "double benefit" or "double deduction."

Housing allowances for retired ministers

Pension payments, retirement allowances, or disability payments paid to a retired minister from an established plan are generally taxable as pension income. However, denominations often designate a housing allowance for retired ministers to compensate them for past services to local churches of the denomination, to the denomination itself, or in denominational administrative positions. The housing allowance designated relates only to payments from the denominationally sponsored retirement program.

Withdrawals from a denominationally sponsored 403(b) plan, also called a tax-sheltered annuity (TSA), or 401(k) plan qualify for designation as a housing allowance. Withdrawals from a 403(b) or 401(k) plan not sponsored by a church are not eligible for designation as a housing allowance.

Retired ministers may also exclude the rental value of a home furnished by a church or a rental allowance paid by a church as compensation for past services.

> **Remember**
> Payments from denominational retirement plans are generally allowed to be designated as housing allowance. While a local church may designate a housing allowance for a retired minister, it is unclear if the IRS will honor the designation on the minister's tax return.

Can a local church (as contrasted with a denomination) or a nondenominational local church designate a housing allowance for a retired minister for the church's contributions to a minister's 403(b) plan? While IRS rulings in this area are not specific, a church has a reasonable and supportable position to make the designation. However, it is unclear whether the IRS will accept a housing exclusion on the minister's tax return based on such a designation.

If a denomination or church reports the gross amount of pension or TSA payments on Form 1099-R and designates the housing allowance, the recipient may offset the housing expenses and insert the net amount on page 1, Form 1040. A supplementary schedule such as the following example should be attached to the tax return:

Pensions and annuity income (Form 1040, line 16a)	$10,000
Less housing exclusion	8,000
Form 1040, line 16b	$2,000

For a retired minister, the amount excluded for income tax purposes is limited to the lowest of (1) the amount used to provide a home, (2) the properly designated housing allowance, or (3) the fair rental value of the furnished home, plus utilities.

A surviving spouse of a retired minister cannot exclude a housing allowance from income. If a minister's surviving spouse receives a rental allowance, it is includible in gross income.

Housing allowances for evangelists

Traveling evangelists may treat a portion of an honorarium received as an excludable housing allowance to the extent that the paying church designates all or a portion of the honorarium as a housing allowance in advance of payment. Honoraria payments of $600 or more in a calendar year to an evangelist require the church to issue Form 1099-MISC. The $600 reporting threshold is after excluding any properly designated housing allowances and the net of expense reimbursements based on adequate substantiation.

> **Example:** William Dalton, an ordained evangelist, preaches at Westside Church for ten days. Westside Church paid Mr. Dalton $1,500 consisting of $300 documented travel expenses, a properly designated housing allowance of $500, and a $700 honorarium. Since the non-excludable portion of the honorarium exceeded $600, the church issued Mr. Dalton a Form 1099-MISC for $700.

Housing allowances for teachers or administrators

A minister employed as a teacher or administrator by a church school, college, or university is performing ministerial services for purposes of the housing exclusion. However, if they perform services as a teacher or administrator on the faculty of a nonchurch college, they cannot exclude from their income a housing allowance or the value of a home that is provided to them.

CHAPTER 4 ➤ HOUSING EXCLUSION

Integrity*Points*

- **Properly determining who qualifies for a housing allowance.** The designation of a portion of cash compensation as a housing allowance is only available to certain ministers. Ordination, licensure, or commissioning of a minister alone is not enough.

  The first integrity step for a church or parachurch organization is to determine whether an individual qualifies for the designation of a housing allowance. The various rules for ministers serving a local church, serving as evangelists or missionaries, assigned by a church, or functioning in other service positions are discussed in chapter 1.

- **Applying the limits on the exclusion.** The designation of a housing allowance for a qualified minister is an action required by the employer (usually a church), formally and prospectively. However, it is the minister's responsibility to determine how much of the housing allowance designation qualifies for exclusion from federal, and perhaps state, income taxes. Remarkably, the IRS does not require the reporting of the application of the housing exclusion limits. But the law and integrity require the limits be applied.

  For the vast majority of ministers, the most overlooked test is the fair rental value, including furnishings, plus utilities. The housing allowance designation by the church or parachurch organization (see first IntegrityPoint) is only the starting point.

  The fair rental value, including furnishings, plus utilities is admittedly a "soft" number because the guidance provided by the IRS is vague on this topic. But an honest effort to reasonably determine this number is essential.

  The excess housing allowance, which is the designated housing allowance less the lowest of the housing exclusion limitations (see page 59–60), must be reported on Form 1040, line 7. This results in the excess housing allowance being subjected to federal, and perhaps state, income taxes.

65

Housing Exclusion Worksheet
Minister Living in a Parsonage
Owned by or Rented by the Church

Minister's name:_____

For the period _____, 20___ to _____, 20_____

Date designation approved _____, 20___

Allowable Housing Expenses *(expenses paid by minister from current income)*

	Estimated Expenses	Actual
Utilities *(gas, electricity, water)* and trash collection	$_____	$_____
Local telephone expense *(base charge)*	_____	_____
Decoration and redecoration	_____	_____
Structural maintenance and repair	_____	_____
Landscaping, gardening, and pest control	_____	_____
Furnishings *(purchase, repair, replacement)*	_____	_____
Personal property insurance on minister-owned contents	_____	_____
Personal property taxes on contents	_____	_____
Umbrella liability insurance	_____	_____
Subtotal	_____	
10% allowance for unexpected expenses	_____	
TOTAL	$_____	$_____ (A)
Properly designated housing allowance		$_____ (B)

The amount excludable from income for federal income tax purposes is the lower of A or B (or reasonable compensation).

Housing Exclusion Worksheet
Minister Living in Home
Minister Owns or Is Buying

Minister's name:_____

For the period _____, 20____ to _____, 20_____

Date designation approved _____, 20____

Allowable Housing Expenses *(expenses paid by minister from current income)*

	Estimated Expenses	Actual
Down payment on purchase of housing	$_____	$_____
Housing loan principal and interest payments	_____	_____
Real estate commission, escrow fees	_____	_____
Real property taxes	_____	_____
Personal property taxes on contents	_____	_____
Homeowner's insurance	_____	_____
Personal property insurance on contents	_____	_____
Umbrella liability insurance	_____	_____
Structural maintenance and repair	_____	_____
Landscaping, gardening, and pest control	_____	_____
Furnishings *(purchase, repair, replacement)*	_____	_____
Decoration and redecoration	_____	_____
Utilities *(gas, electricity, water)* and trash collection	_____	_____
Local telephone expense *(base charge)*	_____	_____
Homeowner's association dues/condominium fees	_____	_____

Subtotal _____

10% allowance for unexpected expenses _____

TOTAL $_____ $_____ (A)

Properly designated housing allowance $_____ (B)

Fair rental value of home, including furnishings, plus utilities $_____ (C)

The amount excludable from income for federal income tax purposes is the lowest of A, B, or C (or reasonable compensation).

Housing Exclusion Worksheet
Minister Living in Home Minister Is Renting

Minister's name:_____

For the period _____, 20___ to _____, 20_____

Date designation approved _____, 20___

Allowable Housing Expenses *(expenses paid by minister from current income)*

	Estimated Expenses	Actual
Housing rental payments	$_____	$_____
Personal property insurance on minister-owned contents	_____	_____
Personal property taxes on contents	_____	_____
Umbrella liability	_____	_____
Structural maintenance and repair	_____	_____
Landscaping, gardening, and pest control	_____	_____
Furnishings *(purchase, repair, replacement)*	_____	_____
Decoration and redecoration	_____	_____
Utilities *(gas, electricity, water)* and trash collection	_____	_____
Local telephone expense *(base charge)*	_____	_____
Other rental expenses	_____	_____
Subtotal	_____	
10% allowance for unexpected expenses	_____	
TOTAL	$_____	$_____ (A)
Properly designated housing allowance		$_____ (B)

The amount excludable from income for federal income tax purposes is the lower of A or B (or reasonable compensation).

CHAPTER 5

Business Expenses

In This Chapter

- Accountable and nonaccountable expense reimbursement plans
- Substantiating and reporting business expenses
- Travel and transportation expenses
- Auto expense deductions
- Home-office rules
- Other business expenses
- Allocation of business expenses

Most ministers spend several thousand dollars each year on church-related business expenses. For example, the ministry-related portion of auto expenses is often a major cost. You only have two choices: try to deduct the expenses for tax purposes or have the expenses reimbursed by the church under an accountable expense reimbursement plan. You will almost always save tax dollars if your expenses are reimbursed.

Business and professional expenses fall into three basic categories: (1) expenses reimbursed under an accountable plan, (2) expenses paid under a nonaccountable plan, and (3) unreimbursed expenses. The last two categories are treated the same for tax purposes.

The reimbursement of an expense never changes the character of the item from personal to business. Business expenses are business expenses whether or not they are reimbursed. Personal expenses are always nondeductible and nonreimbursable. If a personal expense is inadvertently reimbursed by the employer, the minister should immediately refund the money to the employer.

To be deductible or reimbursable, a business expense must be both ordinary and necessary. An ordinary expense is one that is common and accepted in your field. A necessary expense is one that is helpful and appropriate for your field. An expense does not have to be indispensable to be considered necessary.

> **Key Issue**
> Combining an accountable expense reimbursement plan with a housing allowance or any other fringe benefit plan is not permissible. These concepts are each covered under separate sections of the tax law and cannot be commingled.

Accountable and Nonaccountable Expense Reimbursement Plans

An accountable plan is a reimbursement or expense allowance arrangement established by the church that requires (1) a business purpose for the expenses, (2) substantiation of expenses to the employer, and (3) the return of any excess reimbursements. A sample plan is included in the 2018 edition of the *Zondervan Church and Nonprofit Tax & Financial Guide*.

The substantiation of expenses and the return of excess reimbursements must be handled within a reasonable time. The following methods meet the "reasonable time" definition:

- ▶ The fixed date method applies if:
    - ☐ an advance is made within 30 days of when an expense is paid or incurred
    - ☐ an expense is substantiated to the employer within 60 days after the expense is paid or incurred
    - ☐ any excess amount is returned to the church within 120 days after the expense is paid or incurred

- ▶ The periodic statement method applies if:
    - ☐ the employer provides employees with a periodic statement that sets forth the amount paid that is more than substantiated expenses under the arrangement
    - ☐ the statements are provided at least quarterly
    - ☐ the employer requests that the employee provide substantiation for any additional expenses that have not yet been substantiated and/or return any amounts remaining unsubstantiated within 120 days of the statement

> **Caution**
> Documentation for business expenses must be submitted to the church or other employer on a timely basis—within 60 days after the expense was paid or incurred. While the 60 days is a timeliness "safe harbor" vs. a fixed time limit, it is clear that documentation submitted semiannually or annually should not be reimbursed under an accountable plan.

If a minister substantiates business expenses and any unused payments are returned, expense reimbursements have no impact on their taxes. The expenses reimbursed are not included on Form W-2 or deducted on your tax return.

Example 1: The church adopts an accountable reimbursement plan using the "fixed date method." The church authorizes salary of $76,000 and in a separate action, without an indication that the reimbursements are being funded out of what otherwise would be the minister's salary, agrees to pay business expenses up to $10,000.

During the year, the minister substantiates $9,000 of expenses under the accountable guidelines. The church provides a Form W-2 reflecting compensation of $76,000. The substantiated expenses of $9,000 are not reported to the IRS by the church or on the minister's tax return.

The church retains the $1,000 difference between the amount budgeted by the church and the amount reimbursed to the minister. (See pages 72–74 for an example where the church pays the balance in the expense reimbursement plan to the minister.)

Example 2: The church authorizes a salary of $63,000 and additionally authorizes allowances of $5,000 for auto expenses and $3,000 for other business expenses. The church does not require or receive any substantiation for the auto or other business expenses. This is a nonaccountable reimbursement plan.

The church should provide a Form W-2 reflecting compensation of $71,000. The minister may be able to claim the auto and other business expenses on Form 2106 (2106-EZ) and Schedule A as miscellaneous deductions if reporting as an employee for income tax purposes.

The IRS disallows deductions for a portion of unreimbursed business expenses on the premise that the expenses can be allocated to the minister's excludable housing allowance (see allocation of business expenses on pages 91–93). This is another reason that every minister should comply with the accountable expense reimbursement rules. The goal should be to eliminate all unreimbursed business expenses.

Accountable expense reimbursement plans should not be combined with other fringe benefit plans or a housing allowance. Too often, ministers have been advised that the church can establish a general reimbursement account to cover business expenses, housing expenses, dependent care expenses, and educational expenses. While all of these items can be handled in a tax beneficial manner for a minister, they are subject to separate rules in the tax law. Some of the items are subject to the nondiscrimination rules, while others are not. Dollar limits must be separately established in some instances, but not in others. Housing expenses for a minister-owned home are not reimbursable at all.

The timing of documenting expenses for reimbursement is of utmost importance. Under the fixed date method (see page 70), the IRS provides a safe harbor of 60 days after the expense is paid or incurred. In other words, the IRS will contest a reimbursement, based on timeliness of submitting the documentation, if the documentation is provided to the employer. Does this mean that the IRS will disallow expenses reimbursed on the 61st day? Not necessarily. It simply means 60 days is a safe harbor as a "reasonable time."

Example: A church approves $75,000 of compensation for the pastor and says to let the church know at the end of the year how much has been spent on business expenses, and they will show the net amount on Form W-2. Is this valid? No. The salary must be established separately from expense reimbursements. Further, even if an accountable expense reimbursement plan is used, the annual submission of expense documentation would fail the timeliness test for expenses incurred in all but the last portion of the year.

Nonaccountable expense reimbursement plans

If a minister does not substantiate expenses to the church, or if the amount of the reimbursement exceeds the actual expenses and the excess is not returned to the employer within a reasonable period, the minister's tax life becomes more complicated.

Nonaccountable reimbursements and excess reimbursements over IRS mileage or per diem limits must be included in your gross income and reported as wages on Form W-2. If the church pays an "allowance" for certain business expenses, it represents taxable compensation. The term "allowance" implies that the payment is not based upon documented expenses, does not meet the adequate accounting requirements for an accountable plan, and must be included in the minister's income.

> **Warning**
>
> Many ministers are paid expense "allowances." These payments accomplish nothing in terms of good stewardship. "Allowances" are fully taxable for income and social security tax purposes. Ministers must then resort to trying to deduct their expenses—much of which will be limited by the tax law—instead of receiving a full reimbursement.

Unreimbursed expenses or expenses reimbursed under a nonaccountable plan can be deducted only as itemized miscellaneous deductions and only to the extent that they, with other miscellaneous deductions, exceed 2% of the adjusted gross income. Unreimbursed expenses are not deductible if the minister is an employee for income tax purposes and does not itemize.

The unused "balance" in an accountable expense reimbursement plan

If the church pays the unused balance in an accountable expense reimbursement plan (perhaps calling the payment of the balance a "bonus"), the expense reimbursement plan becomes nonaccountable for the entire year. (This is also referred to as a "recharacterization of income.") All payments under a nonaccountable plan are reportable as compensation on Form W-2.

Example: A church sets the minister's salary at $60,000 and agrees to reimburse business expenses under an accountable plan for up to $10,000. The reimbursed expenses are $9,000, and the church gave a bonus for the $1,000 difference. Because of the "bonus" arrangement, all reimbursements made under the plan are generally considered to be nonaccountable. The entire $70,000 must be reported by the church as compensation on Form W-2.

> **Caution**
>
> The best expense reimbursement plan for a minister is one that pays 100% of church-related expenses. Too often, churches place dollar limits on these plans. With a dollar limit, any money left in the plan at the end of the year must stay with the church for reimbursements to be tax-free. If the balance is paid to the minister, all payments for the year become taxable.

CHAPTER 5 ➤ BUSINESS EXPENSES

Substantiating and Reporting Business Expenses

Substantiating business expenses

For expenses to be allowed as deductions, a minister must show that money was spent and that it was spent for a legitimate business reason. To prove that the money was spent, generally documentary evidence must be provided that can be confirmed by a third party. Canceled checks, credit card, or other receipts are an excellent starting point. To the IRS, third-party verification is important; if business expenses are paid in cash, be sure to get a receipt.

Documenting a business expense can be time-consuming. The IRS is satisfied if the five Ws are noted on the back of the credit card slip or other receipt:

> **Remember**
> When a minister provides a listing of business expenses to the church or other employer—this is only a report, not documentation. Documentary evidence is much more than a report. It involves hard-copy support of the five Ws (why, what, when, where, and who).

- ➤ Why (business purpose)
- ➤ What (description, including itemized accounting of cost)
- ➤ When (date)
- ➤ Where (location)
- ➤ Who (names of those for whom the expense was incurred, e.g., Pastor Mark Smith)

The only exception to the documentation rules is if the individual outlays for business expenses, other than for lodging, which come to less than $75. The IRS does not require receipts for such expenses, although the five Ws are still required for adequate substantiation. A receipt for lodging expenses will always be needed, regardless of the amount. An employer may apply a documentation threshold lower than $75.

Use of a church credit card can be helpful to charge church-related business expenses. However, the use of a credit card does not automatically provide substantiation without additional documentation of the expense; e.g., business purpose and business relationship.

When a minister is traveling out of town as an employee, the church may use a per diem for reimbursements instead of actual costs of meals (see page 77). The per diem is not subject to the 50% limitation on meal and entertainment expenses.

For more detailed information, refer to IRS Publication 463, *Travel, Entertainment, Gift and Car Expenses*.

Forms on which expenses are reportable

Only the portion of business and professional expenses directly attributable to Schedule C (C-EZ) income (self-employment activities) should be deducted on Schedule C (C-EZ). The portion of these expenses related to activities as an employee of the church should be deducted on Form 2106 (2106-EZ). If the minister receives reimbursement for any business or professional expenses and adequately accounts to the church under an accountable plan, he or she should not report the expenses on Form 2106 (2106-EZ) or Schedule C (C-EZ).

CASH EXPENSE REPORT

Name: Pastor Frank Morris
Address: 3801 North Florida Avenue
Miami, FL 33168
Period Covered: From: 7/1/17 To: 7/14/17

DATE	City	Purpose of Travel	Brkfast	Lunch	Dinner	Snack	Lodging	Trans.	Description	Amount	ACCOUNT to be Charged
7/2/17									Lunch w/Bob Cox	18.21	544-20
7/6/17	Atlanta, GA	Continuing Ed. Sem.		10.80	13.40	2.10	90.50	265.08	Tips	8.00	549-20
7/6/17	"	" " "	6.40								544-20
7/6/17									Lunch w/Al Lane	12.80	544-80
7/14/17									Lunch w/Sam Lee	11.12	544-40
		TOTAL CASH EXPENSES	6.40	10.80	13.40	2.10	90.50	265.08		50.13	

*If this is entertainment, please use the entertainment worksheet on the back of this form.

Signature (person requesting reimbursement): Frank Morris Date: 7/16/17
Approved by: Bob Davis Date: 7/16/17

Total cash expenses: 438.41
Personal auto business mileage: 106.47
(Complete worksheet on the back of this form.)
199 miles × 53.5¢ per mile
Less travel advance: (300.00)
Balance due: 244.88
Refund due organization:

Travel and Transportation Expenses

The terms "travel" and "transportation" are often used interchangeably, but each has a distinct meaning for tax purposes. Travel is the broader category, including not only transportation expenses, but the cost of meals, lodging, and incidental expenses as well. To deduct travel expenses—including expenses incurred for meals, phone calls, cab fares, and so forth—the business purpose must take the minister away from home overnight or require a rest stop. If the minister does not spend the night, he or she can deduct only transportation costs.

Travel expenses

Many different expenses can add up on a business trip: air and taxi fares, costs of lodging, baggage charges, rental cars, tips, laundry and cleaning, and telephone expenses. The minister can deduct 100% of these unreimbursed expenses plus 50% of the meal and entertainment expenses incurred while he or she was away, provided certain guidelines are met:

- The trip must have a business purpose.
- The expenses cannot be "lavish and extravagant."
- The time away from home is long enough to require sleep or rest.

Deriving some personal pleasure from a trip doesn't disqualify it from being deductible. The IRS does, however, apply some important limitations to the tax treatment of foreign travel expenses.

> **Key Issue**
> Travel expenses must be divided between your self-employment activities reported on Schedule C (C-EZ) and activities as an employee reported on Form 2106 (2106-EZ). Any unreimbursed travel expense that is also a meal or entertainment expense is subject to the 50% limitation for business meals and entertainment.

If the travel is within the United States, all transportation costs can be deducted, plus the costs of business-related meals (subject to the 50% limit) and lodging, if business was the primary reason for the trip. If a Saturday night stay is needed to get a lower airfare, the hotel and meal expenses for Saturday will generally be deductible. If the trip is primarily personal, none of the transportation costs can be deducted, but other business-related travel expenses can be deducted.

If the minister is reimbursed for travel expenses and adequately accounts to the church, he or she should not report travel expenses on Form 2106 (2106-EZ). Further, the minister is not subject to the 50% limitation for business meals and entertainment.

International travel

Costs are deductible if a minister takes an international trip for business reasons. If the trip is seven days or less, he or she can deduct the entire airfare even if most of the time is spent on personal activities. If some days are spent for personal reasons, the hotel, car rental, and meal costs are not deductible for those days. If the trip is more than seven days and more than 25% of the time is spent on personal activities, all expenses must be allocated between business and personal time.

Trips to the Holy Land

Ministers often travel to the Holy Land to more closely identify with the area where Christ taught, preached, and ministered. In spite of all the obvious ministerial advantages of visiting the Holy Land, the applicability of tax deductions or tax-free reimbursements for such trips is not as clear.

Generally, no deduction or reimbursement is allowed for travel as a form of education. However, travel expense may be deductible or reimbursable if the travel is necessary to engage in an activity that gives rise to a business deduction relating to education.

A number of factors must be considered before the tax status of a Holy Land trip may be determined. To qualify as a deductible or reimbursable ministry-related expense, the trip must meet the general educational expense rules outlined on pages 88–89. Holy Land trips are also subject to the international travel rules as described above.

If the answer to the following questions is "Yes," the expenses more likely qualify for reimbursement or as a deduction:

➤ Did the employing church require or strongly suggest that the minister make the trip to the Holy Land?

➤ Is this the minister's first trip to the Holy Land? If he or she has a pattern of making the pilgrimage every few years, the trip is less likely to qualify as an educational expense.

➤ Will the minister be receiving college credit for the trip from a recognized educational institution? Is there a course syllabus?

➤ Is the trip organized for the purpose of study in the Holy Land and led by a Bible scholar?

➤ Did the minister take notes and pictures of places visited? If most of the photos include family members and friends, the trip is less likely to qualify as an education expense.

A tax deduction or reimbursement by a church for a minister's trip to the Holy Land should be made only after careful consideration of the facts and circumstances and the applicable tax rules.

Furlough travel

A missionary on furlough may qualify for travel status. The purpose of the travel must be primarily business, such as deputation (resource-raising), reporting to constituents, or education, and the missionary's primary residence must remain in another country. Incidental costs for personal travel such as vacation, nonbusiness spousal costs, and travel costs of children are not deductible. If these expenses are paid by a church or missions organization, they should be included in compensation on Form W-2.

Travel expenses of the minister's spouse or children

If the minister's spouse or children accompany him or her on the business trip, their expenses are nonreimbursable and nondeductible unless they qualify for employee treatment and

➤ the travel of the spouse or dependent is for a bona fide business purpose; and

➤ the employee substantiates the time, place, amount, and business purpose of the travel under an accountable business expense reimbursement plan.

If there is not a bona fide purpose or the payments are not made under an accountable plan, the expenses are includible as income on your Form W-2.

The IRS and the courts evaluate the following criteria to determine whether a bona fide business purpose exists:

➤ The spouse's function must be necessary; i.e., results in desired business (ministry) benefits to the church.

➤ The spouse's contributions to the church must be those which cannot be efficiently performed (or performed at all) by the minister-employee alone.

➤ The spouse's services must augment the minister's purpose for the trip.

➤ The benefit to the church must be substantial.

> **Remember**
>
> Spouses and children often accompany ministers to Christian conferences and other work-related meetings. Their expenses are reimbursable under an accountable plan or deductible only if you can document a business (ministry) purpose (for example, a minister's wife attends certain meetings at a conference and reports to the church on those meetings).

Per diem allowance

The IRS has provided per diem allowances under which the amount of away-from-home meals and lodging expenses may be substantiated. These rates may not be used to claim deductions for unreimbursed expenses. Higher per diem rates apply to certain locations annually identified by the IRS. For more information on these rates, see IRS Publication 1542.

Travel expenses for pastors with interim appointments

Many ministers accept or are appointed to temporary ministerial positions with churches. For example, a semiretired minister may own his or her own home and decide not to relocate for a temporary assignment. So the minister drives 60 miles each week to serve a church that does not have a resident minister. Or, a minister may have secular employment in a city where he or she lives and is invited to preach each Sunday on an interim basis for a church located 30 miles from his or her home. The minister is able to maintain the secular job and fill the ministerial assignment with periodic trips to the church.

If a minister temporarily changes his or her job location, the minister's tax home does not change to the new location. This means that the minister can deduct or be reimbursed for his or her travel expenses (auto or public transportation expense and meals) to and from the temporary location. If the

> **Caution**
>
> Ministers often drive significant distances each week to serve their churches. Auto expenses become a major issue. Transportation expenses are deductible or reimbursable only if the period of employment is for a temporary period. Simply being classified as an "interim" minister by a church does not justify temporary status.

minister stays overnight at the temporary location, food and lodging expenses at the temporary location become deductible or reimbursable.

When is a job location temporary? A minister will be treated as being temporarily away from home during any period of employment that is realistically expected to last and actually does last a year or less. Daily transportation expenses are deductible or reimbursable by the church if the minister qualifies for temporary work status. These rules may also apply to a minister serving more than one church (a circuit arrangement).

However, if employment away from home is realistically expected to last for more than one year, the employment will be treated as indefinite, regardless of whether it actually exceeds one year. In this case, daily transportation expenses are not deductible or reimbursable by the church.

> **Example 1:** A minister lives in town A and accepts an interim pulpit assignment in town B, which is 60 miles away from town A. The assignment in town B is realistically expected to be completed in 18 months, but in fact it was completed in 10 months. The employment in town B is indefinite because it was realistically expected that the work in town B would last longer than one year, even though it actually lasted less than a year. Accordingly, travel expenses paid or incurred in town B are nondeductible.

If employment away from home in a single location initially is realistically expected to last for one year or less, but at some later date the employment is realistically expected to exceed one year, that employment will be treated as temporary (in the absence of facts and circumstances indicating otherwise) until the date that the minister's realistic expectation changes.

> **Example 2:** An interim assignment began as a temporary assignment (a six-month assignment that was extended for a second six-month period), but at the 365th day of employment it was apparent that the contract would be extended for an additional period. At that time, the minister no longer has a realistic expectation that his or her employment would last for one year or less. Thus, the expenses the minister incurred after that 365th day were not deductible.

When a minister's realistic expectation changes—i.e., when the minister realistically expects the initially temporary employment to exceed one year—the employment becomes indefinite for the *remaining* term of employment. In other words, the employment can become indefinite before the end of the one-year period if, before the end of that period, the minister realistically expects that his or her employment will exceed one year.

> **Example 3:** A minister accepted a temporary ministerial assignment, which the minister realistically expected would be completed in nine months. After eight months, the minister was asked to remain for seven more months (for a total stay of 15 months). Although the minister's employment is temporary for the first eight months and travel expenses during that period are deductible, the minister's employment for the remaining seven months is indefinite, and the

minister's travel expenses for that seven-month period are not deductible. If, after working on the assignment only three months, the minister was asked to extend his or her employment for 10 months, only the travel expenses incurred during the first three months would be deductible.

In effect, the IRS takes the position that part of a period of employment that is more than a year will still be treated as temporary if the taxpayer reasonably expected that the employment would last for a year or less when the employment started. The employment won't be treated as indefinite until the taxpayer's expectation changes.

If a minister is not told how long an assignment is expected to last, other factors will have to be taken into account to determine whether it can reasonably be expected to last more than one year. Merely being classified as an interim minister by a church does not justify indefinite status. Also, the fewer connections that a minister keeps with his or her former work location, the less likely it is that the new assignment will be treated as merely temporary.

Auto Expense Deductions

A minister's car expenses are deductible or reimbursable to the extent that they are for business rather than personal use. Generally, only those expenses that are necessary to drive and maintain a car that is used to go from one workplace to another are deductible. However, in some limited situations, the expense of driving between home and a workplace is deductible (see pages 83–85).

Business-related auto expenses incurred by an employee and reimbursed under an accountable plan are excludable from the employee's gross income. Generally, unreimbursed employee business-related auto expenses may be claimed only as a miscellaneous itemized deduction on Schedule A, subject to the 2% AGI floor.

Mileage and actual expense methods

In determining the deduction for the business use of a personal car, a minister may use one of two methods to figure the deduction: (1) the standard mileage rate, or (2) the actual expense method. Generally, the minister can choose the method that gives the greater deduction. If he or she uses the actual expense method and accelerated depreciation for the first year his or her car was placed in service, the minister may not use the standard mileage method in a subsequent year. However, if the standard mileage method is used for the first year the car was placed in service, either method may be used in subsequent years.

Standard mileage rate method

If the minister is paid the maximum mileage rate of 53.5 cents per mile (2017 rate), and he or she provides the time, place, and business purpose of the driving, the minister has made an adequate accounting of the automobile expenses.

If the church does not reimburse the minister for auto expenses or reimburses under a nonaccountable plan, the minister may deduct business miles on Form 2106 (2106-EZ). The total from Form 2106 (2106-EZ) is carried to Schedule A, Miscellaneous Deductions.

The standard mileage rate, which includes depreciation and maintenance costs, is based on the government's estimate of the average cost of operating an automobile. Depending upon the make, age, and cost of the car, the mileage rate may be more or less than your actual auto expense. If you use the mileage rate, you may also deduct parking fees and tolls and the business portion of personal property tax. All auto-related taxes must be claimed on Schedule A for employees.

> **Remember**
> The standard mileage rate may generate a lower deduction than using actual expenses in some instances. But the simplicity of the standard mileage method is a very compelling feature.

If the minister uses the standard mileage rate for the business use of his or her car, depreciation is included in that rate. The rate of depreciation that is allowed in the standard mileage rate may be found in IRS Publication 463.

The standard mileage rate may also be used for leased autos (see page 83 for additional information, "Leasing your car").

➤ **Conditions on use of mileage rate.** The mileage rate may not be used if:

☐ the minister has claimed depreciation under Modified Accelerated Cost Recovery (MACRS), Accelerated Cost Recovery (ACRS), or another accelerated method

☐ the minister has claimed first-year expenses under Section 179 of the tax code

➤ **Use of mileage rate in first year.** If the minister chooses the standard mileage rate for the first year the car is in service, he or she may use the standard mileage rate or actual expense method in later years. If the minister does not choose the standard mileage rate in the first year, he or she may not use it for that car in any following year.

> **Warning**
> You have an important decision to make the first year you put a car into service. You will generally want to use the standard mileage rate in that first year. If you do not use the standard mileage rate in the first year, you may not use it for that car in any following year.

By choosing to use the mileage rate in the first year the car is in service, the minister may not use the MACRS method of depreciation for the car in a later year. Also, he or she may not claim a deduction under Section 179. If the minister switches to the actual expense method in a later year before the automobile is fully depreciated, he or she must use the straight-line method of depreciation.

Actual expense method

The actual expense method is a permitted alternative method for ministers. This method may be preferential when operating costs exceed the deduction allowed under the standard mileage rate method. However, even when the actual expense method exceeds the mileage method, the simplicity of the mileage method may outweigh the tax savings.

If accurate records have been kept, determining the deduction for most expenses should be straightforward. Generally, the amount of depreciation the minister may claim and the method used to calculate it depend on when the auto was purchased and was first used for ministerial purposes.

Under the actual expense method, the minister can use either accelerated or straight-line depreciation. As the names imply, the accelerated method front-loads the depreciation, giving larger deductions sooner. The straight-line method gives the same depreciation deduction every year.

> **Tip**
> While the actual expense method is one of your options for obtaining a reimbursement or taking a deduction for auto expenses, it requires significantly more recordkeeping than the standard mileage method. For example, you still need to maintain a mileage log so you can prorate costs between business and personal miles.

Driving an employer-provided vehicle

When a church provides a car to a minister, the church must report the personal use of the car as income on Form W-2 or 1099-MISC. However, when a minister pays the church the fair market value of the personal use of the car, no income tax impact to the minister. Partial payment to the church reduces the minister's taxable income by the amount of the payment.

When a car is used for both business and personal purposes, an allocation between the two types of use must be made on the basis of the number of miles driven. The amount included in the minister's compensation is generally based on one of the following valuation rules (for more information, see the 2018 edition of the *Zondervan Church and Nonprofit Tax & Financial Guide*):

> **Cents-per-mile valuation rule.** Generally, this rule may be used if the employer reasonably expects that the vehicle will be regularly used in the employer's trade or business and if the vehicle is driven at least 10,000 miles a year and is primarily used by employees. This valuation rule is available only if the fair market value of the vehicle, as of the date the vehicle was first made available for personal use by employees, does not exceed a specified value set by the IRS. For 2017, this value is $15,900 (passenger automobile) or $17,800 (truck or van).
>
> The value of the personal use of the vehicle is computed by multiplying the number of miles driven for personal purposes by the current IRS standard mileage rate (53.5 cents

per mile for 2017). For this valuation rule, personal use is "any use of the vehicle other than use in the employer's trade or business of being an employee of the employer."

➤ **Commuting valuation rule.** This rule may be used to determine the value of personal use only where the following conditions are met:

- ☐ The vehicle is owned or leased by the employer and is provided to one or more employees for use in connection with the employer's trade or business and is used as such.

- ☐ The employer requires the employee to commute to and/or from work in the vehicle for bona fide noncompensatory business reasons. One example of a bona fide noncompensatory business reason is the availability of the vehicle to an employee who is on-call and must have access to the vehicle when at home.

> **Caution**
> One of the best fringe benefits for a minister is when the church or other employer provides a vehicle. However, unless the car is parked at the church when not in use, it still requires maintaining a mileage log. Personal (including commuting) miles driven must either be reimbursed to the employer or the tax-value must be placed on Form W-2.

- ☐ The employer has a written policy that prohibits employees from using the vehicle for personal purposes other than for commuting or *de minimis* personal use such as a stop for a personal errand on the way home from work.

- ☐ The employee required to use the vehicle for commuting is not a "control" employee of the employer. A control employee is generally defined as any director or employee who is an officer of the employer whose compensation equals or exceeds $105,000 (2017 rate).

The personal use of an employer-provided vehicle that meets the above conditions is valued at $1.50 per one-way commute, or $3.00 per day.

➤ **Annual lease valuation rule.** Under this rule, the fair market value of a vehicle is determined, and that value is used to determine the annual lease value amount by referring to an annual lease value table published by the IRS. The annual lease value corresponding to this fair market value, multiplied by the personal use percentage, is the amount to be added to the employee's gross income. If the organization provides the fuel, 5.5 cents per mile must be added to the annual lease value. Amounts reimbursed by the employee are offset.

The fair market value of a vehicle owned by an employer is generally the employer's cost of purchasing the vehicle (including taxes and fees). The fair market value of a vehicle leased by an employer is generally either the manufacturer's suggested retail price less 8%, the dealer's invoice plus 4%, or the retail value as reported in a nationally recognized publication that regularly reports automobile retail values.

Leasing your car

A minister who leases a car and uses it in connection with the work of the church is generally able to deduct part or all of lease payments as a rental deduction. However, business use is typically less than 100%. Therefore, the rental deduction is scaled down in proportion to the personal use. For example, a minister who uses a leased car 80% for business may deduct only 80% of the lease payments.

Additionally, the tax law is designed to bring lease payments in line with the "luxury auto" limits (annually determined by the IRS) placed on depreciation deductions for purchased cars (most cars meet the "luxury" definition). So, leasing a "luxury" car may not give you a tax break over buying one. However, nontax considerations may be important in the lease vs. buy decision.

The mileage method may also be used for the deduction or reimbursement of expenses for a leased car.

Commuting

Personal mileage is never deductible. Commuting expenses are nondeductible personal expenses.

Unless a minister's home-office qualifies as a home-office under the tax law (see pages 85–87), travel to and from home and church (a regular work location) for church services and other work at the church is commuting and is not deductible or reimbursable. The same rule applies to multiple trips made in the same day.

> **Key Issue**
>
> Churches (and other employers) and ministers often struggle to define commuting miles. It is a very important issue because commuting miles should not be reimbursed by an employer or deducted by a minister. The key to understanding commuting miles is defining regular and temporary work locations.

On the other hand, the cost of traveling between home and a temporary work location is generally deductible or reimbursable. Once the

---

Business Miles Do Not Start at Home If—

- ❏ You have a personal computer in your home office and you or another member of your family occasionally uses the personal computer for personal use.
- ❏ Your home office is in your bedroom, your living room, or any other room where the space is shared for church work and family living.
- ❏ The church has an adequate office. You do most of your work there but work at home once in a while.
- ❏ The church expects you to use the church office for your work, but you prefer to work at home because it is convenient to you.

minister arrives at the first work location, temporary or regular, he or she may deduct trips between work locations.

A regular place of business is any location at which the minister works or performs services on a regular basis. These services may be performed every week, for example, or merely on a set schedule. A temporary place of business is any location at which services are performed on an irregular or short-term basis.

If a minister makes calls in a certain hospital or nursing home nearly every day, it qualifies as a regular work location. However, if he or she only visits the hospital or nursing home a few days each month, it generally qualifies as a temporary work location.

> **Example 1:** A minister, not qualifying for an office at home, drives from home to the church. This trip is commuting and treated as personal mileage.
>
> The minister leaves the church and drives to a hospital to call on a member. From the hospital, the minister drives to the home of a prospect to make a call. These trips qualify for business mileage regardless of whether the hospital qualifies as a regular or a temporary work location.
>
> From the prospect's house, the minister drives home. This trip is also deductible since the minister is driving from a temporary work location.
>
> **Example 2:** A minister, not qualifying for an office at home, drives from home to a hospital to call on a member. The hospital is typically a temporary work location. This trip is deductible.
>
> The minister then drives to a member's office to make a call and then returns to the minister's office at the church. The trips to this point are deductible as

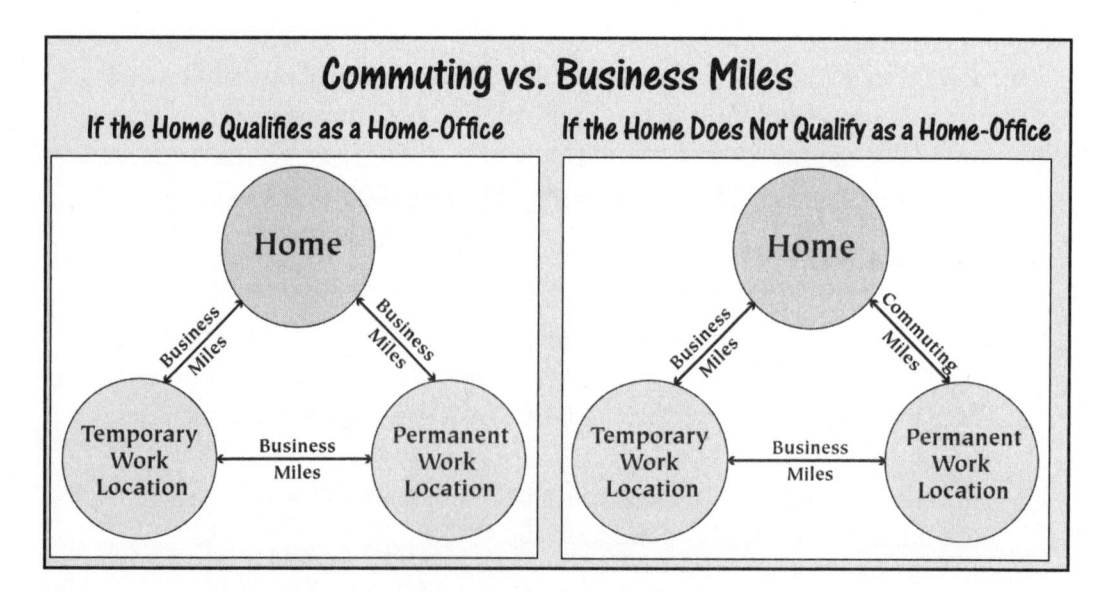

Commuting vs. Business Miles

If the Home Qualifies as a Home-Office

Home ↔ Temporary Work Location (Business Miles)
Home ↔ Permanent Work Location (Business Miles)
Temporary Work Location ↔ Permanent Work Location (Business Miles)

If the Home Does Not Qualify as a Home-Office

Home ↔ Temporary Work Location (Business Miles)
Home ↔ Permanent Work Location (Commuting Miles)
Temporary Work Location ↔ Permanent Work Location (Business Miles)

business expenses because they are all trips between work locations. The minister then drives to his home. This trip is commuting and is not deductible because the minister is driving from a regular work location to a nonwork location.

Documentation of auto expenses

To support the automobile expense deduction or reimbursement, automobile expenses must be substantiated by adequate records. A weekly or monthly mileage log that identifies dates, destinations, business purposes, and odometer readings in order to allocate total mileage between business and personal use is a basic necessity if the minister uses the mileage method. If he or she uses the actual expense method, a mileage log and supporting documentation of expenses are required.

Reporting auto expenses

If the minister is reimbursed for automobile expenses under an accountable expense plan, he or she should not report travel expenses on Form 2106 (2106-EZ). This type of reimbursement eliminates the need for income or social security tax reporting by the church or the minister. If the minister does not have an accountable expense reimbursement plan, automobile expenses are reported on Form 2106 (2106-EZ) for minister-employees.

Remember
For your records to withstand an IRS audit, use a daily mileage log to document business vs. personal mileage. Whether you keep a notepad in the car or track the data on your smartphone, some type of log is the best approach to submitting data for reimbursement from your employer or for taking a tax deduction.

Home-Office Rules

Under the home-office rules, a minister must meet the following qualifications to achieve home-office status:

➤ A specific portion of the taxpayer's home must be used *exclusively* and on a *regular basis* for business activity.

➤ The home office is used for the convenience of the employer or is necessary for the business of the employer. Use of the home that is merely appropriate and helpful to the church is not sufficient to meet the convenience test. Similarly, use of the home for the minister's convenience or because the minister can get more work done at home also will not suffice.

➤ The home office must be the minister's principal place of business. Conducting administrative or management activities of the church in the home office are examples of qualifying work.

➤ The home office is used for the convenience of the employer, and the employer has no other fixed location where the minister conducts *substantial* administrative or management activities. ***Note:*** Insubstantial administrative or management activities that take place outside the home office will not necessarily preclude the minister from qualifying.

For many ministers, the key is to determine if they are performing work outside the home office that is so substantial that they fail the last test (see above). A minister may do minimal paperwork at another fixed location, like the church, and meet the insubstantial test. Also, ministers conducting substantial non-administrative or nonmanagement business activities at fixed locations other than their home offices will not be prevented from qualifying for a home office. For example, counseling sessions with individuals at the church will not preclude home-office status.

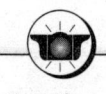

> **Caution**
>
> To qualify for home-office status, there are rigorous tests the minister must pass. One of the toughest is the test that requires a specific portion of the taxpayer's home to be used exclusively and on a regular basis for business activity. This is difficult for many ministers when a computer in the office area is not used exclusively for business purposes.

The rules do not define if sermon preparation time qualifies as administrative or management activities. However, it seems that sermon preparation is a program activity of the church and is not administrative or management. The following activities would likely qualify as administrative or management: communication with church vendors; time spent in planning and communication with church staff or congregational leaders regarding issues such as project assignments, personnel issues, financial matters, planning for annual or quarterly congregational meetings, and planning for periodic meetings of the top governing body or committees of the church.

If a minister does not substantially perform all of his or her administrative and management activities in the home office, the relative importance or time tests must be met:

➤ The relative importance test considers the importance of the activities undertaken at each place of business. The activities are compared to determine which location serves as a base for the most important functions.

➤ The time test considers the actual time spent at respective business locations. A minister would meet this test if he or she spent more than half of his or her time working in the home office.

Ministers should keep proper records to document the required regular and exclusive business use of the home office, even if the office is only a portion of a room. They should keep a daily log of meetings related to church activities at the home office. They should also make videos or take photographs to show there are no personal items in that part of the home. They also need to ensure that no personal or family activities occur in the home office. It will also be helpful if the church has a written policy explaining the need for the minister to have a home office.

Rarely is it advantageous or even appropriate for a minister to claim office-in-the-home deductions (Form 8829). Churches often provide an office on the church premises for the minister, so the necessity of an office in the home is generally questioned closely by the IRS. Furthermore, since the total cost to provide the home is used in computing the exempt housing allowance, home-office deductions for taxes, insurance, mortgage interest and the like are duplications of expenses eligible for exclusion from income for income tax purposes. (Also, note that itemized deductions are allowable for mortgage interest and taxes even if these expenses are excluded from income under the housing allowance provisions.)

Even if there is no home-office expense deduction or reimbursement available to a minister, qualifying under the home-office rules will permit a minister to treat otherwise personal commuting mileage as business mileage (see IRS Publication 587, *Business Use of Your Home*).

If a minister qualifies for home-office status, the starting (first business trip of the day) and ending (last business trip of the day) points for business miles can be the home. But ministers not qualifying under the home-office rules can only deduct or be reimbursed for miles from the minister's home to a temporary work location (a hospital, nursing home, member's home, etc.) and/or miles from a temporary work location to the minister's home. The miles between the minister's residence and the church (home to a permanent work location) are personal commuting miles—nondeductible, nonreimbursable—regardless of the number of trips made each day unless home-office status applies. Even without home-office status, when a minister has reached a work location (either permanent or temporary), trips between work locations are deductible or reimbursable.

> **Idea**
> The tax law provides for a home-office deduction. However, with housing expenses excluded from income by the housing allowance, ministers generally do not qualify for the home-office deduction. The home-office rules may still benefit some ministers by allowing them to start claiming business miles from their home instead of first requiring them to reach the church or other business location.

The IRS has provided a simplified option for claiming a home-office deduction. Under the "safe harbor" method, taxpayers can easily calculate the home-office deduction by multiplying the square footage of the area of the home that is used strictly for business purposes by the prescribed rate of $5 per square foot. While the safe harbor method has its benefits, a taxpayer might have to accept sacrifices, too. Specifically, depreciation of the space allocated to the qualified home office cannot be deducted. Taxpayers can opt for the safe harbor method or the regular method on a year-to-year basis; however, once the election is made for any given tax year, it is irrevocable.

Other Business Expenses

In addition to travel and transportation expenses, there are other business and professional expenses that may be deductible if unreimbursed or submitted to the church for reimbursement under an accountable plan:

➤ **Business gifts.** Up to $25 per donee can be deducted for ministry gifts to any number of individuals every year. Incidental costs, such as for engraving, gift wrapping, insurance, and mailing, do not need to be included in determining whether the $25 limit has been exceeded.

The gifts must be related to the ministry. Gifts to church staff or board members would generally be deductible, subject to the $25 limit. Wedding and graduation gifts generally do not qualify as business expenses.

➤ **Cell phones.** The IRS treats the value of a church-provided cell phone and similar telecommunications equipment (including the value of any personal use by the employee) as excludible from the employee's income, as long as the cell phone is provided to the employee primarily for a noncompensatory business reason (such as the employer's need to contact the employee at all times for work-related emergencies). Providing a cell phone to promote morale or goodwill, to attract a prospective employee, or to furnish additional compensation to an employee is evidence that there is no noncompensatory business reason.

Church staff may be reimbursed for the business use of a cell phone, but the church should probably require the employee to submit a copy of the monthly bill and evidence that the bill has been paid.

> **Warning**
> The one-time equipment write-off cannot be used as part of a minister's accountable expense reimbursement plan. If a minister personally owns a computer that is partially used for his or her employer, the business portion of the computer can be reimbursed under an accountable plan based on annual depreciation. The business portion of the cost of the computer cannot be reimbursed in one year under the one-time write-off rules.

If a church does not have a substantial noncompensatory business reason for providing a cell phone to an employee or reimbursing the employee for business use of his or her personal cell phone, then the value of the use of the phone or the amount of the reimbursement is includible in gross income, reportable on Forms 941 and W-2, and for lay employees is subject to federal and state employment tax withholding.

Cell phones a minister owns and uses more than 50% for ministry may be depreciated (or reimbursed) as five-year recovery property or deducted under Section 179. The business portion of depreciation may be reimbursed under an accountable expense reimbursement plan, if the 50% business, "convenience of the church," and "condition of employment" tests are met.

As a minister-employee, the use of a cell phone must be for the "convenience of the church" and required as a "condition of employment." The "convenience of the church" test will generally be met if the cell phone is furnished for substantial "noncompensatory business reasons." Whether a minister (or other church employee) passes the "condition of employment" test is based on all the facts and circumstances and is not determined merely by an employer's statement that the use of the cell phone is a condition of employment.

If a minister meets the "convenience of the employer" and "condition of employment" tests but does not use the cell phone more than 50% of the time for work, he or she must depreciate it using the straight-line method. The minister may be reimbursed (or deduct as unreimbursed business expenses on Schedule A) the business-related phone call charges and the business-related portion of the monthly fees. If the minister qualifies under the home-office rules (see pages 85–87), the 50% test does not apply.

> **Remember**
> For a cell phone to be excludible from an employee's income, the phone must be provided primarily for noncompensatory business reasons.

➤ **Clothing.** The cost of clothing is deductible or reimbursable if the church requires the clothes and they are not suitable as normal apparel. For example, a regular suit worn into the pulpit on Sunday is not deductible or reimbursable, but vestments are deductible or reimbursable.

➤ **Education.** There are two types of deductions for educational expenses. First, up to $2,500 of interest paid during the tax year on any qualified education loan is deductible as an adjustment to gross income on Form 1040, line 33. The debt must be incurred by the taxpayer solely to pay qualified higher educational expenses.

Second, the taxpayer's own educational expenses may also be deducted as a business expense, even if they lead to a degree, if the education:

- ☐ is required by the church to keep the minister's salary status or job (and serves a business purpose of the church), or
- ☐ maintains or improves skills in the minister's present employment.

> **Caution**
> If the education is required to meet the minimum educational requirements of your work, educational expenses are not deductible.

Even though the above requirements are met, expenses do not qualify if the education is:

- ☐ required to meet the minimum educational requirements of the minister's work or
- ☐ part of a program of study that will qualify the minister for a new occupation.

Deductible educational expenses include the cost of tuition, books, supplies, fees, correspondence courses, and travel and transportation expenses. Expenses under a written "qualified educational assistance program" are discussed on page 35.

➤ **Entertainment.** Meal and entertainment expenses are deductible or reimbursable if they are ordinary and necessary and are either directly related to, or associated with, your ministerial responsibilities.

Do personal meals qualify when the minister is entertaining? Personal expenses are not deductible or reimbursable since the minister would be eating anyway. Granted, he or she might not be spending $10 for lunch, but he or she would be eating. Only the amount over what is normally spent for breakfast, lunch, or dinner is deductible or reimbursable. But the IRS has decided not to enforce this part of the tax law. Unless a taxpayer is deducting outrageous amounts of personal expenses, 50% of the cost of unreimbursed meals while entertaining is generally allowed.

Certain entertainment expenses incurred in the minister's home may be deductible or reimbursable if a ministry relationship can be shown. Since it is difficult to precisely document the cost of meals served in the home, a reasonable cost per meal is generally allowable (for the minister and guests). The minister should keep a log including date(s), names of guests, ministry purpose, and estimated cost. Some ministers claim deductions or reimbursements for providing overnight lodging for church-related guests based on the value of motel lodging. Such deductions or reimbursements are not allowable.

➤ **Interest expense.** For a minister-employee, all auto-related interest expense is personal interest, which is not deductible.

➤ **Moving expenses.** Certain moving expenses reimbursed by a church to a minister-employee are excludable from gross income.

For minister-employees, when moving expense reimbursements have been excluded from income, there is no requirement to add these amounts to determine a minister's net earnings from self-employment, and therefore they are not subject to self-employment tax.

Moving expense reimbursements or payments are excludable only to the extent that they would qualify for a moving expense deduction if they had been paid by the minister and not reimbursed. The definition of deductible moving expenses is very restrictive. For example, meals while traveling and living in temporary quarters near the new workplace are not deductible. If a minister is reimbursed for nondeductible moving expenses, the amounts paid are additional taxable compensation.

➤ **Personal computers.** Personal computers a minister owns and uses more than 50% for ministry may be depreciated (or reimbursed) as five-year recovery property or deducted (but not reimbursed) under Section 179. The business portion of depreciation may be reimbursed under an accountable expense reimbursement plan if the 50% business, "convenience of the church," and "condition of employment" tests are met (see the discussion of these topics under "Cell phones" on pages 88–89).

If a computer is provided by the church in the church office but the minister prefers to work at home on a personal computer, it is not being used for the church's convenience. If the minister meets the "convenience of employer" and "condition of employment"

Warning

If a minister purchases a computer and uses it primarily for church work and meets the "condition" and "convenience" tests, only the depreciation on the business portion of the computer can be reimbursed by the church, not the business portion of the cost, based on the Section 179 first-year write-off rules.

tests but does not use the computer (and related equipment) more than 50% of the time for work, he or she must depreciate these items using the straight-line method and you cannot take the Section 179 write-off. If the minister qualifies under the home-office rules (see pages 85–87), the 50% test does not apply.

Adequate records of the business use of a personal computer should be maintained to substantiate deductions.

➤ **Section 179 deductions.** In the year of purchase, a minister may choose to deduct the cost of tangible personal property used for business up to the annual Section 179 limits determined by the IRS. While Section 179 may be used by ministers to deduct expenses, the deduction is not includible under an accountable expense reimbursement plan.

➤ **Subscriptions and books.** Subscriptions to ministry-related periodicals are deductible or reimbursable. If the information in a periodical relates to your ministerial preparation, news magazines may even qualify.

The cost of books related to the ministry with a useful life of one year or less may be deducted. The cost of books (such as commentaries) with a useful life of more than one year may be depreciated over the useful life. Books with a useful life of more than one year may generally be deducted in the year of purchase under Section 179, but they are not eligible for reimbursement by your church (also see page 50).

Allocation of Business Expenses

The IRS takes the position that the deduction of unreimbursed business expenses is limited to the extent that they are allocable to an excluded housing allowance or the fair rental value of church-provided housing. The IRS applies what is often referred to as the "Deason rule" (referring to a 1964 Tax Court Memorandum).

IRS Publication 517, *Social Security and Other Information for Members of the Clergy and Religious Workers*, explains this topic in detail and includes the concept in a completed tax return example. The most recent *Tax Guide for Churches and Other Religious Organizations* and *Minister Audit Technique Guide*, both issued by the IRS, clearly apply the expense allocation concept.

Since the housing allowance is not tax-exempt for self-employment purposes, the IRS takes the position in their *Minister Audit Technique Guide* that the Deason rule does not apply to the computation of a minister's self-employment taxes.

Under the IRS guidelines, if you exclude a housing allowance or are provided housing by your church, you cannot deduct expenses that are allocable to your excluded rental or parsonage allowance. Home mortgage interest and real estate taxes are still deductible on Schedule A as itemized deductions even though the same amounts are excluded for income tax purposes under the housing allowance rules.

A statement containing all the following information should be attached to your tax return:

- A list of each item of taxable ministerial income by source (such as wages, salary, honoraria from weddings, baptisms, etc.) plus the amount
- The amount of excluded housing allowance or the fair rental value of church-provided housing
- A list of each item of unreimbursed ministerial expense plus the amount
- A statement that the other deductions on your tax return are not allocable to the excluded housing allowance

> **Key Issue**
> Tax Court cases and a recent guide provided by the IRS to their examiners have reinforced the power of the IRS to reduce unreimbursed expense deductions for income tax purposes.

This limitation requires the following calculation:

1. Housing allowance (the fair rental value of a church-provided parsonage and the housing allowance excluded from gross income; this may be less than the church-designated housing allowance) $_____

2. Total income from ministry:

    Salary (including the fair rental value of a church-provided parsonage and the housing allowance excluded from gross income) $_____

    Fees   _____

    Allowances (nonaccountable plan)   _____

        $_____

3. Divide line 1 amount by line 2 amount = % of nontaxable income   _____ %

4. Total unreimbursed business and professional expenses, less 50% of meals and entertainment expenses $_____

5. Multiply line 4 total by line 3 percentage (these are nondeductible expenses allocable to tax-exempt income) $_____

6. Subtract line 5 amount from line 4 amount (these are deductible expenses for federal income tax purposes on Form 2106 [2106-EZ] or Schedule C [C-EZ]) $_____

The following are examples concerning the application of the allocation of business expenses concept:

Example 1: Pastor Fulton receives a salary of $36,000, excludes $18,000 from income under a housing allowance (the church designated $18,000 of the pastor's cash compensation as a housing allowance, and $18,000 was excluded from income since $18,000 was the lowest of the designation, the amount actually spent on housing, and the fair rental value of the home furnished plus utilities), and an auto expense allowance of $6,000 (these expenses were not substantiated to the church under the accountable expense reimbursement rules) for his services as an ordained minister.

Pastor Fulton incurred the following business expenses: Auto, $7,150; vestments, $350; dues, $120; publications and supplies, $300; totaling $7,920. His nondeductible expenses are computed as follows:

Step 1: $18,000 housing allowance/nontaxable income divided by $60,000 total ministry income ($36,000 salary, $18,000 housing and $6,000 car allowance) equals 30% nontaxable income percentage.

Step 2: Total business expenses of $7,920 times 30%, the nontaxable percentage equals $2,376 of nondeductible expenses.

Total expenses of $7,920 less the nondeductible expenses of $2,376 equals the deductible expenses of $5,544.

Pastor Fulton's deductible expenses of $5,544 are reported on Form 2106 and carried forward to Schedule A miscellaneous deductions, since the church considers him an employee and issues a Form W-2. These expenses, along with any other miscellaneous deductions, are subject to a further reduction of 2% of his adjusted gross income.

Example 2: Pastor Geitz received a salary of $12,000, excludes $9,000 from income under a properly designated housing allowance, and earned $3,000 for various speaking engagements, weddings, funerals, etc., all related to her ministry. She reports her salary as wages on page 1 of Form 1040 and fees on Schedule C. Because her actual housing costs ($6,000) were less than the housing allowance and the fair rental value of her home for the year, she must include $3,000 of her housing allowance as "other income" for income tax purposes. Her total business expenses are $4,500. The computation of deductible expenses is shown below:

Step 1: $6,000 (housing allowance actually exempt from income tax) divided by $24,000 total ministry income ($12,000 salary plus $9,000 housing plus $3,000 fees) equals 25% nontaxable income.

Step 2: Total expenses $4,500 times 25% nontaxable income percentage equals $1,125 nondeductible expenses. Total expenses of $4,500 less $1,125 equals $3,375 deductible expenses.

Note that this $3,375 would further be allocable between Schedule A miscellaneous deductions (related to salary) and Schedule C (related to other fees).

This allocation does not change the pastor's self-employment tax, since all ministry income and ministry expenses are included in the compensation, regardless of where they are reported on the return for income tax purposes.

Integrity Points

- **Personal vs. business expenses.** Integrity in expense reimbursements or deductions starts by determining if the expenses are truly business expenses. A business expense must be ordinary (one that is common and accepted in a particular field) and necessary (one that is helpful and appropriate for a particular field). The law and integrity require the faithful application of the "ordinary" and "necessary" rule.

  The reimbursement of an expense never affects the character of the expense. Simply reimbursing an expense does not change its character from personal to business. Personal expenses are always nondeductible and not eligible for reimbursement.

- **An accountable expense reimbursement plan.** The reimbursement of business expenses is much better stewardship for the minister and the employing congregation or parachurch organization. A reimbursement is a dollar-for-dollar tax-free payment. A deduction only benefits the minister if he or she reaches the itemized deduction threshold, and then only by the marginal income tax rates.

  A formal plan is the fundamental starting point. The plan provides the boundaries for compliance with the tax law for business expense reimbursements.

- **Substantiation vs. reporting of expenses.** Substantiating business expenses, either for reimbursement or deduction, is much more rigorous than simply reporting expenses. Substantiation generally involves providing documentary evidence that can be confirmed by a third party. Canceled checks, credit card, or other receipts are an excellent starting point. But the substantiation is not complete without the "why" (business purpose), "what" (description, including itemized account of cost), "when" (date), "where" (location), and "who" (names of those for whom the expense was incurred, e.g., Pastor Mark Smith).

- **Reimbursing 100% of a minister's business expenses.** This is very important from the congregation's stewardship standpoint *and* from a minister's tax deductions viewpoint. The IRS is taking a more consistent stand on disallowing a portion of unreimbursed business expenses that, in its view, are related to the nontaxable element of a housing allowance (see pages 91–93). The loss of these deductions can be avoided through proper compensation planning.

CHAPTER 6: Retirement and Social Security

In This Chapter

- Preparing for retirement
- The fundamentals of social security
- Taking out your retirement money
- The two social security tax systems
- Computing the self-employment tax
- Both spouses are ministers
- Self-employment tax deductions
- Use of income tax withholding to pay social security taxes
- Opting out of social security
- Working after you retire
- Canada Pension Plan

Age 65 was entrenched as the finish line for our careers. But this false endpoint was gradually disappearing even before the Great Recession. We are living longer, the social security retirement age is increasing, and stock market fluctuations have significantly impacted our retirement plans. In fact, the stock market slump left many ministers focused on their nest eggs to the exclusion of all else in their retirement planning.

Medicare still generally becomes effective at age 65. But this program for the elderly and disabled doesn't pay for prescription drugs, and it does not pay for long-term care costs.

For many ministers, the word "retirement" means freedom. Retirement is the end to stressful deadline pressure and setting your alarm clock. But it's also the end to regular paychecks. For ministers who have lived in church-owned parsonages all their lives, retirement brings significant housing challenges.

Retirement is a transition period. God never intended for retirement to be an end in itself. And instead of kicking back at age 60 or 65, by starting a second career, shifting to part-time work, or simply continuing to work full-time, some can allow their retirement portfolio to expand by compounding returns for a greater period of time.

There is danger in trying to be too precise in planning your nest egg with elaborate worksheets or powerful computer programs. Life isn't that precise. Think about what will constitute a successful retirement. Most people would be better off investing more of their efforts in the things money cannot buy:

- deepening one's relationship with the Lord
- building relationships with family and friends
- remaining in good health—weight and stress management are vital
- participating in gratifying and fulfilling activities

Preparing for Retirement

How much income will be needed?

Being financially prepared for retirement is simply a function of time and money: the less we have of one, the more we need of the other.

What is the biggest excuse ministers use when they are not saving for retirement? They say they need every penny to pay their bills now—but they'll start saving once the bills are paid off. Paying off debts is a worthy goal, but most people never pay them all off.

Most ministers cannot save a fortune by the time they reach retirement. On a minister's pay, it is difficult to squirrel away as much as many experts insist is needed for a comfortable retirement. But there is one inescapable truth: The sooner we start saving, the better. Saving for retirement isn't like climbing one great peak. It's really like climbing several smaller ones.

Many financial planners suggest 70% to 80% pre-retirement income is needed. But ministers may be able to significantly reduce the income requirement just by moving from an area with a high cost of living to a lower-cost one.

How long is retirement going to be?

The major concern of retirees today is the fear of outliving their income. Today, a 66-year-old male is expected to live 18 more years, and a female is expected to live 24 more years. But life expectancies are averages, and planning on an "average" retirement can be dangerously shortsighted for anyone in good health. It makes sense for healthy people from long-lived families to plan for a retirement stretching at least to age 85, and women are likely to live longer than men.

Investing for retirement

The best advice for ministers is the simplest: Put as much into a 403(b) tax-sheltered annuity plan as possible. Whether the payments are church-funded or funded by a salary reduction, the contributions are tax-deferred for income tax purposes and are not subject to self-employment social security taxes. When benefits are received

> **Idea**
> Few ministers contribute up to the limits of their retirement plans. With the changes in retirement plan contribution limits, ministers can contribute more than ever before.

from a tax-sheltered annuity plan in retirement, the payments are not subject to self-employment social security taxes.

If the plan was sponsored by a church denomination, the benefits qualify for housing allowance treatment, subject to the regular housing allowance limitations (see pages 83–84). Most financial planners recommend ministers pay off their mortgage before they retire. But if the minister is a good money manager, he or she may want to arrange indebtedness so there are mortgage payments during at least the early years of retirement.

What if the minister has already contributed the maximum to a tax-sheltered annuity plan? A $5,500 contribution to a nondeductible Roth IRA or a regular deductible IRA is a good option for the next retirement savings dollars. How to decide? Young ministers will tend to benefit more from a Roth IRA because it thrives on long-term compounding. If the minister is nearing retirement and is in a 25% or higher income tax bracket, but believes he or she will drop to the 10% bracket at retirement, he or she should stay with a deductible IRA.

When the options have been exhausted, the minister may consider a taxable investment. The key to choosing taxable investments for retirement savings is to keep expenses down and get the most benefit from the 15% maximum capital gains rate (minimum rate for most taxpayers).

Asset allocation—the division of savings among different investment vehicles—is a key part of any retirement strategy. Not only is it necessary to decide what kind of investment account to use, the minister must also decide which specific investments go into which account.

Proper diversification entails much more than simply spreading contributions evenly among the available choices. It is influenced strongly by how long the minister will continue to work and how much has already been invested elsewhere. In general, the more time the minister has, the more aggressive he or she can afford to be in asset allocation.

Insurance choices as retirement approaches

When he or she is approaching retirement, the minister's insurance needs are often different from when he or she was in his or her 30s and 40s. Here are some insurance policies that may be needed and policies that can probably be done without:

> **Life insurance.** The need for life insurance usually declines or disappears once the minister is in or near retirement. The minister's children are probably financially independent. And by now enough assets may have been accumulated to cover the spouse's future needs. This means the minister might want to drop some of life insurance coverage.
>
> If life insurance is needed for estate planning or to protect dependents financially for at least 15 years, the minister should probably buy cash-value insurance so he or she can lock in the premium. If the minister owns a term life policy that is no longer needed, he or she can stop paying premiums and let the policy lapse.

Countdown to Retirement

This table can help ministers make the timely decisions that ensure a comfortable retirement. Since only the minister knows when he or she plans to call it quits, it is organized according to the number of years until then. If plans change, this checklist can be compressed into the time available.

CATEGORY	FIVE YEARS BEFORE RETIREMENT	TWO YEARS BEFORE RETIREMENT	THREE MONTHS BEFORE RETIREMENT	IN RETIREMENT
BUDGET	Draw up two budgets, current expenses and expected expenses in retirement. Plan to pay off debts by retirement.	Update your current and future budgets.	Merge your two budgets, deleting career expenses and adding any new retiree expenses.	Fine-tune your budget every year so that your projected spending matches your actual spending.
PENSION Defined-benefit plan	Ask your pension office to project your pension monthly and in a lump sum.	Decide how to take your pension; if as a lump sum, decide how to invest it.	Set up the investments you have chosen for your lump sum.	Invest your lump sum immediately to avoid the tax consequences.
403(b), 401(k) plans	Put the maximum in your plan. Wait as long as possible to tap the money so earnings grow tax deferred.	Keep contributing the maximum. If you will take a lump sum, ask an accountant how to minimize taxes.	Decide how to take your money. At 59½ you may start penalty-free lump-sum withdrawals.	At 70½ you may have to start minimum withdrawals from tax-deferred retirement plans.
SOCIAL SECURITY	Set up a "my Social Security" account at www.ssa.gov/myaccount/ to check your earnings and be sure your employers contributed the right amounts.	Double-check your "my Social Security" account.	Decide when after age 62 to start receiving social security.	At retirement age, there is no limit on the income you can earn without reducing your social security benefits.
INVESTMENTS	Meet with a financial planner to discuss your goals and adjust your asset mix to meet them.	Adjust the balance between growth and income investments to reduce your market risk and increase income.	Make further reductions in market risk.	Generally, keep some of your money in stocks to offset inflation.
EMERGENCY FUND	Stash an amount equal to three months' expenses in a money market fund.	Set up (or renew) a home-equity line of credit that you can tap in case of an emergency.	Your cash and home-equity line of credit should amount to one full year of expenses.	Keep one year's expenses in the fund; tap it only when you must.
HOUSE Sell vs. keep	Decide whether to keep your present house or sell it. If you sell, decide whether to buy another or rent.	If you plan to move after retiring, visit potential locations during vacations.	If you are selling, put your house on the market three to six months before retirement.	Your gain on the house is tax-free up to $500,000 (married), $250,000 (single).
Repairs and improvements	Renovate now; it's easier to borrow if you're employed.	Budget now for any big-ticket repairs you may need after you retire.		
MEDICAL INSURANCE	Ask your pension office what your medical benefits will be in retirement.	If you need individual coverage, start shopping for it now.	Apply for the coverage one month prior to retiring.	Medicare starts at 65. Six months before then, shop for Medigap insurance.

CHAPTER 6 > RETIREMENT AND SOCIAL SECURITY

> **Long-term care insurance.** Long-term care (LTC) insurance is a way to pay for nursing home costs while protecting your financial assets. LTC policies have improved significantly in recent years, but they are expensive.
>
> Long-term care policies cover nursing home stays only, home care only, or both. A good LTC policy will cover skilled or intermediate care, or custodial help in any type of facility, with no prior hospitalization required.

Remember
Consider long-term care plans that provide the same coverage for home health care and nursing facilities. The employer can pay or reimburse LTC premiums tax-free. The premiums are generally the minister's responsibility from after-tax dollars after he or she retires.

> **Medical insurance.** The minister's medical insurance may stop when he or she becomes eligible for Medicare at full retirement age, currently age 65. If the minister is old enough for Medicare, call social security to enroll. The minister may be eligible to remain in a group policy for 18 months after leaving your current employment, if the plan is based on COBRA rules.

The Fundamentals of Social Security

Ignore scare stories about social security not being there at retirement. The truth is, the benefits for most ministers will survive largely intact for many years. And Congress is likely to take steps to shore up the program in the next few years.

The age for collecting the full social security benefit used to be 65—but no longer. Full retirement gradually increases from age 65 to 67. Here, by year of birth, is the age at which ministers can expect to collect the full social security retirement benefit:

Year of Birth	Age for Collecting Full Retirement Benefit
Before 1938	65
1938	65 and two months
1939	65 and four months
1940	65 and six months
1941	65 and eight months
1942	65 and ten months
1943–1954	66
1955	66 and two months
1956	66 and four months
1957	66 and six months
1958	66 and eight months
1959	66 and ten months
1960 and later	67

Filing Tip
If the minister works while receiving social security benefits, social security and Medicare taxes are still paid regardless of age. Additional earnings can result in increasing the benefit if the earnings are higher than those of an earlier year used in the previous calculation.

Income taxes on benefits

Social security benefits are income-tax-free for the majority of beneficiaries. However, those with high total incomes must include up to 85% of their benefits as income for federal income tax purposes. Special step-rate "thresholds" determine the amount which may be taxed:

➤ Single persons: $25,000 and $34,000

➤ Married couples filing a joint return: $32,000 and $44,000

Working after reaching retirement age

If the minister is under full retirement age (FRA), he or she loses $1 of social security benefits for every $2 earned over a certain limit, which increases annually ($16,920 in 2017). Once FRA is reached, one can earn as much as desired with no cut in benefits. The earnings test looks only at money you earn from a job or self-employment, not income from investments or other sources. Dollars from income excluded because of the housing allowance are included in the earnings test.

Checking on benefits

It is recommended to complete a request for an earnings and benefit estimate statement every three years. This information can be accessed by setting up an account at www.ssa.gov/myaccount. The Social Security Agency should be notified of any discrepancies.

Ministers should not overlook the possibility of errors in the church retirement plan, either. It is wise to get a summary plan description from the church pension board, and look over the annual statement summary.

Taking Out Retirement Money

Ministers spend their entire lives putting money into retirement plans. When and how money is withdrawn from tax-deferred retirement plans are among the most important financial decisions.

Capital builds up in retirement plans, free of taxes. But the federal, state, and local governments are looking for their share when money is withdrawn. And Congress has devised a host of hurdles and penalties:

➤ Workers cannot start withdrawing until they retire at age 55 or reach 59½. If they do, they have to pay a 10% tax penalty on top of the standard income tax rates. The Roth IRA is an exception because money can be withdrawn without penalty if the funds are left in the Roth IRA for at least five years.

➤ For church plans, the minister must start withdrawals at age 70½ or the date of retirement, whichever is later. For other retirement plans, withdrawals must start when the minister reaches age 70½. If not, the minister will have to pay a walloping 50% penalty tax. There is no age requirement for starting to withdraw funds from a Roth IRA.

The Two Social Security Tax Systems

Social security taxes are collected under two systems. Under the Federal Insurance Contributions Act (FICA), the employer pays one-half of the tax and the employee pays the other half. Under the Self-Employment Contributions Act (SECA), the self-employed person pays all the tax (self-employment tax) as calculated on the taxpayer's Schedule SE. IRS Publications 517 and 1828 provide information on social security taxes for ministers.

Ministers are always self-employed for social security purposes, subject to SECA under the tax law with respect to services performed in the exercise of their ministry, whether employed by a church, integral agency of a church, or a parachurch organization. Ministers are self-employed for social security purposes regardless of how their employer categorizes them for income tax purposes. Ministers are not subject to FICA-type social security taxes, even though they report their income taxes as employees and receive a Form W-2 from their employer.

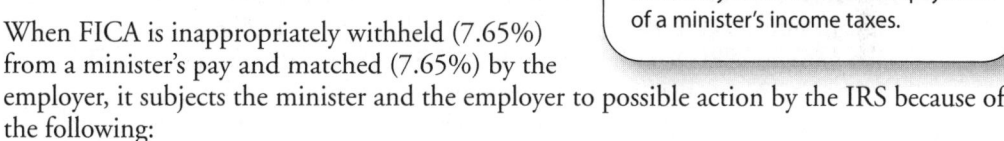

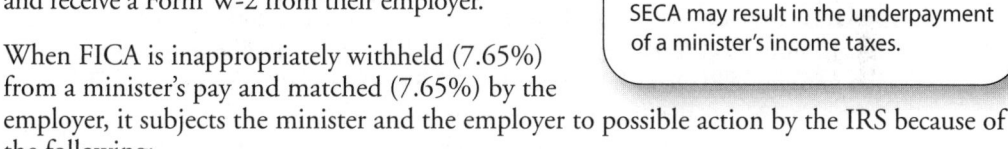

Warning

Churches and other employers commonly subject ministers to the wrong type of social security. If a minister qualifies for a housing allowance, he or she is not subject to FICA-type social security. The inappropriate use of FICA instead of SECA may result in the underpayment of a minister's income taxes.

When FICA is inappropriately withheld (7.65%) from a minister's pay and matched (7.65%) by the employer, it subjects the minister and the employer to possible action by the IRS because of the following:

> The minister has often underpaid his or her income taxes. The 7.65% match that was paid by the church is really compensation that is avoiding income tax because it is not being reported in Box 1 of the Form W-2. Additionally, the minister is paying FICA instead of SECA, and the IRS could require that this be corrected retroactively.

> The employer is underreporting the employee's income by the 7.65% FICA match. Also, the employer is reporting FICA social security taxes when it should not. The IRS could require the employer to retroactively correct Forms 941 and W-2.

> **Example:** A church hires and pays you to perform ministerial services, subject to the church's control. Under the common-law rules (pages 9–14), you are an employee of the church while performing those services. The church reports your wages on Form W-2 for income tax purposes, but no social security taxes are withheld. You are self-employed for social security purposes. You must pay self-employment tax (SECA) on those wages yourself unless you request and receive an exemption from self-employment tax. On Form W-2, Boxes 3 through 6 are left blank.

SOCIAL SECURITY SYSTEMS

FICA (Federal Insurance Contributions Act)	SECA (Self-Employment Contributions Act)
Non-minister employees of a church are all subject to FICA. 　Employee pays　　　7.65% 　Employer pays　　　7.65% 　　　　　　　　　　15.30%	All qualified ministers are subject to SECA (unless they have opted out of social security). Self-employed individuals pay the full 15.3%.
The 15.3% is paid on a wage base of up to $127,200 for 2017.	The 15.3% is paid on a wage base of up to $127,200 for 2017.
Medicare taxes still apply to wages in excess of $127,200.	Medicare taxes still apply to wages in excess of $ 127,200.

Many churches reimburse ministers for a portion or all of their SECA liability. SECA reimbursements represent additional taxable compensation in the year paid to the minister for both income and social security tax purposes.

Because of the SECA deductions (see page 46–47), a full SECA reimbursement is effectively less than the gross 15.3% rate.

> **Example:** A church provides a cash salary of $35,000 and provides a parsonage that has an annual fair rental value of $15,000. Even though a full reimbursement of the minister's SECA is slightly less than 15.3%, the church decides to reimburse at the 15.3% rate for simplicity. Since the minister has entered into a voluntary withholding arrangement with the church for federal income taxes, the church grosses up the monthly pay by $637.50 (15.3% times $50,000, or $6,650 divided by 12) and withholds federal income tax of $554.17 plus a sufficient amount to cover the minister's estimated federal income tax.

Computing the Self-Employment Tax

When computing the self-employment tax, your net earnings include the gross income earned from performing qualified services minus the deductions related to that income.

This includes church compensation reported in Box 1 of Form W-2 (the designated housing allowance should not be shown in this box), the net

> **Key Issue**
> Unless a minister has opted out of social security, the net ministerial income plus the excluded housing allowance and the fair rental value of church-provided housing is subject to self-employment social security tax. This is true even if the minister is retired and receiving social security benefits. There is no age limit on paying social security tax.

profit or loss from Schedule C or C-EZ (relating to clergy income), any housing allowance excluded from Box 1 of Form W-2, the fair rental value of church-provided housing, and amounts that should have been included in Box 1 of Form W-2, such as business expense reimbursements made under a nonaccountable plan, a self-employment social security tax reimbursement or allowance, love offerings, etc.

The following tax rates apply to net earnings from self-employment of $400 or more each year:

Year	Tax Rate OASDI	Tax Rate Medicare	Maximum Earnings Base OASDI	Maximum Earnings Base Medicare
2015	12.4%	2.9%	$118,000	no limit
2016	12.4%	2.9%	118,500	no limit
2017	12.4%	2.9%	127,200	no limit
2017	12.4%	2.9%	128,700	no limit

OASDI = Old-age, survivors, and disability insurance, or social security

Only business expenses are deductible in determining income subject to SECA. The minister may deduct unreimbursed business expenses for the SECA computation even if deductions are not itemized on Schedule A.

Moving expenses do not qualify as business expenses. Therefore, moving expenses are not deductible in computing self-employment tax. However, for minister-employees, reimbursed moving expenses are excludable from Form W-2. Therefore, the reimbursements are not included for income or social security tax purposes.

Example: You have the following ministerial income and expenses: church salary $50,000 (of which the housing allowance is $12,000); net Schedule C (C-EZ) income related to special speaking engagements, weddings, funerals, etc., $1,350; Schedule A employee business expenses (after offsetting 50% of nondeductible meal and entertainment expenses) $1,800. You do not itemize your deductions on Schedule A since the standard deduction is more beneficial.

Your self-employment income is	
Salary from church	$38,000
Church-designated housing allowance	12,000
Schedule C (C-EZ) net earnings	1,350
Schedule A employee business expenses	(1,800)
Total	**$49,550**

Use the worksheet on page 124 to calculate net earnings from self-employment. Net earnings are transferred to Form SE, page 1, line 2, to calculate the SECA tax.

Self-Employment Social Security Tax Worksheet

Inclusions:

Salary paid by church as reflected on Form W-2, Box 1 $_____

Net profit or loss as reflected on Schedule C or C-EZ (includes speaking honoraria, offerings you receive for marriages, baptisms, funerals, and other fees)   _____

Housing allowance excluded from salary on Form W-2   _____

Fair rental value of church-provided housing (including paid utilities)   _____

Nonaccountable business expense reimbursements (if not included on Form W-2)   _____

Reimbursement of self-employment taxes (if not included on Form W-2)   _____

Other amounts that should have been included on Form W-2, Box 1, such as love offerings   _____

Total inclusions   _____

Deductions:

Unreimbursed ministerial business and professional expenses or reimbursed expenses paid under a nonaccountable plan

    A. Deductible on Schedule A before the 2% of AGI limitation whether or not you itemized,[1] or   _____

    B. Not deductible on Form 2106/2106 EZ or Schedule C/C-EZ because expenses were allocated to taxable/nontaxable income   _____

Total deductions   _____

Net earnings from self-employment (to Schedule SE) $_____

[1] The 50% unreimbursed meal and entertainment expense limitation applies to amounts subject to social security tax. In other words, if some of your meal and entertainment expenses were subjected to the 50% limit, the remainder cannot be deducted here.

Note 1: Your net earnings from self-employment are not affected by the foreign earned income exclusion or the foreign housing exclusion or deduction if you are a U.S. citizen or resident alien who is serving abroad and living in a foreign country.

Note 2: Amounts received as pension payments or annuity payments related to a church-sponsored tax-sheltered annuity by a retired minister are generally considered to be excluded from the social security calculation.

CHAPTER 6 ➤ RETIREMENT AND SOCIAL SECURITY

Both Spouses Are Ministers

If a husband and wife who are both duly ordained, commissioned, or licensed ministers have an agreement with a church that each will perform specific services for which they will receive pay, jointly or separately, they must divide the compensation according to the agreement. Such a division of income would have no impact on their income tax if they filed a joint return. But each of them could obtain social security coverage by dividing the compensation and subjecting the compensation to social security tax.

If the agreement for services is with one spouse only and the other spouse receives no pay for any specific duties, amounts paid for services are included only in the income of the spouse having the agreement.

If a couple has already filed a return and incorrectly divided, or failed to divide, the income for self-employment tax purposes, they may file an amended return showing the corrected amount as self-employment income for each spouse.

> **Caution**
> A minister's spouse who is not duly ordained, commissioned, or licensed as a minister of a church but who receives pay for performing services for the organization should not include the earnings with the minister's self-employment income. The non-minister spouse is generally an employee of the church for federal income tax and social security (FICA) tax purposes.

If one spouse is ordained, commissioned, or licensed and the other is not, the "qualified" minister under the tax law generally receives 100% of the compensation from the church, and the spouse is considered a volunteer. This is true even though they may have been hired as a team and each spouse provides significant services to the church.

However, it may be legitimate to split the compensation from the church based on the duties of each spouse. Pay should never be split merely for the purpose of allowing a spouse to qualify for social security or to avoid exceeding the social security earnings limit for one spouse.

Self-Employment Tax Deductions

Ministers can take an income tax deduction equal to one-half of their self-employment tax liability. The deduction is claimed against gross income on line 27 of Form 1040, page 1.

They may also deduct a portion of their self-employment tax liability in calculating their self-employment tax. This deduction is made on Schedule SE, Section A, line 4 or Section B, line 4a, by multiplying self-employment income by .9235.

> **Idea**
> Because of the deductibility of the self-employment tax in both the income tax and self-employment tax computations, if the church desires to reimburse the minister's entire social security tax obligation, it is effectively less than the gross 15.3% rate. See page 66 for the effective rate at various marginal income tax rates.

105

The purpose of these deductions is to equalize the social security (and income) taxes paid by (and for) employees and self-employed persons with equivalent income.

Use of Income Tax Withholding to Pay Social Security Taxes

Under a voluntary withholding agreement, a minister-employee may ask the church to withhold a sufficient amount to cover federal income taxes plus enough for the self-employment taxes (SECA). The church must report all amounts withheld under such an arrangement as federal income taxes. The other option for the payment of income and social security taxes is to use the Form 1040-ES in paying quarterly estimated taxes.

> **Key Issue**
>
> Ministers should take advantage of opportunities to enter into a voluntary withholding arrangement with their employer to withhold enough federal income tax to cover both their federal income tax and self-employment social security tax obligation. Withholding the proper amount each payday is a very efficient way to pay taxes. You do not run the risk of filing Forms 1040-ES late and incurring underpayment penalties.

Example: A minister projected that he will owe $1,000 of federal income tax for 2017 and $3,000 of self-employment social security tax for a total tax obligation of $4,000. The minister and his spouse will not have withholding from non-church employment. He will not qualify for the earned income tax credit. The minister could enter into a voluntary withholding agreement whereby the church would withhold federal income tax from each paycheck so that by the end of 2017, $4,000 was withheld (this would be reported on Form W-2, Box 2). No FICA-type social security tax is withheld from the minister's pay since he is not subject to that type of social security. Alternately, the minister could file Forms 1040-ES on April 15, 2017; June 15, 2017; September 15, 2017; and January 15, 2018 and submit payments of $1,000 per filing.

Opting Out of Social Security

All ministers are automatically covered by social security (SECA) for services in the exercise of ministry unless an exemption has been received based on the filing with, and approval by, the IRS of Form 4361. You must certify that you oppose, either conscientiously or because of religious principles, the acceptance of any public insurance (with respect to services performed as a minister), including social security benefits. Either opposition must be based on religious belief. This includes an opposition to insurance that helps pay for or provide services for medical care (such as Medicare) and social security benefits.

To claim the exemption from self-employment tax, the minister must:

- file Form 4361
- be conscientiously opposed to public insurance (which includes insurance systems established by the Social Security Act) because of the minister's individual religious considerations (not because of general conscience), or because of the principles of the minister's religious denomination
- file for other than economic reasons
- inform the ordaining, commissioning, or licensing body of the church or order that he or she is opposed to public insurance
- establish that the religious organization that ordained, commissioned, or licensed the minister or his or her religious order is a tax-exempt religious organization
- establish that the organization is a church or a convention or association of churches
- sign and return the statement sent by the IRS to verify that the requested exemption based on the grounds listed on the statement

Warning
Opting out of social security is relatively simple. Form 4361 must be filed by the due date of the minister's tax return for the second year with $400 or more, any portion of which comes from the exercise of ministry. But the simplicity of opting out should not be confused with the significant difficulty of complying with the requirements for opting out.

Tip
Even though a minister signs Form 4361 and certifies that he or she is opposed to accepting public insurance benefits which are based on earnings from services performed in his or her capacity as a minister, the minister can still purchase life insurance or participate in retirement programs administered by nongovernmental institutions.

Deadline for filing for an exemption

The application for exemption from self-employment tax must be filed by the date the tax return is due, including extensions, for the second year in which the minister had net ministerial income of $400 or more. These do not have to be consecutive tax years.

Example 1: A minister ordained in 2016 has net earnings of $400 in 2016 and $500 in 2017. An application for exemption must be filed by April 15, 2018, if no extension has been filed. If the minister does not receive the approved exemption by April 15, 2018, the self-employment tax for 2017 is due by that date.

Example 2: A minister has $300 in net clergy earnings in 2016 but earned $400 in both 2015 and 2017. An application for exemption must be filed by April 15, 2018, if no extension has been filed. If the minister does not receive the approved exemption by April 15, 2018, the self-employment tax for 2017 is due by that date.

Example 3: A minister, ordained in 2015, earned $700 net for that year. In 2016, ministerial compensation was $1,000 and related expenses were $1,000. Therefore, the 2016 net earnings were zero. Also in 2016, $7,000 in net self-employment earnings was received from non-ministerial sources. In 2017, net ministerial earnings were $1,500 and self-employment income of $12,000 was received from non-ministerial sources.

> **Tip**
> If the exemption is approved, it does not apply to non-ministerial wages or to any other self-employment income. For example, a bi-vocational pastor who is employed part-time in a secular job is subject to FICA on the wages from the secular job. If a minister performs independent contractor services unrelated to his ministry, this net profit is subject to social security.

Because the minister had ministerial net earnings in 2015 and 2017 that were more than $400 each year, the application for exemption must be filed by April 15, 2018. If the minister does not receive the approved exemption by April 15, 2018, the self-employment tax for 2017 is due by that date.

Example 4: A minister was ordained in 2016 with $1,000 and $2,000 of net ministerial earnings for 2016 and 2017, respectively. The minister filed Form 4361 in 2017 (this was a timely filing since the last day to file without extensions is April 15, 2018) and the application was approved by the IRS. The minister paid self-employment social security tax on the $1,000 of net ministerial earnings for 2016 since the Form 4361 had not yet been filed. Based on the approval of Form 4361, the minister can file an amended income tax return for 2016 using Form 1040X (see pages 123–24) and receive a refund of the social security tax paid on the net ministerial earnings for that year.

A minister must include with Form 4361 a statement that he has informed the ordaining body of his church of his opposition to the coverage.

A second ordination with a second church generally does not provide a second opportunity for a minister to opt out by filing Form 4361.

Basis of filing for exemption

Neither economics nor any other non-religious reason is a valid basis for the exemption. Many ministers are improperly counseled to opt out of social security because it may not be a "good investment." The minister's view of the soundness of the social security program has absolutely no relationship to the application for exemption.

The first consideration is the minister's ability to sign Form 4361 with a clear conscience. Key words in qualifying for exemption from social security coverage on ministerial earnings

Form **4361** (Rev. January 2011) Department of the Treasury Internal Revenue Service	**Application for Exemption From Self-Employment Tax for Use by Ministers, Members of Religious Orders and Christian Science Practitioners**	OMB No. 1545-0074 **File Original and Two Copies**

File original and two copies and attach supporting documents. This exemption is granted only if the IRS returns a copy to you marked "approved."

Please type or print

1 Name of taxpayer applying for exemption (as shown on Form 1040) Harold T. Baldwin	Social security number 603-42-8941
Number and street (including apt. no.) PO Box 183	Telephone number (optional)
City or town, state, and ZIP code Milton, PA 17647	

2 Check **one** box: ☐ Christian Science practitioner ☒ Ordained minister, priest, rabbi
☐ Member of religious order not under a vow of poverty ☐ Commissioned or licensed minister (see line 6)

3 Date ordained, licensed, etc. (Attach supporting document. See instructions.)
7/1/15

4 Legal name of ordaining, licensing, or commissioning body or religious order
Christian General Conference

Number, street, and room or suite no.
PO Box 5002

Employer identification number
48-9017682

City or town, state, and ZIP code
Nashville, AR 71852

5 Enter the first 2 years after the date shown on line 3 that you had net self-employment earnings of $400 or more, any of which came from services as a minister, priest, rabbi, etc.; member of a religious order; or Christian Science practitioner ▶ 2016 2017

6 If you apply for the exemption as a licensed or commissioned minister and your denomination also ordains ministers, please indicate how your ecclesiastical powers differ from those of an ordained minister of your denomination. Attach a copy of your denomination's bylaws relating to the powers of ordained, commissioned, and licensed ministers.

7 I certify that I am conscientiously opposed to, or because of my religious principles I am opposed to, the acceptance (for services I perform as a minister, member of a religious order not under a vow of poverty, or Christian Science practitioner) of any public insurance that makes payments in the event of death, disability, old age, or retirement; or that makes payments toward the cost of, or provides services for, medical care. (Public insurance includes insurance systems established by the Social Security Act.)

I certify that as a duly ordained, commissioned, or licensed minister of a church or a member of a religious order not under a vow of poverty, I have informed the ordaining, commissioning, or licensing body of my church or order that I am conscientiously opposed to, or because of religious principles I am opposed to, the acceptance (for services I perform as a minister or as a member of a religious order) of any public insurance that makes payments in the event of death, disability, old age, or retirement; or that makes payments toward the cost of, or provides services for, medical care, including the benefits of any insurance system established by the Social Security Act.

I certify that I have never filed Form 2031 to revoke a previous exemption from social security coverage on earnings as a minister, member of a religious order not under a vow of poverty, or Christian Science practitioner.

I request to be exempted from paying self-employment tax on my earnings from services as a minister, member of a religious order not under a vow of poverty, or Christian Science practitioner, under section 1402(e) of the Internal Revenue Code. I understand that the exemption, if granted, will apply only to these earnings. Under penalties of perjury, I declare that I have examined this application and to the best of my knowledge and belief, it is true and correct.

Signature ▶ *Harold T. Baldwin* Date ▶ 1/30/18

Caution: Form 4361 is **not proof** of the right to an exemption from federal income tax withholding or social security tax, the right to a parsonage allowance exclusion (section 107 of the Internal Revenue Code), assignment by your religious superiors to a particular job, or the exemption or church status of the ordaining, licensing, or commissioning body, or religious order.

For Internal Revenue Service Use

☐ Approved for exemption from self-employment tax on ministerial earnings
☐ Disapproved for exemption from self-employment tax on ministerial earnings

By _____ _____
(Director's signature) (Date)

General Instructions

Section references are to the Internal Revenue Code unless otherwise noted.

Purpose of form. File Form 4361 to apply for an exemption from self-employment tax if you have ministerial earnings (defined later) and are:

• An ordained, commissioned, or licensed minister of a church;
• A member of a religious order who has not taken a vow of poverty; or
• A Christian Science practitioner.

Note. If you are a commissioned or licensed minister of a religious denomination or church that ordains its ministers, you may be treated in the same manner as an ordained minister if you perform substantially all the religious functions within the scope of the tenets and practices of your religious denomination or church.

This application must be based on your religious or conscientious opposition to the acceptance (for services performed as a minister, member of a religious order not under a vow of poverty, or Christian Science practitioner) of any public insurance that makes payments for death, disability, old age, or retirement; or that makes payments for the cost of, or provides services for, medical care, including any insurance benefits established by the Social Security Act.

If you are a duly ordained, commissioned, or licensed minister of a church or a member of a religious order not under a vow of poverty, prior to filing this form you must inform the ordaining, commissioning, or licensing body of your church or order that, on religious or conscientious grounds, you are opposed to the acceptance of public insurance benefits based on ministerial service.

For Privacy Act and Paperwork Reduction Act Notice, see page 2. Cat. No. 41586H Form **4361** (Rev. 1-2011)

Caution: Very few ministers qualify to file Form 4361. The filing must be based on the minister's conscience or religious principles, not because of a preference to invest retirement funds elsewhere.

are "religious principles" and "conscientiously opposed to the acceptance of any public insurance." Religious principles do not simply consist of the conviction that perhaps social security will not be there when retirement comes or that a better retirement plan can be purchased through an annuity or other retirement program. The belief must be an integral part of the minister's religious system of beliefs, his or her theology.

Further, this religious principle must be one that would prevent the minister from ever asking for the benefits from such a plan based on the church salary. No basis exists for an objection related to paying the taxes or to the level of the taxes to be paid.

> **Caution**
> Opting out of social security is one of the most abused provisions of the tax law that applies to ministers. Too often ministers have opted out because they are concerned about long-term safety of the program or they feel they have a better way to invest the funds. These reasons do not provide a basis to sign Form 4361.

If a minister opts out and does not have sufficient credits from prior employment or from future non-ministerial employment, neither the minister nor his or her dependents will be covered under social security benefits, survivors' benefits, or Medicare. If a minister opts out of social security, he or she should make alternate plans to provide for catastrophic illness, disability, or death, as well as for retirement.

This is not a decision to be taken lightly. First, the minister must act on religious convictions. Second, he or she must be prepared financially with alternatives to the benefits of social security coverage.

Although a minister may opt out of social security with respect to ministerial income, he or she may still receive social security benefits related to non-ministerial wages or other self-employment income.

Opting back into social security

Until April 15, 2002, ministers could opt back into social security by filing Form 2031. This was a special two-year window based on a law passed in 1999. With the window to opt back into social security closed, there is currently no formal method available for ministers to opt back into social security.

Working After Retirement

There is no retirement earnings test for persons who have attained full retirement age (FRA). But for individuals who have not attained FRA, there is a limit on earnings from current work. The earnings limit is a retirement test and is a separate issue from income taxes.

If the minister earns more than the exempt amount (see below), the benefits to the minister and family members that are based on work record will be reduced. If a family member earns more than the exempt amount, only that person's benefit is reduced.

If the minister is under FRA throughout 2017, he or she can earn $16,920. If the earnings exceed this, then $1 of benefits is withheld for every $2 earned above $16,920. If the earnings exceed this limit, some benefits may still be payable.

If the minister attains FRA in 2017, he or she can earn $44,880 in the period before the month in which FRA is attained with no reduction in benefits. If the minister's earnings exceed this, then $1 in benefits is withheld for every $3 earned above $44,880.

After retirement, ministers may receive special payments for work they did before they started getting social security benefits. Usually, these special payments will not affect their social security benefit if they are compensation for work done before retirement. Examples of special payments include bonuses, accumulated vacation or sick pay, and severance pay.

Canada Pension Plan

Under an agreement between the United States and Canada, a minister is subject to the laws of the country in which the services are performed for the purposes of United States social security and the Canada Pension Plan, respectively. In other words, a Canadian citizen who moves to the United States to pastor a church generally must pay United States social security (SECA) tax.

There is one exception to the general rule if the minister is required by a Canadian employer to transfer to a related organization in the United States on a temporary basis for a period not exceeding 60 months, with the intention of returning to the employment with the Canadian employer at the end of the temporary assignment. In this case, the Canadian employer must complete Form CPT56, Certificate of Coverage Under the Canada Pension Plan Pursuant to Article V of the Agreement on Social Security Between Canada and the United States, which may be obtained at www.ccra-adrc.gc.ca.

Some ministers may work in both the United States and Canada (see Publication IC84-6 Canada-United States Social Security Agreement issued by the Canada Revenue Agency). Each country issues "certificates of coverage" to confirm a particular work is covered under the social security laws of that country.

Integrity**Points**

- **Improperly opting out of social security.** The improper (actually, the word is "illegal," but it is such a harsh word) opting out of social security by ministers is one of the dirty little secrets of the profession.

  Shame on those who have promoted ministers opting out of social security for reasons that are inconsistent with federal law! And, shame on the ministers, many naively by their own admission, who accepted faulty advice.

  It's not a matter of whether it makes good money-sense for a minister to pay into social security. It's simply the right thing to do. Ministers are required to pay social security unless they are one of the rare ministers who are opposed to receiving public insurance (including social security) based on conscientious opposition or religious principles.

  In speaking and otherwise communicating with thousands of ministers across America, we have found only a handful of ministers who opted out of social security for legal reasons. What a blight on the profession, and what a poor example for congregations!

- **Correctly calculating the social security tax.** Paying the self-employment social security tax is often a bitter pill to swallow for ministers—the social security tax usually dwarfs the amount of income tax. But calculating the correct amount of social security tax due is also very challenging.

  The IRS certainly does not give a minister much help in calculating the social security tax. One might think the IRS would have developed a form to help ministers—there's an IRS form for nearly every other purpose!

  Far too many ministers do not include the housing allowance excluded from salary on Form W-2 and/or the fair rental value of congregation-provided housing and the reimbursement of social security tax. On the flip side of the equation, of the amount subject to social security, many ministers forget to exclude unreimbursed ministerial business and professional expenses (or reimbursed expenses paid under a nonaccountable plan [see page 124]).

CHAPTER 7 Paying Taxes

In This Chapter

- Tax withholding
- Estimated tax
- Excess social security withheld (FICA)
- Earned income credit
- Extension of time to file
- Extension of time to pay
- Offers in compromise
- Filing an amended tax return

The federal income tax is a pay-as-you-go tax. Ministers must pay the tax as they earn or receive income during the year. Employees usually have income tax withheld from their pay. However, the pay of qualified ministers is not subject to federal income tax withholding. Ministers who are employees for income tax purposes may enter into a voluntary withholding agreement with the church to cover any income tax and self-employment social security taxes that are due. IRS Publication 505 provides additional information on tax withholding and estimated taxes.

Tax Withholding

Federal income tax withheld from earnings as an employee should be reported to the minister on your Form W-2. The total amount withheld from all sources should be entered on line 64, Form 1040, page 2.

Churches are not required to withhold income taxes from wages paid to ministers for services performed in the exercise of their ministry. The exemption does not apply to non-ministerial church employees such as a secretary, organist, or custodian.

A minister-employee may have a voluntary withholding agreement with the employing church to cover income taxes (the amount may be set high enough to also cover the self-employment social security tax liability). An agreement to withhold income taxes from wages should be in writing. There is no required form for the agreement. It may be as simple as a letter from the minister to the church requesting that a specified amount be withheld as federal income taxes. Or a minister may request voluntary withholding by submitting Form W-4 (Employee's Withholding Allowance Certificate) to the church and indicate an additional amount to be withheld in excess of the tax table amount.

If federal income taxes withheld are sufficient to cover both the minister's income and self-employment social security (SECA) taxes, it is very important that the amounts be reported as "federal income taxes withheld" when the church completes quarterly Forms 941 and annual Forms W-2 and W-3. FICA social security taxes should never be withheld or remitted for qualified ministers.

> **Idea**
> Though not required, churches should offer to withhold federal (and state and local, where applicable) income taxes (never FICA taxes!) from a minister's pay. Filing Forms 1040-ES often means saving up money for the 4/15, 6/15, 9/15, and 1/15 deadlines. Withholding the proper amount each week or payday is so much more efficient.

For personal budgeting purposes, a minister may request the church to withhold amounts from compensation. Coinciding with the Form 1040-ES due dates (April 15, June 15, September 15, and January 15), the church pays the withheld amounts directly to the minister and then the minister uses the funds to make the appropriate estimated tax payments to the IRS. The withholding has no impact on Form W-2.

Example 1: A minister's cash compensation is $40,000 for 2017, and the anticipated income and self-employment social security tax obligation for 2017 is $4,800. The minister uses the estimated tax method to pay income and self-employment social security tax.

Based on an agreement with the minister, a church withholds $400 per month from the minister's compensation in relation to the minister's tax obligation. The church pays the minister $1,200 on April 15, June 15, October 15, and January 15 to provide the amount the minister needs to submit with Form 1040-ES. The $4,800 withheld does not impact the reporting on Form W-2, e.g., Box 1 of Form W-2 shows $40,000. The $4,800 is not included in Box 2 as Federal Income Tax Withheld because no funds were remitted to the IRS for payroll tax purposes.

Example 2: A minister's cash compensation is $40,000 for 2017, and the church and the minister enter into a voluntary withholding arrangement for federal income tax purposes.

Based on the agreement, the church withholds $400 of federal income taxes per month and remits the withheld amounts to the IRS through the payroll tax reporting process. The Form W-2 for 2017 shows compensation in Box 1 of $40,000 and Federal Income Tax Withheld in Box 2 of $4,800.

Estimated Tax

Estimated tax is the method used to pay income and self-employment taxes for income that is not subject to withholding. The estimated tax is the expected tax for the year minus your expected withholding and credits.

If filing a declaration of estimated tax, the worker must complete the quarterly Forms 1040-ES. If the 2018 estimated taxes are $1,000 or less, no declaration of estimated tax is required.

If the estimated tax payments for 2018 equal 90% of the worker's 2018 tax liability, underpayment penalties will be avoided. An option is to make the 2018 estimated tax payments equal to 100% of the worker's 2017 federal and social security taxes (Form 1040, page 2, line 63). This method generally avoids underpayment penalties and is easier to calculate. The estimated tax payments for certain higher income taxpayers must be 110% of the prior year tax.

> **Filing Tip**
> When using the estimated tax method of submitting income and social security tax money to the IRS, pay at least as much as your previous year's total taxes (before offsetting withholding, estimated tax payments, etc.). Spread the payments equally over the four Forms 1040-ES. This will generally avoid underpayment penalties.

Ministers with an adjusted gross income of over $150,000 ($75,000 for married individuals filing separately) may fall under special rules requiring larger estimated tax payments. At this income level, if the estimated tax payments for 2018 equal 110% of the 2017 tax liability, underpayment penalties will be avoided.

In estimating 2018 taxes, net earnings from self-employment should be reduced by 7.65% before calculating the self-employment tax of 15.3%. There is also an income tax deduction for one-half of the self-employment tax (Form 1040, page 1, line 27).

The minister pays one-fourth of his or her total estimated taxes in installments as follows:

For the Period	Due Date
January 1 - March 31	April 15
April 1 - May 31	June 15
June 1 - August 31	September 15
September 1 - December 31	January 15

Estimated tax payments are counted as paid when the IRS receives them. Thus, paying more later does not offset shortfalls from prior installments. Withheld tax is considered as paid evenly throughout the year. Therefore, increasing withholding late in a year offsets earlier underpayments.

Excess Social Security Withheld (FICA)

If a minister worked for two or more employers during 2017 and together they paid him or her more than $127,200 in wages, too much FICA tax was probably withheld from the wages. The minister can claim the extra amount as a credit on line 71 of Form 1040, page 2,

2018 MINISTER'S TAX & FINANCIAL GUIDE

Three Ways to Pay Your Taxes

1

Estimated Taxes

The minister pays federal income taxes and social security taxes (SECA) directly to the IRS.

Form 941-V is filed by the minister on 4/15, 6/15, 9/15, and 1/15.

2

Voluntary Withholding

The church withholds federal income tax and pays quarterly to the IRS. Additional federal income tax may be withheld to cover the minister's social security tax (SECA) liability.

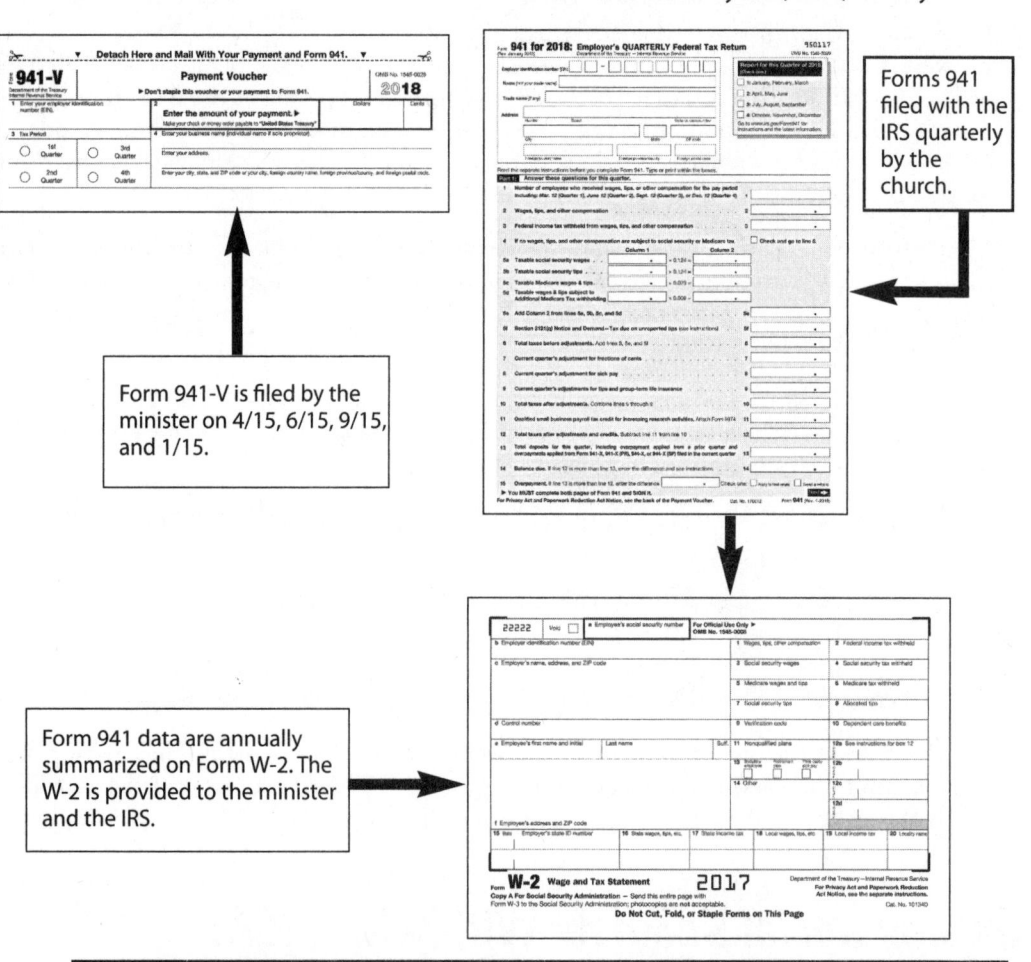

Forms 941 filed with the IRS quarterly by the church.

Form 941 data are annually summarized on Form W-2. The W-2 is provided to the minister and the IRS.

3

Payroll withholding from the minister's pay. The church does not remit the amounts withheld to the IRS. The amounts are paid directly to the minister on or before 4/15, 6/15, 9/15, and 1/15. The minister then files Form 1040-ES and remits the money to the IRS.

CHAPTER 7 > PAYING TAXES

Calculate the Most Important Tax Planning Number of 2018

It is only necessary to pay by December 31 (January 15 if paying estimates) the smallest of the "safe harbor" amounts. Use this worksheet to calculate them to know how much to withhold or pay in estimated taxes.

100% of your 2016 tax liability
(the number on line 63 on your Form 1040): _____

90% of your estimated 2018 tax (federal income tax
and self-employment social security tax) liability.
Recalculate this number at least three times before
October to update changes in your tax circumstances.
(The October date gives you enough time to make
changes in withholdings or your final estimated payment.)

Estimated 2018 tax liability: _____ x 90% = _____

You can also avoid a penalty if you owe less than
$1,000 on April 15 after considering withholdings.
But be careful using this loophole—if you miscalculate
just a little bit, you could be facing a penalty. So
recalculate this at least three times a year as well.

Estimated 2018 tax liability: _____

Minus projected 2018 federal income tax
withholdings: _____

Equals: (must be less than $1,000) _____

Fill in the smallest of these numbers: _____

You only have to pay this amount by the end of the year.

A special rule applies to individuals with adjusted gross income for the previous year in excess of $150,000.

to reduce the income tax when the return is filed. If the social security tax withholding shown in Box 4 of all the Forms W-2 exceeds $7,886.40 for 2017, the worker is entitled to a refund of the excess.

If filing a joint return, the worker cannot add any social security withheld from his or her spouse's income to the amount withheld from his or her income. The worker must figure the excess separately for both himself and his or her spouse to determine if either has excess withholding.

Earned Income Credit

Many ministers qualify for the earned income credit (EIC). The program currently furnishes a basic benefit for families even when there are no dependent children. There are three supplemental benefits to adjust for families with two or more children, those with a newborn child, and those that incur certain health insurance costs for their children.

> **Tip**
> For 2017, a qualifying child was at the end of 2017 under age 19, or under age 24 and a student, or any age and permanently and totally disabled and who lived with you in the United States for more than half of 2017. If the child was married or meets the conditions to be a qualifying child of another person (other than your spouse if filing a joint return), special rules apply. See IRS Publication 596.

Employees may be eligible for the maximum EIC if their 2017 taxable and nontaxable earned income was less than $20,600 if there is no qualifying child; less than $45,207 if there is one qualifying child; less than $50,597 if there are two or more children; and less than $53,930 if there are three or more qualifying children (these rates are based on married filing jointly). The employee cannot claim the EIC unless the investment income is $3,450 or less.

A child is a qualifying child if the child meets three tests: relationship, age, and residency.

- **Relationship.** The child must be either the son, daughter, adopted child, stepchild, eligible foster child of the employee, or any descendant of them.

- **Age.** The child must be under age 19 at the end of 2017, a full-time student under age 24 at the end of 2017, or permanently and totally disabled at any time during 2017, regardless of age.

- **Residency.** The child must have lived with the employee in the United States for more than half of 2017 (all of 2017 if an eligible foster child).

The fair rental value of a parsonage provided by the congregation is includible in the earned income calculation. Plus, a housing allowance designated by the congregation in relation to either a parsonage or minister-provided housing counts as earned income. (Exception: If the minister has opted out of social security, neither the fair rental value of a parsonage or housing allowances designated is includible.) However, fees received from activities such as weddings and funerals are not includible.

CHAPTER 7 ▸ PAYING TAXES

If claiming the EIC, the employee can either have the IRS figure the amount of the credit, or the employee can figure it (he or she must complete and attach Schedule EIC to the return if he or she has at least one qualifying child). If the employee calculates it, he or she must complete a worksheet found in the IRS instructions that determines whether the earned income credit is based on earned income or modified adjusted gross income (generally equal to the adjusted gross income after disregarding certain losses). Then the employee must look up the amount of the credit in an IRS table.

Extension of Time to File

The 2017 return should be filed with the IRS service center and payment made by April 15, 2018, to avoid penalties and interest.

If the worker has applied for an extension of time to file the return, remember that the final payment is still due by April 17, 2018, with the extension application. The extension of time to file is not an extension of the time to pay.

Six-month extension

To receive a six-month extension of time, the worker should file Form 4868, Application for Automatic Extension of Time to File U.S. Individual Income Tax Return. The form must be filed by April 17, 2018.

As an alternative option to filing a paper Form 4868, you can electronically file Form 4868 using a tax software package, through a tax professional, or through other service providers.

Service providers may charge a convenience fee based on the amount of the tax payment being made. Fees

Remember
Obtaining a six-month extension is easy. No reason for late filing is needed. The IRS will automatically grant the extension. However, this is not an extension of time to pay—only an extension of time to file. If the amount you owe on your return will generate an underpayment penalty, filing 4868 will not help you.

Form **4868**
Department of the Treasury
Internal Revenue Service (99)

Application for Automatic Extension of Time To File U.S. Individual Income Tax Return

For calendar year 2017, or other tax year beginning , 2017, ending , 20 .

OMB No. 1545-0074

2017

Part I Identification
1 Your name(s) (see instructions)
Address (see instructions)
City, town, or post office | State | ZIP Code
2 Your social security number | 3 Spouse's social security number

Part II Individual Income Tax
4 Estimate of total tax liability for 2017 . . $
5 Total 2017 payments . . . .
6 **Balance due.** Subtract line 5 from line 4 (see instructions) . . . .
7 Amount you're paying (see instructions) . ▶
8 Check here if you're "out of the country" and a U.S. citizen or resident (see instructions) . . . . ▶ ☐
9 Check here if you file Form 1040NR or 1040NR-EZ and didn't receive wages as an employee subject to U.S. income tax withholding. . . . . ▶ ☐

For Privacy Act and Paperwork Reduction Act Notice, see page 4.   Cat. No. 13141W   Form **4868** (2017)

119

may vary between service providers. The employee will be told what the fee is during the transaction and will have the option to continue or cancel the transaction. The convenience fee can also be determined by calling the providers' toll-free automated customer service numbers or visiting their websites. Do not add the convenience fee to the tax payment.

Penalties

An elaborate system of penalties exists to make sure that tax returns are filed correctly and tax liabilities are paid on time. In addition, interest is charged on many penalties, including the late filing penalty, substantial understatement penalty, overvaluation penalty, negligence penalty, and fraud penalty.

➤ **Failure to pay penalty.** Even if the IRS grants an extension of time to file, if 90% of the tax is not paid on time, the employee will be subject to a penalty of one-half of 1% of the unpaid tax for each month or part of a month that the tax is not paid, to a maximum of 25% of the tax. The penalty can be avoided only if it can be shown that failure to pay is due to reasonable cause and not willful neglect.

> **Tip**
> Ask a professional to look over tax due notices from the IRS. It is not unusual for the IRS to send a penalty notice when no penalty is actually due. Demonstrating that you do not owe a penalty may be as simple as completing Form 2210.

➤ **Penalty computed by the IRS.** If the employee does not want to figure the penalty, the IRS will figure it and send a bill. In certain situations the employee must complete Form 2210 and attach it to the return.

➤ **Form 2210.** If the employee wants to figure the penalty, he or she must complete Part I and either Part II or Part III of Form 2210, Underpayment of Estimated Tax by Individuals and Fiduciaries.

Generally, employees will not have to pay a penalty if any of the following situations apply:

☐ The total of the 2017 withholding and estimated tax payments was at least as much as the 2016 tax, the employee is not subject to the special rule limiting use of prior year's tax, and all required estimated tax payments were on time.

☐ The tax balance on the return is no more than 10% of the total 2017 tax, and all required estimated tax payments were on time.

☐ The total 2017 tax minus withholding is less than $1,000.

☐ The employee did not owe tax for 2017.

Interest

If an employee has not paid the entire tax due by April 17, 2018, he or she must pay interest from then until the date the tax liability is paid. Receiving an automatic extension of time to file the tax return will not relieve the employee of the burden of interest.

State extensions

For states that have a state income tax, check the instruction forms that come with the return to determine how to file an extension. In some states, if no additional tax is owed, there is no need to file a separate state extension. Instead, the state will allow the same extensions that the IRS grants, and a copy of the federal extension should be attached to the state return for filing. Other states may require their own forms.

Extension of Time to Pay

It is important to file the return on time even if it is impossible to pay the tax. Filing on time will avoid late filing penalties which are one-half of 1% per month based on the balance of tax due, up to a maximum penalty of 25%. Filing stops the penalties, not the interest.

If an employee can't pay the full amount due, he or she should pay as much as possible when filing the return. Generally, taxes should not be charged directly to a credit card unless it's a small amount that can be paid off shortly. While an employee might earn frequent flyer miles, he or she will pay interest charges to the credit card company, plus a credit card cost to the IRS of up to 3%, and none of that is deductible.

Installment payments

The IRS may permit a taxpayer to pay the taxes on an installment plan. The request for an installment agreement cannot be turned down if the tax owed is not more than $10,000 and all three of the following apply:

- During the past five tax years, the individual has timely filed all income tax returns and paid any income tax due, and has not entered into an installment agreement for payment of income tax;

- The IRS determines that the individual cannot pay the tax owed in full when it is due and the IRS is given any information needed to make that determination; and

- The individual agrees to pay the full amount owed within three years and to comply with the tax laws while the agreement is in effect.

> **Tip**
> If you want to pay your taxes on an installment plan, ask for a six-month extension of time to pay or make the IRS an offer in compromise. Consider obtaining professional assistance. These are very specialized forms.

When filing the tax return, it is necessary to include Form 9465, Installment Agreement Request. Within a month, the IRS will notify the taxpayer whether the installment payment plan has been approved. But the IRS requires the payments to start within a month. If approved, the taxpayer will have up to 60 months to pay and will still owe the IRS the late-payment penalty plus interest including interest on the penalty. To limit interest and penalty charges, file the return on time and pay as much of the tax as possible with the return. The

121

IRS generally charges any installment agreement user fee of $120. The user fee may be reduced if paid as a direct debit from the taxpayer's bank account.

If the IRS approves the request, they will send a letter explaining how to pay the fee and how to make the first installment payment. They will usually let the taxpayer know within 30 days after they receive the request whether it is approved or denied.

Six-month extension

Even if a six-month extension of time is granted until October 15, 2018 to file the 2017 return by filing Form 4868 (see pages 119–20), generally the taxes must be paid by April 17, 2018.

An employee may be able to put off paying the taxes for six months until October 15, 2018 without a penalty by using Form 1127, Application for Extension of Time for Payment of Tax. Getting this extension is not easy. The employee will have to prove to the IRS that he or she does not have the money to pay the taxes, cannot borrow, and, if forced to pay up, the employee and family will suffer "undue hardship."

Hardship means more than inconvenience. Substantial financial loss must be shown if the tax is paid on the date it is due. This loss could be caused by selling property at a sacrifice price.

If the employee files for this extension, he or she must include a complete statement of all his or her assets and liabilities and an itemized list of money received and spent for three months prior to the request. Plus, the IRS may require security such as a notice of lien, mortgage, pledge, deed of trust of specific property, or personal surety.

Offers in Compromise

An Offer in Compromise (OIC) is an agreement between the taxpayer and the government that settles a tax liability for payment of less than the full amount owed. The IRS will generally accept an OIC when it is unlikely that the tax liability can be collected in full and the amount offered reasonably reflects collection potential.

The IRS may legally compromise for one of the following reasons:

➤ Doubt as to liability—doubt exists that the assessed tax is correct.

➤ Doubt as to collectibility—doubt exists that the taxpayer could ever pay the full amount of tax owed. The IRS will generally consider a doubt as to collectibility offer when the taxpayer is unable to pay the taxes in full either by liquidating assets or through current installment agreement guidelines.

➤ Effective tax administration—there is no doubt the tax is correct and no doubt the amount owed could be collected, but an exceptional circumstance exists that allows

CHAPTER 7 ➢ PAYING TAXES

Form **1127**
(Rev. December 2011)
Department of the Treasury
Internal Revenue Service

Application for Extension of Time for Payment of Tax Due to Undue Hardship

OMB No. 1545-2131

Before you begin: Use the chart on page 3 to see if you should file this form.

Name(s) shown on return

Identifying number

Number, street, and apt., room, or suite no. If you have a P.O. box, see instructions.

City, town, or post office, state, and ZIP code. If you have a foreign address, see instructions.

Part I   Request for Extension

I request an extension from _____ , 20 ____ , to _____ , 20 ____ , to pay tax of $ _____ .
This request is for (check only one box):
☐ The tax shown or required to be shown on Form _____ .
☐ An amount determined as a deficiency on Form _____ .
This request is for calendar year 20 ____ , or fiscal year ending _____ , 20 ____ .

Part II   Reason for Extension

Undue hardship. Enter below a detailed explanation of the undue hardship that will result if your application is denied. (If more space is required, please attach a separate sheet.) To establish undue hardship, you must show that you would sustain a substantial financial loss if forced to pay a tax or deficiency on the due date. For a complete definition of "undue hardship," see the instructions on page 3 under *Who Should File*.

Part III   Supporting Documentation

To support my application, I certify that I have attached (you must check both boxes or your application will not be accepted):
☐ A statement of my assets and liabilities at the end of last month (showing book and market values of assets and whether securities are listed or unlisted), and
☐ An itemized list of my income and expenses for each of the 3 months prior to the due date of the tax.

Signature and Verification

Under penalties of perjury, I declare that I have examined this application, including any accompanying schedules and statements, and to the best of my knowledge and belief, it is true, correct, and complete; and, if prepared by someone other than the taxpayer, that I am authorized to prepare this form.

Signature of taxpayer ▶ _____   Date ▶ _____

Signature of spouse ▶ _____   Date ▶ _____

Signature of preparer other than taxpayer ▶ _____   Date ▶ _____

FOR IRS USE ONLY (Do not detach)

This application is   ☐ Approved   ☐ Denied   ☐ Returned: _____

Reason(s): _____

Signature of authorized official   Date

For Privacy Act and Paperwork Reduction Act Notice, see instructions.   Cat. No. 17238O   Form **1127** (Rev. 12-2011)

123

the IRS to consider the offer. To be eligible for compromise on this basis, the taxpayer must demonstrate that collection of the tax would create an economic hardship or would be unfair and inequitable.

To work out an offer in compromise, the taxpayer must show that paying the whole tax would cause a severe or unusual economic hardship. Examples of economic hardship include:

- ➤ incapability of earning a living because of long-term medical condition, or
- ➤ liquidation of assets would render the taxpayer unable to pay his or her basic living expenses.

The taxpayer should file Form 656, Offer in Compromise, with the district director's office where the liability is pending.

Filing an Amended Tax Return

There may still be time to revise 2014, 2015, and 2016 income tax returns by filing Form 1040X (see page 125). Employees may review these tax returns to determine if they missed out on any tax savings. Or if they find more money is owed, they can pay before the IRS catches up with them and the interest due has increased. Interest or penalties should not be included on Form 1040X; the IRS will adjust them.

Form 1040X should be filed only after the original return is filed. Generally, Form 1040X must be filed within three years, plus extensions, after the date the original return was filed or within two years after the date the tax was paid, whichever is later. If Form 1040 was filed early (before April 15), it is considered filed on the due date. If correcting wages or other employee compensation, attach a copy of all additional or corrected Forms W-2 received after filing the original return. A separate Form 1040X should be filed for each year being amended.

> **Tip**
> You may need to amend your tax return to pay more taxes or to get a refund from the IRS. Your tax returns can generally be amended if you file Form 1040X within three years of the due date, plus extensions, of the year you are amending.

Employees must not forget to amend their state return, if appropriate. The IRS and the state tax authorities exchange information. If an amended federal return is filed without an amended state return when required to do so, the state is likely to find out about the amended data from the IRS.

CHAPTER 7 ➤ PAYING TAXES

Form **1040X** (Rev. January 2018)	Department of the Treasury—Internal Revenue Service **Amended U.S. Individual Income Tax Return** ▶ Go to www.irs.gov/Form1040X for instructions and the latest information.		OMB No. 1545-0074

This return is for calendar year [X] 2017 [ ] 2016 [ ] 2015 [ ] 2014
Other year. Enter one: calendar year _____ or fiscal year (month and year ended): _____

Your first name and initial	Last name	Your social security number
Milton L.	Brown	541 : 16 : 8194
If a joint return, spouse's first name and initial	Last name	Spouse's social security number
Alessia S.	Brown	238 : 49 : 7209
Current home address (number and street). If you have a P.O. box, see instructions.	Apt. no.	Your phone number
418 Trenton Street		
City, town or post office, state, and ZIP code. If you have a foreign address, also complete spaces below (see instructions).		
Springfield, OH 45504		
Foreign country name	Foreign province/state/county	Foreign postal code

Amended return filing status. You **must** check one box even if you are not changing your filing status. **Caution:** In general, you can't change your filing status from a joint return to separate returns after the due date.
[ ] Single
[X] Married filing jointly
[ ] Married filing separately
[ ] Head of household (If the qualifying person is a child but not your dependent, see instructions.)
[ ] Qualifying widow(er)

Full-year coverage.
If all members of your household have full-year minimal essential health care coverage, check "Yes." Otherwise, check "No."
See instructions.
[X] Yes   [ ] No

	Use Part III on the back to explain any changes		A. Original amount or as previously adjusted (see instructions)	B. Net change— amount of increase or (decrease)— explain in Part III	C. Correct amount
	Income and Deductions				
1	Adjusted gross income. If a net operating loss (NOL) carryback is included, check here . . . . ▶ [ ]	1	32,000	(3,000)	29,000
2	Itemized deductions or standard deduction	2	11,400	0	11,400
3	Subtract line 2 from line 1	3	20,600	(3,000)	17,600
4	Exemptions. **If changing, complete Part I on page 2 and enter the amount from line 29**	4	10,950	0	10,950
5	Taxable income. Subtract line 4 from line 3	5	9,650	(3,000)	6,650
	Tax Liability				
6	Tax. Enter method(s) used to figure tax (see instructions): _____	6	965	(300)	665
7	Credits. If a general business credit carryback is included, check here . . . . ▶ [ ]	7			
8	Subtract line 7 from line 6. If the result is zero or less, enter -0- . .	8	965	(300)	665
9	Health care: individual responsibility (see instructions)	9			
10	Other taxes	10	5,500		5,500
11	Total tax. Add lines 8, 9, and 10	11	6,465	(300)	6,165
	Payments				
12	Federal income tax withheld and excess social security and tier 1 RRTA tax withheld. (**If changing**, see instructions.)	12			
13	Estimated tax payments, including amount applied from prior year's return	13	7,000		7,000
14	Earned income credit (EIC)	14			
15	Refundable credits from: [ ] Schedule 8812 Form(s) [ ] 2439 [ ] 4136 [ ] 8863 [ ] 8885 [ ] 8962 or [ ] other (specify): _____	15			
16	Total amount paid with request for extension of time to file, tax paid with original return, and additional tax paid after return was filed	16			
17	Total payments. Add lines 12 through 15, column C, and line 16	17			7,000
	Refund or Amount You Owe				
18	Overpayment, if any, as shown on original return or as previously adjusted by the IRS	18			535
19	Subtract line 18 from line 17 (If less than zero, see instructions.)	19			6,465
20	**Amount you owe.** If line 11, column C, is more than line 19, enter the difference	20			
21	If line 11, column C, is less than line 19, enter the difference. This is the amount **overpaid** on this return	21			300
22	Amount of line 21 you want **refunded to you**	22			300
23	Amount of line 21 you want **applied to your** _____ (enter year): estimated tax .	23			

Complete and sign this form on Page 2.

For Paperwork Reduction Act Notice, see instructions.   Cat. No. 11360L   Form **1040X** (Rev. 1-2018)

Amended returns must be filed within three years of the return due date plus approved extensions (see page 143).

Integrity Points

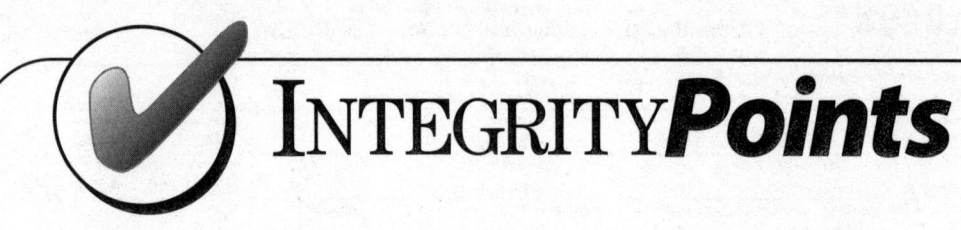

- **Filing your income tax returns and paying the tax due.** Unfortunately, many ministers do not file their tax returns when they are due and/or do not pay the amount of tax due. Few things will bring more shame to a minister and the church.

    One of the few things worse than getting behind on filing tax returns and paying taxes is taking the position that it is not required to file tax returns—an approach taken by tax protesters. There is no validity to such a position.

- **Withholding of income tax by the church.** Take advantage of income tax withholding by the employing church. This is one of the most important decisions a minister can make to ensure timely payment of income tax (and additional income tax may be withheld to cover social security tax).

    True, a church is not required to withhold federal (and state) income tax from the minister's pay—it's voluntary for both the church and the minister. But most churches will gladly handle the small additional paperwork to assist the minister with tax withholding. And if taxes are timely withheld, underpayment penalties can be eliminated, and the minister is more likely to file his or her return—and on time!

- **Properly calculating the earned income tax credit.** While it is sad that a minister would ever qualify for the earned income tax credit (confirming the minister is being paid below the poverty line) from the perspective of adequate compensation, there is no shame in claiming the credit.

    However, there is shame in computing the earned income tax credit based on inaccurate data. The fair rental value of a parsonage provided by the church plus a housing allowance (parsonage or minister-owned housing) is includible in the earned income calculation for this credit (unless the minister has opted out of social security).

Line by Line

Form 1040

There are two short forms, the 51-line 1040A and the super-short, 14-line 1040EZ. Generally, ministers should use the 79-line Form 1040 instead. It accommodates every minister, and there's no penalty for leaving some of the lines blank. Besides, going down the 1040 line by line may jog one's memory about money received or spent in 2017. (Line numbers noted in this summary refer to the Form 1040 and related schedules.)

- **Filing status (lines 1 to 5). Line 2:** If the minister's spouse died in 2017, he or she can still file jointly and take advantage of tax rates that would be lower than if he or she files as a single person or as a head of household.

    Line 3: If the minister is married and lives in a separate-property state, compute the tax two ways—jointly and separately. Then, file the return resulting in the lower tax.

    Line 4: If the minister is single, he or she may qualify as head of household if he or she provided a home for someone else—like a parent. Filing as head of household rather than as a single person can save a bundle on taxes.

    Line 5: If the minister's spouse died in 2015 or 2016 and he or she has a dependent child, there is benefit from joint-return rates as a qualifying widow(er).

- **Exemptions (lines 6a to 6d).** Remember to include a social security number for any dependents. If a child does not have one, obtain Form SS-5, Application for a Social Security Number, at http://www.ssa.gov/online/ssa-5.html. If unable to secure the social security number before the filing deadline, the minister may file for an extension of time to file.

- **Income (lines 7 to 22). Line 7:** If the minister is considered an employee for income tax purposes, he or she should receive Form W-2 from the employer. The total amount of the taxable wages is shown in Box 1 of Form W-2; attach Copy B of the

> **Filing Tip**
> Form 1040, Line 7. All compensation from Form W-2 is reported on line 7. Be sure the church has not included the housing allowance amount in Box 1 of Form W-2.

127

W-2 to your Form 1040. Include the data from other W-2s received for the minister or spouse on this line. If the church erroneously included the housing allowance in Box 1, Form W-2, the minister should ask the church to reissue a corrected Form W-2.

If the cash housing allowance designated and paid by the employer exceeds the lowest of (1) the amount used to provide a home from current ministerial income, (2) the amount properly designated by the employer, or (3) the fair rental value of the home including utilities and furnishings, enter the difference on line 7.

> **Filing Tip**
>
> Form 1040, Line 7. If the housing allowance designated by the employer exceeds the housing allowance exclusion to which the minister is entitled, he or she must include the difference on line 7 with a description "Excess housing allowance." The exclusion is limited by the lower of the fair rental value of a minister-provided home or the actual housing expenses.

Line 8a: Include as taxable-interest income the total amount of earnings on savings accounts, certificates of deposit, credit union accounts, corporate bonds and corporate bond mutual funds, U.S. treasuries and U.S. government mutual funds, and interest paid to the minister for a belated federal or state tax refund (whether or not a Form 1099-INT has been received). If the statements due have not yet been received, call the issuer to get them. If more than $1,500 of taxable interest income was received in 2017, Schedule B must also be completed.

Line 8b: Here's where to note any tax-exempt interest from municipal bonds or municipal bond funds. Don't worry—that income is not taxable. But social security recipients must count all their tax-exempt interest when computing how much of their social security benefits will be taxable.

Line 9a: Enter as dividend income only ordinary dividends, not capital-gains dividends paid by mutual funds, which are reported on Schedule D. Form 1099-DIV statements show the amount and type of ordinary dividends received during 2017. If more than $1,500 in dividend income was received in 2017, Schedule B must be completed. Remember: earnings from a money-market mutual fund are considered dividend income, not interest income.

Line 10: If a refund of a state or local tax was received in 2017 that was deducted on Schedule A in a prior year, include the refund here.

Line 12: Even when filing as an employee for income tax purposes, there will probably be some honoraria or fee income from speaking engagements, weddings, funerals, and so on.

> **Filing Tip**
>
> Form 1040, Line 12. The only ministerial income that should be reported on line 12 is fees from weddings, funerals, speaking engagements, and similar income. Unreimbursed expenses related to this income should be deducted on Schedule C or Schedule C-EZ.

➤ FORM 1040 – LINE BY LINE

This income, less related expenses (see page 18), should be reported on Schedule C or C-EZ and entered on this line.

Line 13: Enter capital-gains dividends here if there were no other capital gains or losses in 2017.

Line 15a: Report as IRA distributions even amounts that were rolled over tax-free in 2017 from one IRA into another. On line 15b, you will report as taxable the amount of any IRA distributions that were not rolled over minus any return of nondeductible contributions.

Line 16a: It is likely that only a portion of the total pensions and annuities received is taxable. Form 1099-R will show the taxable amount, which should be entered on line 16b. If pensions and annuities were received from a denominationally sponsored plan, the minister may be eligible to exclude a portion or all of these payments as a housing allowance.

Line 20a: No more than 85% of social security benefits can be taxed for 2017 and none at all if the provisional income is below $32,000 on a joint return, $25,000 for singles. If the income doesn't exceed the threshold, leave this line blank. If it does, use the worksheet on Form 1099-SSA to compute taxes on the benefits.

- **Adjustments to income (lines 23 to 37). Line 25:** Health Savings Account deduction. Contributions made by a taxpayer to a health savings account (HSA) up to $3,400 for an individual plan and $6,750 for a family plan are deductible on this line. Individuals who have reached age 55 by the end of the tax year are allowed to increase their annual contribution for years after 2017.

Line 26: If the employer paid directly or reimbursed the minister for qualified moving costs incurred in 2017, these amounts would not be included as compensation on Form W-2. Therefore, the minister would have no moving expenses to deduct on line 26. However, if part or all of the moving costs were not paid directly or reimbursed, deduct these expenses here.

Line 27: One-half of the social security tax that is deductible for income tax purposes is reflected on this line. This number comes from Schedule SE, Section A, line 6, or Section B, line 13.

Line 33: Interest paid on a qualifying student loan may be deducted on this line. The maximum deductible amount of interest is $2,500, and it is phased out at high income levels.

Line 36: If a minister is employed as a chaplain or any other minister-employee of a nonreligious organization, use this line for the deduction of 403(b) contributions that were sent directly to the plan. On the dotted line next to line 36, enter the amount of the deduction and identify it as indicated.

- **Tax computation (lines 38 to 56). Line 40:** Claim the standard deduction only if the amount exceeds what could be written off in itemizing expenses on Schedule A. For 2017, the standard deduction is $12,700 joint, $9,500 head of household, and $6,350 single. The amounts are higher if the minister or spouse is 65 or older or legally blind.

    Line 51: Taxpayers with adjusted gross income of $50,000 or less may claim a credit on this line equal to a certain percentage of the employee contributions made to a retirement account or IRA (must complete Form 8880).

    > **Filing Tip**
    > Form 1040, Line 51. If contributions were made to a 403(b) or 401(k) plan, and the adjusted gross income was $50,000 or less, the minister may be eligible for the retirement savings contributions credit. The credit is also available for contributions to either a traditional or a Roth IRA. The excluded portion of minister's housing does not reduce this credit.

    Line 52: If the minister has a dependent child (a child under the age of 17 at the end of the tax year), he or she should complete Schedule 8812 to claim up to a maximum credit of $1,000 per qualifying child. This nonrefundable child tax credit can reduce the actual taxes owed dollar-for-dollar, but only down to zero.

- **Other taxes (lines 57 to 63). Line 57:** If the taxpayer is a qualified minister (see pages 2–9) and has not opted out of social security (see pages 106–110), he or she is self-employed for social security tax purposes. Social security is not withheld by the church but is calculated on Schedule SE if there were net earnings of $400 or more and paid with Form 1040. The tax is 15.3% of the first $127,200 of 2017 self-employment income. If the total wages and self-employment earnings were less than $127,200, time and headaches can probably be saved by filing the Short Schedule SE on the front of the SE form.

    Line 59: The minister will owe the tax on qualified plans plus the 10% penalty on the amount withdrawn from the IRA or another retirement plan if the minister was under 59½, unless certain exceptions are met.

- **Payments (lines 64 to 74). Line 64:** Did the minister have a voluntary withholding arrangement whereby the employing church withheld federal income tax from the minister's compensation? Then show the amount of federal income tax the church withheld (from the W-2, Box 2) along with other federal income tax withholding from other employment of the minister or spouse here. Also include tax withheld on the other Forms 1099 and W-2. The amount withheld should be shown in Box 6 of Form 1099-SSA and Box 4 of other Forms 1099.

    Line 65: Don't get confused: Even though the fourth-quarter 2017 estimated tax payment was made in January 2018, it's counted on the 2017 return.

    Line 66: Enter the earned income tax credit here or let the IRS calculate it. If the minister has a qualifying child, Schedule EIC must be completed.

> FORM 1040 – LINE BY LINE

- **Refund or amount owed (lines 75 to 79). Line 79:** The IRS assumes the taxpayer must pay the estimated tax penalty if he or she owes $1,000 or more beyond what has been paid through withholding or estimated tax and the amount due is more than 110% of the 2016 tax bill. The minister may qualify for one of several exceptions, however. Use Form 2210 to prove this case.

Schedule A (Itemized Deductions)

If the minister lives in church-provided housing, he or she often cannot itemize. But run down Schedule A just to see whether there might be more write-offs than the standard deduction will permit.

- **Medical and dental expenses (lines 1 to 4).** Don't overlook the cost of getting to and from the doctor or pharmacist. Write off 17 cents per mile plus the cost of parking. If the taxpayer didn't drive, deduct any bus, train, or taxi fares. The cost of trips to see out-of-town specialists and as much as $50 a day for the cost of lodging when out of town to get medical care count toward the 10% limit of adjusted gross income (or 7.5% if the taxpayer or spouse is 65 or older). Include all health insurance premiums, as well as Medicare Part B premiums for 2017.

- **Taxes you paid (lines 5 to 9).** Even though real estate taxes are a housing expense excludable under the housing allowance, they may still be deducted (even for multiple properties if not deducted elsewhere on the return) on line 6 as an itemized deduction—one of the few "double benefits" allowed in the tax law.

> **Filing Tip**
> **Schedule A, Lines 6, 10-12.** These lines relate to the most significant tax break available to ministers who own their own homes. Even though real estate taxes, mortgage interest, and points are excludable under the housing allowance, subject to certain limits, the same amounts are deductible as itemized deductions.

- **Interest you paid (lines 10 to 15). Line 10:** If the minister bought a house during 2017, review all escrow or settlement papers for any mortgage interest paid that was not shown on the lender's year-end statement. If interest was paid on a second mortgage or line of credit secured by the minister's home, include the interest expense here.

  As with real estate taxes, it is possible to deduct mortgage interest as an itemized deduction even if the interest is included in housing expenses subject to a housing allowance. Interest paid on a secured mortgage is deductible on Schedule A regardless of how the proceeds of the loan are used. However, the only mortgage interest properly includible as housing expense under a housing allowance is when the loan proceeds were used to provide housing. For example, interest on a second mortgage used to finance a child's college education is deductible on Schedule A but does not qualify as a housing expense for housing allowance purposes.

Don't overlook points paid to get the mortgage. All of the points are generally deductible as interest here. Points paid for a refinancing must be amortized over the life of the loan. But it is permissible to deduct on the 2017 return the portion of all points paid that correspond with the percentage of refinancing used for home improvements.

- **Gifts to charity (lines 16 to 19). Line 16:** For gifts you made in 2017, there must be written acknowledgments from the charity of any single gifts of $250 or more and for all gifts of cash.

    Line 17: Deduct charitable mileage for any volunteer work at the rate of 14 cents a mile.

- **Job expenses and other miscellaneous deductions (lines 21 to 27).** Don't assume it's impossible to surmount the 2% adjusted gross income (AGI) floor on these miscellaneous deductions. A wealth of employee business, investment, and tax-related expenses—from job-hunting costs to tax preparation fees—are deductible here. And if the minister bought business equipment required by the employer and he or she was not reimbursed, the minister can write off its entire cost up to the 2017 limit. (However, see the allocation of expense rules, pages 91–93.)

> **Filing Tip**
> **Schedule A, Line 21.** Since the deduction for meal and entertainment expense is limited on Form 2106, expenses claimed on lines 21 to 23 are reduced by 2% of your adjusted gross income. The standard deduction may be advantageous for you, and using an accountable expense reimbursement plan to reduce or eliminate unreimbursed expenses is generally a wise move.

Schedule C (C-EZ)

Nearly every minister should file Schedule C or Schedule C-EZ. While a minister should receive Form W-2 for employment compensation and report the amount in Box 1 of Form W-2 on Form 1040, line 7, most ministers have some income from honoraria or fees related to weddings or funerals. Additionally, a minister may have speaking fees unrelated to the employer, product royalties, and other self-employment income reportable on Schedule C (C-EZ).

Only expenses related to the income reported on Schedule C (C-EZ) may be deducted on the form. For example, if a minister received honoraria of $500 for speaking at a church other than where employed, the $500 is reported on Schedule C (C-EZ) and the travel and other expenses related to the speaking engagement are deductible on the form.

> **Filing Tip**
> **Schedule C-EZ, Line 2.** Only business expenses related to the income reported on line 1 may be reported on line 2. A minister's housing expenses are not deducted on this form (or generally any other form). Expenses related to employee compensation must be reported on Form 2106.

Expenses related to a minister's primary employment (compensation that was reported on Form W-2) must be deducted on Form 2106 and carried forward to Schedule A. If using Schedule C-EZ, reflect the data as follows:

- **Gross receipts. Line 1:** Include income from honoraria, fees, product royalties, and other income earned as an independent contractor.
- **Total expenses. Line 2:** Only include business expenses related to the income on line 1.

Schedule SE

Most ministers will need to file Schedule SE to report income subject to self-employment taxes. Most frequently, a minister will be able to utilize the short-form (page 1 of the form), but the decision matrix at the top of the form will indicate if a minister may need to utilize the long form (page 2 of the form).

When computing the self-employment tax, net earnings include the gross income earned from performing qualified services minus the deductions related to that income. See Self-Employment Social Security Tax Worksheet on page 104.

Form 2106-EZ

While the goal of every minister should be to minimize unreimbursed business expenses, there are often some unreimbursed expenses to file on Form 2106 or 2106-EZ. Ministers may use Form 2106-EZ only if all of the following apply:

- ☐ The minister is an employee deducting expenses attributable to his or her job.
- ☐ The minister does not get reimbursed by your church for any expenses. (Nonaccountable reimbursements from the church included in Box 1 of your Form W-2 are not considered reimbursements for this purpose.)
- ☐ If the minister is claiming vehicle expense, he or she is using the standard mileage rate for 2017.

- **Vehicle expense. Line 1:** Multiply the business miles by the 2017 standard business mileage rate of 53.5 cents per mile. Commuting miles to and from work are excluded, regardless of how many trips per day.
- **Parking fees, tolls, and transportation. Line 2:** Enter business-related parking fees, tolls, and transportation that did not involve overnight travel or commuting to and from work.
- **Travel expense while away from home overnight. Line 3:** Enter lodging and transportation expenses connected with overnight travel away from the minister's tax home. The minister cannot deduct expenses for travel away from his or her tax home for any period of temporary employment of more than one year.

- **Business expenses not included on lines 1 through 3. Line 4:** Enter other job-related expenses not listed on any other line of this form. Include expenses for business gifts, education (tuition and books), trade publications, etc.

> **Filing Tip**
> The minister may be able to take a credit for his or her educational expenses instead of a deduction on line 4. See Form 8863 Educational Credits for details.

- **Meals and entertainment expenses. Line 5:** Generally, only 50% of business meals and entertainment expenses may be deducted, including meals incurred while away from home on business. Instead of actual cost, the minister may be able to claim the standard meal allowance (see page 77) for daily meals and incidental expenses.

Form 2441

If the minister paid someone to care for his or her child or other qualifying person so he or she (and spouse, if filing a joint return) could work or look for work in 2017, the minister may be able to take the credit for child and dependent care expenses.

- **Qualifying person (Line 2[a]).** A qualifying person is any child under age 13 who can be claimed as a dependent. If the child turned 13 during the year, the child is a qualifying person for the part of the year he or she was under age 13.

- **Qualified expenses (Line 2[c]).** These include amounts paid for household services and care of the qualifying person while the taxpayer worked or looked for work. Child support payments are not qualified expenses. Household services include the services of a cook, maid, babysitter, housekeeper, or cleaning person if the services were partly for the care of the qualifying person.

Form 8962

The premium tax credit is for those that were enrolled in health insurance through a state marketplace. The credit provides financial assistance to pay the premiums. This form reconciles whether there is a refund owed to a taxpayer or whether the taxpayer owes additional taxes related to an advance payment of the premium tax credit. There is an example of this form in use on page 171, which includes an excess advance payment of the premium tax credit.

- **Part I.** This section determines the annual contribution amount one is required to pay out of pocket.

- **Part II.** This section reconciles how much one has paid based on Form 1095-A and how much should be paid based on actual income as determined in Part I.

- **Part III.** This section is used to determine any necessary repayment of excess advance payment of a premium tax credit.

> FORM 1040 – LINE BY LINE

- **Parts IV & V.** Use these parts to make allocations as it may relate to divorces, married filing separately, marriages, or where a policy is shared between two tax families. See the Instructions to 8962 for further details.

Form 8863

Education credits maybe taken if the minister, spouse, or a dependent claimed on the taxpayer's return was a student enrolled at or attending an eligible educational institution.

- **American Opportunity Credit (Part I).** The minister may be able to take a credit of up to $2,500 for qualified expenses paid in 2017 for each student who qualifies for the credit (see instructions for Form 8863).

> **Tip**
> It does not matter whether the education expenses were paid in cash, by check, by credit card, or with borrowed funds.

- **Lifetime learning credit (Part II).** The maximum lifetime learning credit for 2017 is $2,000, regardless of the number of students. The lifetime learning credit cannot be taken for any student for whom the American Opportunity Credit is being taken.

- **Qualified expenses (Line 1[c] or Line 4[c]).** Generally, qualified expenses are amounts paid in 2017 for tuition and fees required for the student's enrollment or attendance at an eligible educational institution. Qualified expenses do not include amounts paid for room and board, insurance, medical expenses, transportation, or course-related books, supplies, and equipment.

Form 8889

The minister may be required to file Form 8889 if he or she participated in a Health Savings Account (HSA) in 2017.

- **HSA distributions (Line 14).** Amounts withdrawn from the HSA in 2017 are reflected on this line. There is generally no tax impact of HSA withdrawals unless they exceed unreimbursed medical expenses.

> **Tip**
> There is no requirement to file Form 8889 if HSA withdrawals for the year do not exceed unreimbursed medical expenses.

- **Unreimbursed medical expenses (Line 15).** Medical expenses that were not reimbursed by your medical insurance may generally be included on this line.

The 1040 Challenge

Completing Form 1040 can be very challenging and take hours to complete. Although it may not seem entirely logical, the 1040 and its accompanying schedules can be used to walk through the process of figuring the income and deductions and computing the tax.

Exemptions reduce the income by letting taxpayers subtract a fixed amount of money for themselves, their spouse, and each dependent.

Total Income includes:

Compensation from the church paid to the minister-employee for income tax purposes shown on Form W-2.

Net earnings from Schedule C (C-EZ) for income from speaking engagements, marriages, and funerals. (Schedule C will include all ministerial income and expenses if the minister is reporting as self-employed for income tax purposes.)

Adjustments

Adjusted Gross Income (AGI)

The 1040 Challenge

[Image of Form 1040 (2017), Page 2, with annotations pointing to sections:]

- Itemized or Standard Deductions
- Exemptions
- Taxable Income
- Gross Income Tax
- Credits
- **Other Taxes.** All ministers must show their social security tax due on line 57.
- Tax Already Paid
- Refund or Tax Payment Due

137

The 1040 Challenge

Schedule A

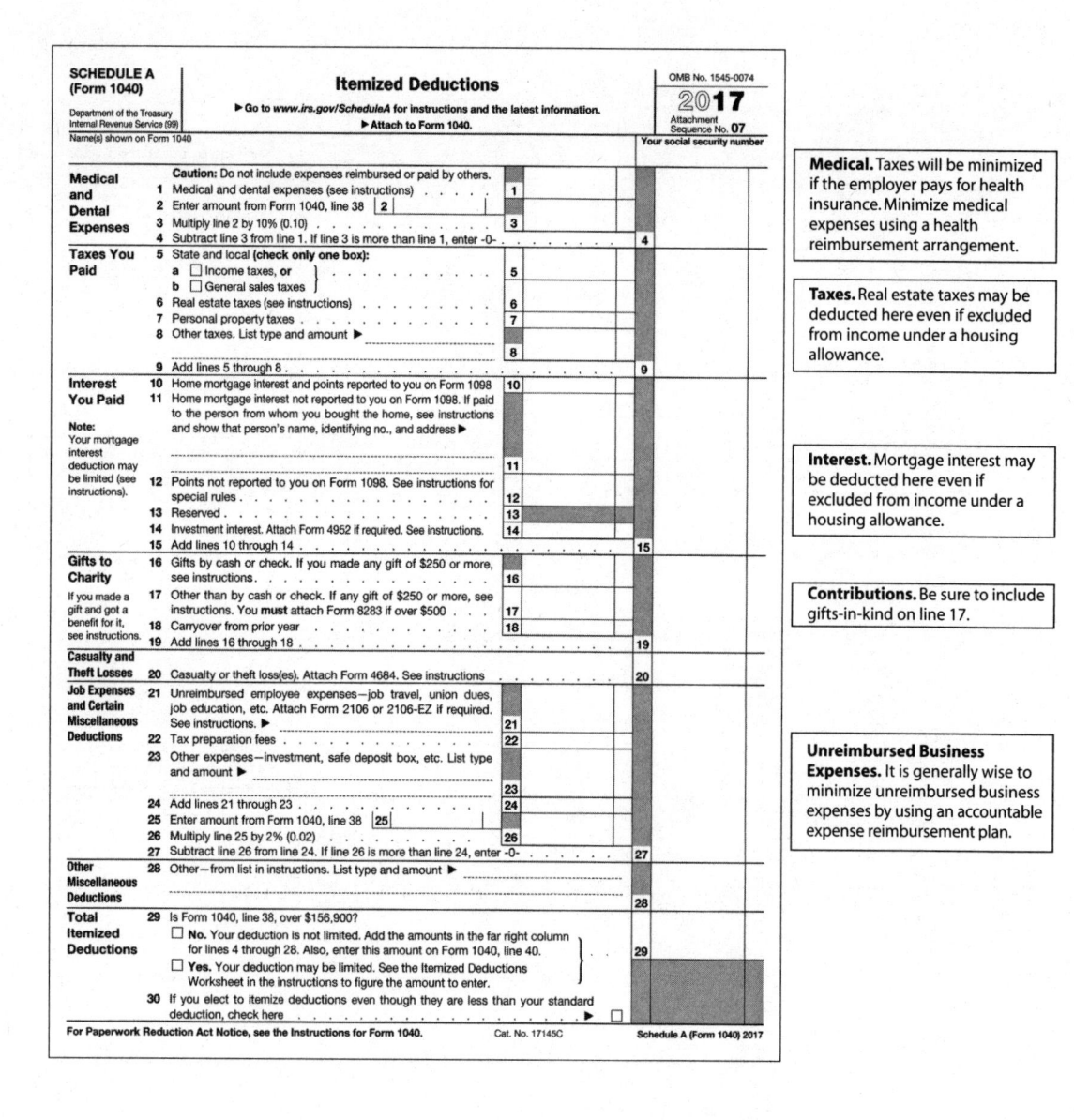

SCHEDULE A (Form 1040)
Department of the Treasury
Internal Revenue Service (99)

Itemized Deductions
▶ Go to *www.irs.gov/ScheduleA* for instructions and the latest information.
▶ Attach to Form 1040.

OMB No. 1545-0074
2017
Attachment Sequence No. 07

Name(s) shown on Form 1040 | Your social security number

Medical and Dental Expenses
Caution: Do not include expenses reimbursed or paid by others.
1 Medical and dental expenses (see instructions)
2 Enter amount from Form 1040, line 38
3 Multiply line 2 by 10% (0.10)
4 Subtract line 3 from line 1. If line 3 is more than line 1, enter -0-

Taxes You Paid
5 State and local (check only one box):
   a ☐ Income taxes, or
   b ☐ General sales taxes
6 Real estate taxes (see instructions)
7 Personal property taxes
8 Other taxes. List type and amount ▶
9 Add lines 5 through 8

Interest You Paid
Note: Your mortgage interest deduction may be limited (see instructions).
10 Home mortgage interest and points reported to you on Form 1098
11 Home mortgage interest not reported to you on Form 1098. If paid to the person from whom you bought the home, see instructions and show that person's name, identifying no., and address ▶
12 Points not reported to you on Form 1098. See instructions for special rules
13 Reserved
14 Investment interest. Attach Form 4952 if required. See instructions.
15 Add lines 10 through 14

Gifts to Charity
If you made a gift and got a benefit for it, see instructions.
16 Gifts by cash or check. If you made any gift of $250 or more, see instructions.
17 Other than by cash or check. If any gift of $250 or more, see instructions. You **must** attach Form 8283 if over $500
18 Carryover from prior year
19 Add lines 16 through 18

Casualty and Theft Losses
20 Casualty or theft loss(es). Attach Form 4684. See instructions.

Job Expenses and Certain Miscellaneous Deductions
21 Unreimbursed employee expenses—job travel, union dues, job education, etc. Attach Form 2106 or 2106-EZ if required. See instructions. ▶
22 Tax preparation fees
23 Other expenses—investment, safe deposit box, etc. List type and amount ▶
24 Add lines 21 through 23
25 Enter amount from Form 1040, line 38
26 Multiply line 25 by 2% (0.02)
27 Subtract line 26 from line 24. If line 26 is more than line 24, enter -0-

Other Miscellaneous Deductions
28 Other—from list in instructions. List type and amount ▶

Total Itemized Deductions
29 Is Form 1040, line 38, over $156,900?
   ☐ **No.** Your deduction is not limited. Add the amounts in the far right column for lines 4 through 28. Also, enter this amount on Form 1040, line 40.
   ☐ **Yes.** Your deduction may be limited. See the Itemized Deductions Worksheet in the instructions to figure the amount to enter.
30 If you elect to itemize deductions even though they are less than your standard deduction, check here ▶ ☐

For Paperwork Reduction Act Notice, see the Instructions for Form 1040.   Cat. No. 17145C   Schedule A (Form 1040) 2017

Medical. Taxes will be minimized if the employer pays for health insurance. Minimize medical expenses using a health reimbursement arrangement.

Taxes. Real estate taxes may be deducted here even if excluded from income under a housing allowance.

Interest. Mortgage interest may be deducted here even if excluded from income under a housing allowance.

Contributions. Be sure to include gifts-in-kind on line 17.

Unreimbursed Business Expenses. It is generally wise to minimize unreimbursed business expenses by using an accountable expense reimbursement plan.

The 1040 Challenge
Schedule C-EZ

SCHEDULE C-EZ (Form 1040)
Department of the Treasury
Internal Revenue Service (99)

Net Profit From Business
(Sole Proprietorship)
▶ Partnerships, joint ventures, etc., generally must file Form 1065 or 1065-B.
▶ Attach to Form 1040, 1040NR, or 1041. ▶ See instructions on page 2.

OMB No. 1545-0074
2017
Attachment Sequence No. **09A**

Name of proprietor | Social security number (SSN)

Part I — General Information

You May Use Schedule C-EZ Instead of Schedule C Only If You:
- Had business expenses of $5,000 or less,
- Use the cash method of accounting,
- Did not have an inventory at any time during the year,
- Did not have a net loss from your business,
- Had only one business as either a sole proprietor, qualified joint venture, or statutory employee,

And You:
- Had no employees during the year,
- Do not deduct expenses for business use of your home,
- Do not have prior year unallowed passive activity losses from this business, and
- Are not required to file Form 4562, Depreciation and Amortization, for this business. See the instructions for Schedule C, line 13, to find out if you must file.

A Principal business or profession, including product or service

B Enter business code (see page 2)

C Business name. If no separate business name, leave blank.

D Enter your EIN (see page 2)

E Business address (including suite or room no.). Address not required if same as on page 1 of your tax return.
   City, town or post office, state, and ZIP code

F Did you make any payments in 2017 that would require you to file Form(s) 1099? (see the Instructions for Schedule C) ☐ Yes ☐ No

G If "Yes," did you or will you file required Forms 1099? ☐ Yes ☐ No

Part II — Figure Your Net Profit

1 **Gross receipts.** Caution: If this income was reported to you on Form W-2 and the "Statutory employee" box on that form was checked, see *Statutory employees* in the instructions for Schedule C, line 1, and check here ▶ ☐ | 1

2 **Total expenses** (see page 2). If more than $5,000, you **must** use Schedule C | 2

3 **Net profit.** Subtract line 2 from line 1. If less than zero, you **must** use Schedule C. Enter on both Form 1040, line 12, and Schedule SE, line 2, or on Form 1040NR, line 13, and Schedule SE, line 2 (see page 2). (Statutory employees **do not** report this amount on Schedule SE, line 2.) Estates and trusts, enter on Form 1041, line 3 | 3

Part III — Information on Your Vehicle. Complete this part **only** if you are claiming car or truck expenses on line 2.

4 When did you place your vehicle in service for business purposes? (month, day, year) ▶

5 Of the total number of miles you drove your vehicle during 2017, enter the number of miles you used your vehicle for:
   a Business _____ b Commuting (see page 2) _____ c Other _____

6 Was your vehicle available for personal use during off-duty hours? ☐ Yes ☐ No

7 Do you (or your spouse) have another vehicle available for personal use? ☐ Yes ☐ No

8a Do you have evidence to support your deduction? ☐ Yes ☐ No

b If "Yes," is the evidence written? ☐ Yes ☐ No

For Paperwork Reduction Act Notice, see the separate instructions for Schedule C (Form 1040).   Cat. No. 14374D   Schedule C-EZ (Form 1040) 2017

Income. Include honoraria and fee income.

Expenses. Only include expenses related to income on line 1.

Net Profit. Include in income on page 1 and on Schedule SE.

The 1040 Challenge
Schedule SE

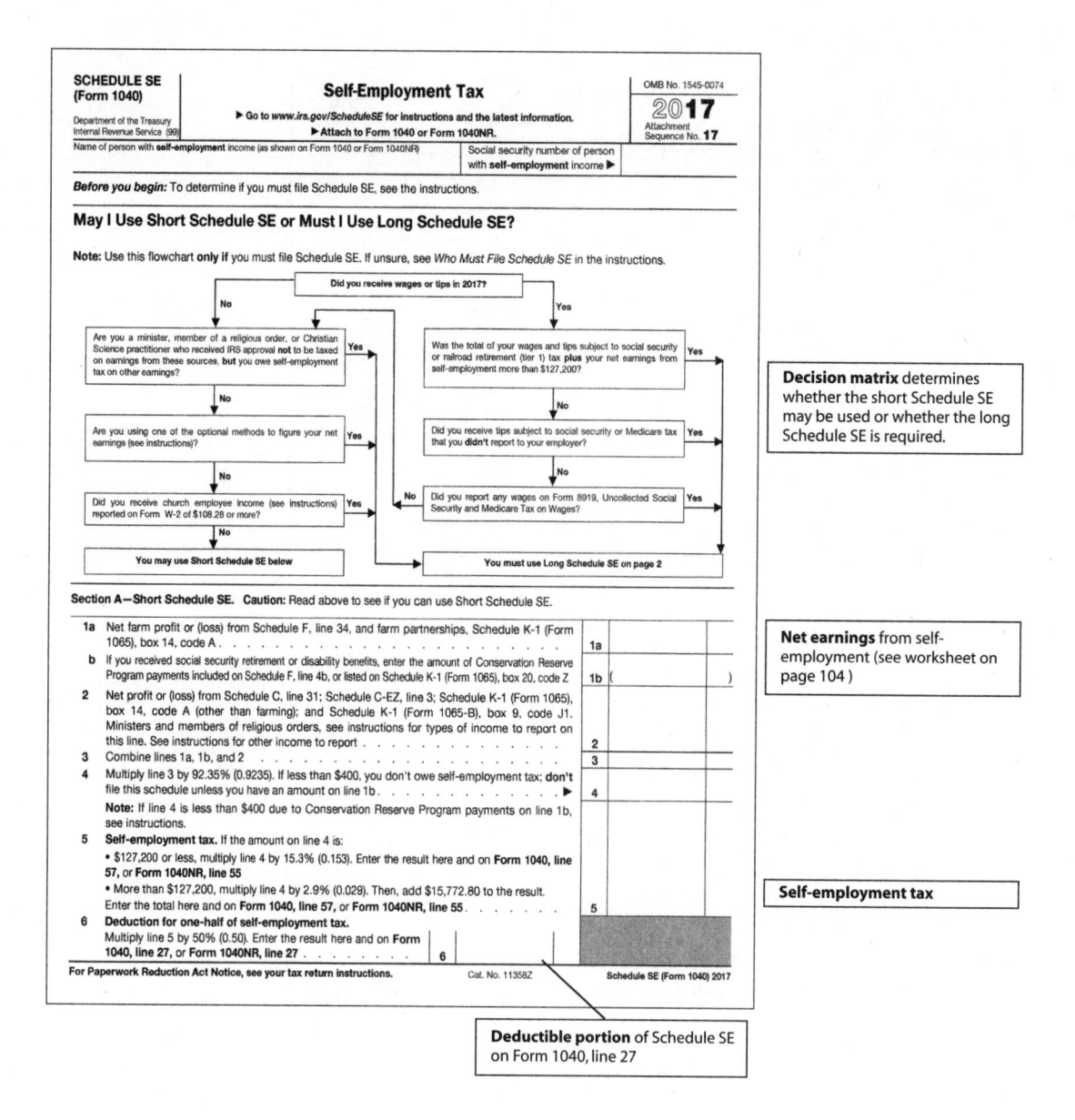

Annotations on the form:
- **Decision matrix** determines whether the short Schedule SE may be used or whether the long Schedule SE is required.
- **Net earnings** from self-employment (see worksheet on page 104)
- **Self-employment tax**
- **Deductible portion** of Schedule SE on Form 1040, line 27

140

The 1040 Challenge
Long Schedule SE

Schedule SE (Form 1040) 2017

Name of person with **self-employment** income (as shown on Form 1040 or Form 1040NR)

Social security number of person with **self-employment** income ▶

Attachment Sequence No. **17** Page **2**

Section B—Long Schedule SE
Part I Self-Employment Tax

Note: If your only income subject to self-employment tax is **church employee income**, see instructions. Also see instructions for the definition of church employee income.

A If you are a minister, member of a religious order, or Christian Science practitioner **and** you filed Form 4361, but you had $400 or more of **other** net earnings from self-employment, check here and continue with Part I . . . . ▶ ☐

1a Net farm profit or (loss) from Schedule F, line 34, and farm partnerships, Schedule K-1 (Form 1065), box 14, code A. **Note:** Skip lines 1a and 1b if you use the farm optional method (see instructions) — **1a**

b If you received social security retirement or disability benefits, enter the amount of Conservation Reserve Program payments included on Schedule F, line 4b, or listed on Schedule K-1 (Form 1065), box 20, code Z — **1b** ( )

2 Net profit or (loss) from Schedule C, line 31; Schedule C-EZ, line 3; Schedule K-1 (Form 1065), box 14, code A (other than farming); and Schedule K-1 (Form 1065-B), box 9, code J1. Ministers and members of religious orders, see instructions for types of income to report on this line. See instructions for other income to report. **Note:** Skip this line if you use the nonfarm optional method (see instructions) **2**

3 Combine lines 1a, 1b, and 2 . . . . **3**

4a If line 3 is more than zero, multiply line 3 by 92.35% (0.9235). Otherwise, enter amount from line 3 — **4a**
Note: If line 4a is less than $400 due to Conservation Reserve Program payments on line 1b, see instructions.

b If you elect one or both of the optional methods, enter the total of lines 15 and 17 here . . **4b**

c Combine lines 4a and 4b. If less than $400, **stop;** you don't owe self-employment tax.
Exception: If less than $400 and you had **church employee income**, enter -0- and continue ▶ **4c**

5a Enter your **church employee income** from Form W-2. See instructions for definition of church employee income . . . **5a**

b Multiply line 5a by 92.35% (0.9235). If less than $100, enter -0- **5b**

6 Add lines 4c and 5b **6**

7 Maximum amount of combined wages and self-employment earnings subject to social security tax or the 6.2% portion of the 7.65% railroad retirement (tier 1) tax for 2017 . . . . . . **7** 127,200 00

8a Total social security wages and tips (total of boxes 3 and 7 on Form(s) W-2) and railroad retirement (tier 1) compensation. If $127,200 or more, skip lines 8b through 10, and go to line 11 — **8a**

b Unreported tips subject to social security tax (from Form 4137, line 10) — **8b**

c Wages subject to social security tax (from Form 8919, line 10) — **8c**

d Add lines 8a, 8b, and 8c **8d**

9 Subtract line 8d from line 7. If zero or less, enter -0- here and on line 10 and go to line 11 ▶ **9**

10 Multiply the **smaller** of line 6 or line 9 by 12.4% (0.124) **10**

11 Multiply line 6 by 2.9% (0.029) **11**

12 **Self-employment tax.** Add lines 10 and 11. Enter here and on **Form 1040, line 57,** or **Form 1040NR, line 55** **12**

13 Deduction for one-half of self-employment tax.
Multiply line 12 by 50% (0.50). Enter the result here and on
Form 1040, line 27, or **Form 1040NR, line 27** . . . | **13**

Part II Optional Methods To Figure Net Earnings (see instructions)

Farm Optional Method. You may use this method **only** if **(a)** your gross farm income[1] wasn't more than $7,800, **or (b)** your net farm profits[2] were less than $5,631.

14 Maximum income for optional methods **14** 5,200 00

15 Enter the **smaller** of: two-thirds (²⁄₃) of gross farm income[1] (not less than zero) **or** $5,200. Also include this amount on line 4b above **15**

Nonfarm Optional Method. You may use this method **only** if **(a)** your net nonfarm profits[3] were less than $5,631 and also less than 72.189% of your gross nonfarm income,[4] **and (b)** you had net earnings from self-employment of at least $400 in 2 of the prior 3 years. **Caution:** You may use this method no more than five times.

16 Subtract line 15 from line 14 . . . . **16**

17 Enter the **smaller** of: two-thirds (²⁄₃) of gross nonfarm income[4] (not less than zero) **or** the amount on line 16. Also include this amount on line 4b above **17**

[1] From Sch. F, line 9, and Sch. K-1 (Form 1065), box 14, code B.
[2] From Sch. F, line 34, and Sch. K-1 (Form 1065), box 14, code A—minus the amount you would have entered on line 1b had you not used the optional method.
[3] From Sch. C, line 31; Sch. C-EZ, line 3; Sch. K-1 (Form 1065), box 14, code A; and Sch. K-1 (Form 1065-B), box 9, code J1.
[4] From Sch. C, line 7; Sch. C-EZ, line 1; Sch. K-1 (Form 1065), box 14, code C; and Sch. K-1 (Form 1065-B), box 9, code J2.

Schedule SE (Form 1040) 2017

Annotations:
- **Net earnings** from self-employment (see worksheet on page 104)
- **Self-employment tax**
- **Deductible portion** of Schedule SE on Form 1040, line 27.

The 1040 Challenge

Form 2106-EZ

Form 2106-EZ — Unreimbursed Employee Business Expenses
Department of the Treasury — Internal Revenue Service (99)
► Attach to Form 1040 or Form 1040NR.
► Go to www.irs.gov/Form2106EZ for the latest information.
OMB No. 1545-0074
2017
Attachment Sequence No. 129A

Your name | Occupation in which you incurred expenses | Social security number

You Can Use This Form Only if All of the Following Apply.

- You are an employee deducting ordinary and necessary expenses attributable to your job. An ordinary expense is one that is common and accepted in your field of trade, business, or profession. A necessary expense is one that is helpful and appropriate for your business. An expense doesn't have to be required to be considered necessary.
- You **don't** get reimbursed by your employer for any expenses (amounts your employer included in box 1 of your Form W-2 aren't considered reimbursements for this purpose).
- If you are claiming vehicle expense, you are using the standard mileage rate for 2017.

Caution: You can use the standard mileage rate for 2017 **only if: (a)** you owned the vehicle and used the standard mileage rate for the first year you placed the vehicle in service, **or (b)** you leased the vehicle and used the standard mileage rate for the portion of the lease period after 1997.

Part I — Figure Your Expenses

1. Complete Part II. Multiply line 8a by 53.5¢ (0.535). Enter the result here **1**
2. Parking fees, tolls, and transportation, including train, bus, etc., that **didn't** involve overnight travel or commuting to and from work **2**
3. Travel expense while away from home overnight, including lodging, airplane, car rental, etc. **Don't** include meals and entertainment **3**
4. Business expenses not included on lines 1 through 3. **Don't** include meals and entertainment. **4**
5. Meals and entertainment expenses: $ _____ × 50% (0.50). (Employees subject to Department of Transportation (DOT) hours of service limits: Multiply meal expenses incurred while away from home on business by 80% (0.80) instead of 50%. For details, see instructions.) **5**
6. Total expenses. Add lines 1 through 5. Enter here and on **Schedule A (Form 1040), line 21** (or on **Schedule A (Form 1040NR), line 7**). (Armed Forces reservists, fee-basis state or local government officials, qualified performing artists, and individuals with disabilities: See the instructions for special rules on where to enter this amount.) **6**

Part II — Information on Your Vehicle. Complete this part **only** if you are claiming vehicle expense on line 1.

7. When did you place your vehicle in service for business use? (month, day, year) ► ___/___/___
8. Of the total number of miles you drove your vehicle during 2017, enter the number of miles you used your vehicle for:
   - a Business _____ b Commuting (see instructions) _____ c Other _____
9. Was your vehicle available for personal use during off-duty hours? .... ☐ Yes ☐ No
10. Do you (or your spouse) have another vehicle available for personal use? .... ☐ Yes ☐ No
11a. Do you have evidence to support your deduction? .... ☐ Yes ☐ No
  b. If "Yes," is the evidence written? .... ☐ Yes ☐ No

For Paperwork Reduction Act Notice, see your tax return instructions. Cat. No. 20604Q Form **2106-EZ** (2017)

Mileage. Deduct unreimbursed business mileage on line 1. It is almost always advantageous to reimburse business miles under an accountable expense reimbursement plan.

Meals and entertainment. Although deductible on this line at 50%, meals and entertainment are 100% reimbursable under an accountable expense reimbursement plan.

The 1040 Challenge
Form 2441

Form **2441**	**Child and Dependent Care Expenses**		OMB No. 1545-0074
Department of the Treasury Internal Revenue Service (99)	▶ Attach to Form 1040, Form 1040A, or Form 1040NR. ▶ Go to www.irs.gov/Form2441 for instructions and the latest information.	1040 1040A 1040NR 2441	**2017** Attachment Sequence No. **21**

Name(s) shown on return   Your social security number

Part I   **Persons or Organizations Who Provided the Care**—You **must** complete this part.
(If you have more than two care providers, see the instructions.)

1	(a) Care provider's name	(b) Address (number, street, apt. no., city, state, and ZIP code)	(c) Identifying number (SSN or EIN)	(d) Amount paid (see instructions)

> **Care provider.** If the care provider is an individual, the social security number must be provided. Otherwise, insert the employer identification number.

Did you receive dependent care benefits?
- No ▶ Complete only Part II below.
- Yes ▶ Complete Part III on the back next.

Caution: If the care was provided in your home, you may owe employment taxes. If you do, you can't file Form 1040A. For details, see the instructions for Form 1040, line 60a, or Form 1040NR, line 59a.

Part II   **Credit for Child and Dependent Care Expenses**

2   Information about your **qualifying person(s)**. If you have more than two qualifying persons, see the instructions.

(a) Qualifying person's name (First / Last)	(b) Qualifying person's social security number	(c) Qualified expenses you incurred and paid in 2017 for the person listed in column (a)

> **Qualifying persons.** Only children under age 13, a disabled spouse, or disabled dependents may be listed here.

3   Add the amounts in column (c) of line 2. **Don't** enter more than $3,000 for one qualifying person or $6,000 for two or more persons. If you completed Part III, enter the amount from line 31 . . . .   **3**

4   Enter your **earned income**. See instructions **4**

5   If married filing jointly, enter your spouse's earned income (if you or your spouse was a student or was disabled, see the instructions); **all others**, enter the amount from line 4 .   **5**

6   Enter the **smallest** of line 3, 4, or 5 . . . .   **6**

7   Enter the amount from Form 1040, line 38; Form 1040A, line 22; or Form 1040NR, line 37 . . . . .   **7**

8   Enter on line 8 the decimal amount shown below that applies to the amount on line 7

If line 7 is:			If line 7 is:		
Over	But not over	Decimal amount is	Over	But not over	Decimal amount is
$0	—15,000	.35	$29,000	—31,000	.27
15,000	—17,000	.34	31,000	—33,000	.26
17,000	—19,000	.33	33,000	—35,000	.25
19,000	—21,000	.32	35,000	—37,000	.24
21,000	—23,000	.31	37,000	—39,000	.23
23,000	—25,000	.30	39,000	—41,000	.22
25,000	—27,000	.29	41,000	—43,000	.21
27,000	—29,000	.28	43,000	—No limit	.20

  8   X .

9   Multiply line 6 by the decimal amount on line 8. If you paid 2016 expenses in 2017, see the instructions **9**

10   Tax liability limit. Enter the amount from the Credit Limit Worksheet in the instructions **10**

11   **Credit for child and dependent care expenses.** Enter the **smaller** of line 9 or line 10 here and on Form 1040, line 49; Form 1040A, line 31; or Form 1040NR, line 47 . . . .   **11**

For Paperwork Reduction Act Notice, see your tax return instructions.   Cat. No. 11862M   Form **2441** (2017)

The 1040 Challenge
Form 8863

Form 8863
Department of the Treasury
Internal Revenue Service (99)

Education Credits
(American Opportunity and Lifetime Learning Credits)
▶ Attach to Form 1040 or Form 1040A.
▶ Go to www.irs.gov/Form8863 for instructions and the latest information.

OMB No. 1545-0074
2017
Attachment Sequence No. **50**

Name(s) shown on return | Your social security number

⚠ **CAUTION** Complete a separate Part III on page 2 for each student for whom you're claiming either credit before you complete Parts I and II.

Part I — Refundable American Opportunity Credit

1. After completing Part III for each student, enter the total of all amounts from all Parts III, line 30 . . . **1**
2. Enter: $180,000 if married filing jointly; $90,000 if single, head of household, or qualifying widow(er) **2**
3. Enter the amount from Form 1040, line 38, or Form 1040A, line 22. If you're filing Form 2555, 2555-EZ, or 4563, or you're excluding income from Puerto Rico, see Pub. 970 for the amount to enter . . . **3**
4. Subtract line 3 from line 2. If zero or less, **stop**; you can't take any education credit **4**
5. Enter: $20,000 if married filing jointly; $10,000 if single, head of household, or qualifying widow(er) **5**
6. If line 4 is:
   • Equal to or more than line 5, enter 1.000 on line 6 . . . .
   • Less than line 5, divide line 4 by line 5. Enter the result as a decimal (rounded to at least three places) . . . . ▶ **6**
7. Multiply line 1 by line 6. **Caution:** If you were under age 24 at the end of the year **and** meet the conditions described in the instructions, you **can't** take the refundable American opportunity credit; skip line 8, enter the amount from line 7 on line 9, and check this box ▶ ☐ **7**
8. **Refundable American opportunity credit.** Multiply line 7 by 40% (0.40). Enter the amount here and on Form 1040, line 68, or Form 1040A, line 44. Then go to line 9 below. **8**

Part II — Nonrefundable Education Credits

9. Subtract line 8 from line 7. Enter here and on line 2 of the Credit Limit Worksheet (see instructions) **9**
10. After completing Part III for each student, enter the total of all amounts from all Parts III, line 31. If zero, skip lines 11 through 17, enter -0- on line 18, and go to line 19 . . . . **10**
11. Enter the smaller of line 10 or $10,000 . . . . **11**
12. Multiply line 11 by 20% (0.20) **12**

> **Qualified expenses.** Only tuition and fees required for enrollment or attendance at an eligible educational institution are includible here.

Form 8863 (2017) Page **2**
Name(s) shown on return | Your social security number

⚠ **CAUTION** Complete Part III for each student for whom you're claiming either the American opportunity credit or lifetime learning credit. Use additional copies of page 2 as needed for each student.

Part III — Student and Educational Institution Information. See instructions.

20. Student name (as shown on page 1 of your tax return)
21. Student social security number (as shown on page 1 of your tax return)

22. Educational institution information (see instructions)

a. Name of first educational institution | b. Name of second educational institution (if any)

(1) Address. Number and street (or P.O. box). City, town or post office, state, and ZIP code. If a foreign address, see instructions. | (1) Address. Number and street (or P.O. box). City, town or post office, state, and ZIP code. If a foreign address, see instructions.

(2) Did the student receive Form 1098-T from this institution for 2017? ☐ Yes ☐ No | (2) Did the student receive Form 1098-T from this institution for 2017? ☐ Yes ☐ No

(3) Did the student receive Form 1098-T from this institution for 2016 with box 2 filled in and box 7 checked? ☐ Yes ☐ No | (3) Did the student receive Form 1098-T from this institution for 2016 with box 2 filled in and box 7 checked? ☐ Yes ☐ No

If you checked "No" in **both (2) and (3)**, skip **(4)**. However, you must complete **(4)** if you're claiming the American opportunity credit. | If you checked "No" in **both (2) and (3)**, skip **(4)**. However, you must complete **(4)** if you're claiming the American opportunity credit.

(4) If you checked "Yes" in **(2)** or **(3)**, enter the institution's employer identification number (from Form 1098-T). | (4) If you checked "Yes" in **(2)** or **(3)**, enter the institution's employer identification number (from Form 1098-T).

23. Has the Hope Scholarship Credit or American opportunity credit been claimed for this student for any 4 tax years before 2017? | ☐ Yes — **Stop!** Go to line 31 for this student. ☐ No — Go to line 24.

24. Was the student enrolled at least half-time for at least one academic period that began or is treated as having begun in 2017 at an eligible educational institution in a program leading towards a postsecondary degree, certificate, or other recognized postsecondary educational credential? | ☐ Yes — Go to line 25. ☐ No — **Stop!** Go to line 31 for this student.

> **Eligible educational institution.** An eligible institution is generally any accredited public, nonprofit, or private college, university, vocational school, or other post-secondary institution.

The 1040 Challenge
Form 8880

Form 8880 — Credit for Qualified Retirement Savings Contributions
Department of the Treasury
Internal Revenue Service

▶ Attach to Form 1040, Form 1040A, or Form 1040NR.
▶ Go to www.irs.gov/Form8880 for instructions and the latest information.

OMB No. 1545-0074
2017
Attachment Sequence No. 54

Name(s) shown on return | Your social security number

CAUTION: You **cannot** take this credit if **either** of the following applies.
- The amount on Form 1040, line 38; Form 1040A, line 22; or Form 1040NR, line 37 is more than $31,000 ($46,500 if head of household; $62,000 if married filing jointly).
- The person(s) who made the qualified contribution or elective deferral **(a)** was born after January 1, 2000, **(b)** is claimed as a dependent on someone else's 2017 tax return, or **(c)** was a **student** (see instructions).

		(a) You	(b) Your spouse
1	Traditional and Roth IRA (including *myRA*) contributions for 2017. **Do not** include rollover contributions		
2	Elective deferrals to a 401(k) or other qualified employer plan, voluntary employee contributions, and 501(c)(18)(D) plan contributions for 2017 (see instructions)		
3	Add lines 1 and 2		
4	Certain distributions received **after** 2014 and **before** the due date (including extensions) of your 2017 tax return (see instructions). If married filing jointly, include **both** spouses' amounts in **both** columns. See instructions for an exception		
5	Subtract line 4 from line 3. If zero or less, enter -0-		
6	In each column, enter the **smaller** of line 5 or $2,000		
7	Add the amounts on line 6. If zero, **stop**; you cannot take this credit		
8	Enter the amount from Form 1040, line 38*; Form 1040A, line 22; or Form 1040NR, line 37		
9	Enter the applicable decimal amount shown below.		

If line 8 is—		And your filing status is—		
Over—	But not over—	Married filing jointly	Head of household	Single, Married filing separately, or Qualifying widow(er)
		Enter on line 9—		
---	$18,500	.5	.5	.5
$18,500	$20,000	.5	.5	.2
$20,000	$27,750	.5	.5	.1
$27,750	$30,000	.5	.2	.1
$30,000	$31,000	.5	.1	.1
$31,000	$37,000	.5	.1	.0
$37,000	$40,000	.2	.1	.0
$40,000	$46,500	.1	.1	.0
$46,500	$62,000	.1	.0	.0
$62,000	---	.0	.0	.0

9 | X .

Note: If line 9 is zero, **stop**; you cannot take this credit.

10	Multiply line 7 by line 9	
11	Limitation based on tax liability. Enter the amount from the Credit Limit Worksheet in the instructions	
12	**Credit for qualified retirement savings contributions.** Enter the **smaller** of line 10 or line 11 here and on Form 1040, line 51; Form 1040A, line 34; or Form 1040NR, line 48	

*See Pub. 590-A for the amount to enter if you are filing Form 2555, 2555-EZ, or 4563 or you are excluding income from Puerto Rico.

For Paperwork Reduction Act Notice, see your tax return instructions. Cat. No. 33394D Form **8880** (2017)

Sample Return No. 1

- Accountable expense reimbursement plan
- Minister owns residence
- Pays federal taxes through voluntary withholding
- Church reimbursed nonqualifying moving expenses
- Housing fair rental value test applied
- 403(b) contribution by salary reduction and employer contributions
- Application of Deason Rule

Minister considered to be an employee for income tax purposes with an accountable business expense plan.

The Browns live in a home they are personally purchasing. Pastor Brown has entered into a voluntary withholding agreement with the church, and $12,000 of federal income taxes are withheld.

Income, Benefits, and Reimbursements:

Church salary	$64,850
Christmas and other special occasion gifts paid by the church based on designated member-gifts to the church	750
Honoraria for performing weddings, funerals, and baptisms	650
Honorarium for speaking as an evangelist at another church	1,000
Mutual fund dividend income:	
Capital gain distributions	150
Interest income:	
Taxable	175
Reimbursement of self-employment tax	12,000

SAMPLE RETURN NO. 1 ▷ MINISTER-EMPLOYEE FOR INCOME TAX PURPOSES (ACCOUNTABLE PLAN)

Business Expenses, Itemized Deductions, Housing, and Other Data:

100% of church-related expenses (including 9,412 business miles) paid personally were reimbursed by the church under an accountable expense plan, based on timely substantiation of the expenses.

Expenses related to honoraria income:	
Parking	$ 25
Travel – 929 x 53.5¢ per mile	497
Meals and entertainment	50
Other	200
Potential itemized deductions:	
Unreimbursed doctors, dentists, and drugs	1,500
State and local income taxes:	
2016 taxes paid in 2017	400
Withheld from salary	1,600
Real estate taxes on home	1,000
Home mortgage interest	14,850
Cash contributions	8,200
Noncash contributions – household furniture/fair market value	266
Tax preparation fee	200
Student loan interest	1,906
Housing data:	
Designation	26,00
Actual expenses	25,625
Fair rental value including utilities	25,000
403(b) pre-tax contributions for Pastor Brown:	
Voluntary employee contributions made under a salary reduction agreement	500
Nonvoluntary employer contributions	2,000
Moving expenses reimbursed under a nonqualified plan (see page 152)	6,750

2018 MINISTER'S TAX & FINANCIAL GUIDE

Form 1040 Department of the Treasury—Internal Revenue Service (99)
U.S. Individual Income Tax Return 2017 OMB No. 1545-0074 IRS Use Only—Do not write or staple in this space.

For the year Jan. 1–Dec. 31, 2017, or other tax year beginning , 2017, ending , 20 See separate instructions.

Your first name and initial: **Milton L.**	Last name: **Brown**
Your social security number: **541 16 8194**	
If a joint return, spouse's first name and initial: **Alessia S.**	Last name: **Brown**
Spouse's social security number: **238 49 7249**	
Home address (number and street): **418 Trenton Street**	Apt. no.
City, town or post office, state, and ZIP code: **Springfield, OH 45504**	

▲ Make sure the SSN(s) above and on line 6c are correct.

Presidential Election Campaign
Check here if you, or your spouse if filing jointly, want $3 to go to this fund. Checking a box below will not change your tax or refund. ☐ You ☐ Spouse

Filing Status
Check only one box.
1. ☐ Single
2. ☒ Married filing jointly (even if only one had income)
3. ☐ Married filing separately. Enter spouse's SSN above and full name here. ▶
4. ☐ Head of household (with qualifying person). (See instructions.) If the qualifying person is a child but not your dependent, enter this child's name here. ▶
5. ☐ Qualifying widow(er) (see instructions)

Exemptions
6a ☒ Yourself. If someone can claim you as a dependent, **do not** check box 6a.
b ☒ Spouse
Boxes checked on 6a and 6b: **2**

c Dependents:
(1) First name Last name	(2) Dependent's social security number	(3) Dependent's relationship to you	(4) ✓ if child under age 17 qualifying for child tax credit
Charles Brown	514 43 9196	Son	☒

No. of children on 6c who:
• lived with you: **1**
• did not live with you due to divorce or separation (see instructions)
Dependents on 6c not entered above

If more than four dependents, see instructions and check here ▶ ☐

d Total number of exemptions claimed **3**

Income

Attach Form(s) W-2 here. Also attach Forms W-2G and 1099-R if tax was withheld.

If you did not get a W-2, see instructions.

7	Wages, salaries, tips, etc. Attach Form(s) W-2 **Incl. Excess Housing Allow. $1,000**	7	58,850
8a	Taxable interest. Attach Schedule B if required	8a	175
b	Tax-exempt interest. **Do not** include on line 8a . . 8b		
9a	Ordinary dividends. Attach Schedule B if required	9a	
b	Qualified dividends . . 9b		
10	Taxable refunds, credits, or offsets of state and local income taxes	10	
11	Alimony received	11	
12	Business income or (loss). Attach Schedule C or C-EZ	12	1,120
13	Capital gain or (loss). Attach Schedule D if required. If not required, check here ▶ ☒	13	150
14	Other gains or (losses). Attach Form 4797	14	
15a	IRA distributions . 15a b Taxable amount	15b	
16a	Pensions and annuities 16a b Taxable amount	16b	
17	Rental real estate, royalties, partnerships, S corporations, trusts, etc. Attach Schedule E	17	
18	Farm income or (loss). Attach Schedule F	18	
19	Unemployment compensation	19	
20a	Social security benefits 20a b Taxable amount	20b	
21	Other income. List type and amount	21	
22	Combine the amounts in the far right column for lines 7 through 21. This is your **total income** ▶	22	60,295

Adjusted Gross Income

23	Educator expenses	23	
24	Certain business expenses of reservists, performing artists, and fee-basis government officials. Attach Form 2106 or 2106-EZ	24	
25	Health savings account deduction. Attach Form 8889	25	
26	Moving expenses. Attach Form 3903	26	
27	Deductible part of self-employment tax. Attach Schedule SE	27	5,988
28	Self-employed SEP, SIMPLE, and qualified plans	28	
29	Self-employed health insurance deduction	29	
30	Penalty on early withdrawal of savings	30	
31a	Alimony paid b Recipient's SSN ▶	31a	
32	IRA deduction	32	
33	Student loan interest deduction	33	1,906
34	Reserved for future use	34	
35	Domestic production activities deduction. Attach Form 8903	35	
36	Add lines 23 through 35	36	7,894
37	Subtract line 36 from line 22. This is your **adjusted gross income** ▶	37	52,401

For Disclosure, Privacy Act, and Paperwork Reduction Act Notice, see separate instructions. Cat. No. 11320B Form **1040** (2017)

Line 7 – See page 153 for calculation of the excess housing allowance.
Line 27 – See pages 105–6 for explanation of the self-employment tax deduction.

SAMPLE RETURN NO. 1 ➤ **MINISTER-EMPLOYEE FOR INCOME TAX PURPOSES (ACCOUNTABLE PLAN)**

	38	Amount from line 37 (adjusted gross income)	38	52,401
Tax and Credits	39a	Check if: ☐ You were born before January 2, 1953, ☐ Blind. ☐ Spouse was born before January 2, 1953, ☐ Blind. Total boxes checked ▶ 39a		
	b	If your spouse itemizes on a separate return or you were a dual-status alien, check here ▶ 39b ☐		
Standard Deduction for— • People who check any box on line 39a or 39b or who can be claimed as a dependent, see instructions. • All others: Single or Married filing separately, $6,350 Married filing jointly or Qualifying widow(er), $12,700 Head of household, $9,350	40	Itemized deductions (from Schedule A) or your standard deduction (see left margin)	40	26,316
	41	Subtract line 40 from line 38	41	26,085
	42	Exemptions. If line 38 is $156,900 or less, multiply $4,050 by the number on line 6d. Otherwise, see instructions	42	12,150
	43	Taxable income. Subtract line 42 from line 41. If line 42 is more than line 41, enter -0-	43	13,935
	44	Tax (see instructions). Check if any from: a ☐ Form(s) 8814 b ☐ Form 4972 c ☐	44	1,378
	45	Alternative minimum tax (see instructions). Attach Form 6251	45	
	46	Excess advance premium tax credit repayment. Attach Form 8962	46	
	47	Add lines 44, 45, and 46 ▶	47	1,378
	48	Foreign tax credit. Attach Form 1116 if required	48	
	49	Credit for child and dependent care expenses. Attach Form 2441	49	
	50	Education credits from Form 8863, line 19	50	
	51	Retirement savings contributions credit. Attach Form 8880	51	
	52	Child tax credit. Attach Schedule 8812, if required	52	1,000
	53	Residential energy credit. Attach Form 5695	53	
	54	Other credits from Form: a ☐ 3800 b ☐ 8801 c ☐	54	
	55	Add lines 48 through 54. These are your total credits	55	1,000
	56	Subtract line 55 from line 47. If line 55 is more than line 47, enter -0- ▶	56	378
Other Taxes	57	Self-employment tax. Attach Schedule SE	57	11,975
	58	Unreported social security and Medicare tax from Form: a ☐ 4137 b ☐ 8919	58	
	59	Additional tax on IRAs, other qualified retirement plans, etc. Attach Form 5329 if required	59	
	60a	Household employment taxes from Schedule H	60a	
	b	First-time homebuyer credit repayment. Attach Form 5405 if required	60b	
	61	Health care: individual responsibility (see instructions) Full-year coverage ☒	61	
	62	Taxes from: a ☐ Form 8959 b ☐ Form 8960 c ☐ Instructions; enter code(s)	62	
	63	Add lines 56 through 62. This is your total tax ▶	63	12,353
Payments	64	Federal income tax withheld from Forms W-2 and 1099	64	
	65	2017 estimated tax payments and amount applied from 2016 return	65	12,000
If you have a qualifying child, attach Schedule EIC.	66a	Earned income credit (EIC)	66a	
	b	Nontaxable combat pay election 66b		
	67	Additional child tax credit. Attach Schedule 8812	67	
	68	American opportunity credit from Form 8863, line 8	68	
	69	Net premium tax credit. Attach Form 8962	69	
	70	Amount paid with request for extension to file	70	
	71	Excess social security and tier 1 RRTA tax withheld	71	
	72	Credit for federal tax on fuels. Attach Form 4136	72	
	73	Credits from Form: a ☐ 2439 b ☐ Reserved c ☐ 8885 d ☐	73	
	74	Add lines 64, 65, 66a, and 67 through 73. These are your total payments ▶	74	12,000
Refund	75	If line 74 is more than line 63, subtract line 63 from line 74. This is the amount you overpaid	75	
	76a	Amount of line 75 you want refunded to you. If Form 8888 is attached, check here ▶ ☐	76a	
Direct deposit? See instructions.	b	Routing number ▶ c Type: ☐ Checking ☐ Savings		
	d	Account number		
	77	Amount of line 75 you want applied to your 2018 estimated tax ▶ 77		
Amount You Owe	78	Amount you owe. Subtract line 74 from line 63. For details on how to pay, see instructions ▶	78	353
	79	Estimated tax penalty (see instructions) 79		

Third Party Designee Do you want to allow another person to discuss this return with the IRS (see instructions)? ☐ Yes. Complete below. ☐ No

Sign Here Your signature: *Milton L. Brown* Date: 4/15/18 Your occupation: Minister
Spouse's signature: *Alessia S. Brown* Date: 4/15/18 Spouse's occupation: Housewife

Paid Preparer Use Only

Form **1040** (2017)

Line 44 – If applicable, be sure to use "Qualified Dividends and Capital Gain Tax Worksheet" in the instructions to Form 1040.

Line 64 – The minister had income tax withheld under a voluntary withholding agreement with the church. Notice that income tax was withheld relating to both the income and social security tax liability.

149

2018 MINISTER'S TAX & FINANCIAL GUIDE

SCHEDULE A **(Form 1040)** Department of the Treasury Internal Revenue Service (99)		**Itemized Deductions** ▶ Go to *www.irs.gov/ScheduleA* for instructions and the latest information. ▶ Attach to Form 1040.			OMB No. 1545-0074 **2017** Attachment Sequence No. **07**
Name(s) shown on Form 1040 Milton L. and Alessia S. Brown					Your social security number 541-16-8194

Medical and Dental Expenses		**Caution:** Do not include expenses reimbursed or paid by others.			
	1	Medical and dental expenses (see instructions)	1	1,500	
	2	Enter amount from Form 1040, line 38 | 2 | 52,401 |			
	3	Multiply line 2 by 10% (0.10)	3	5,240	
	4	Subtract line 3 from line 1. If line 3 is more than line 1, enter -0-			4 0
Taxes You Paid	5	State and local **(check only one box):** a ☒ Income taxes, **or** b ☐ General sales taxes	5	2,000	
	6	Real estate taxes (see instructions)	6	1,000	
	7	Personal property taxes	7		
	8	Other taxes. List type and amount ▶ _____	8		
	9	Add lines 5 through 8			9 3,000
Interest You Paid **Note:** Your mortgage interest deduction may be limited (see instructions).	10	Home mortgage interest and points reported to you on Form 1098	10	14,850	
	11	Home mortgage interest not reported to you on Form 1098. If paid to the person from whom you bought the home, see instructions and show that person's name, identifying no., and address ▶ _____	11		
	12	Points not reported to you on Form 1098. See instructions for special rules	12		
	13	Reserved	13		
	14	Investment interest. Attach Form 4952 if required. See instructions.	14		
	15	Add lines 10 through 14			15 14,850
Gifts to Charity If you made a gift and got a benefit for it, see instructions.	16	Gifts by cash or check. If you made any gift of $250 or more, see instructions	16	8,200	
	17	Other than by cash or check. If any gift of $250 or more, see instructions. You **must** attach Form 8283 if over $500	17	266	
	18	Carryover from prior year	18		
	19	Add lines 16 through 18			19 8,466
Casualty and Theft Losses	20	Casualty or theft loss(es). Attach Form 4684. See instructions			20
Job Expenses and Certain Miscellaneous Deductions	21	Unreimbursed employee expenses—job travel, union dues, job education, etc. Attach Form 2106 or 2106-EZ if required. See instructions. ▶ _____	21		
	22	Tax preparation fees	22	200	
	23	Other expenses—investment, safe deposit box, etc. List type and amount ▶ _____	23		
	24	Add lines 21 through 23	24	200	
	25	Enter amount from Form 1040, line 38 | 25 | 52,401 |			
	26	Multiply line 25 by 2% (0.02)	26	1,048	
	27	Subtract line 26 from line 24. If line 26 is more than line 24, enter -0-			27 0
Other Miscellaneous Deductions	28	Other—from list in instructions. List type and amount ▶ _____			28
Total Itemized Deductions	29	Is Form 1040, line 38, over $156,900? ☒ **No.** Your deduction is not limited. Add the amounts in the far right column for lines 4 through 28. Also, enter this amount on Form 1040, line 40. ☐ **Yes.** Your deduction may be limited. See the Itemized Deductions Worksheet in the instructions to figure the amount to enter.			29 26,316
	30	If you elect to itemize deductions even though they are less than your standard deduction, check here ▶ ☐			

For Paperwork Reduction Act Notice, see the Instructions for Form 1040. Cat. No. 17145C Schedule A (Form 1040) 2017

Lines 6 and 10 – The real estate taxes and home mortgage interest are deducted on this form plus excluded from income on line 7, Form 1040, page 1 as a housing allowance.

Line 21 – There are no unreimbursed employee expenses to deduct since the church reimbursed all the professional expenses under an accountable expense reimbursement plan.

SAMPLE RETURN NO. 1 ▷ MINISTER-EMPLOYEE FOR INCOME TAX PURPOSES (ACCOUNTABLE PLAN)

SCHEDULE C-EZ
(Form 1040)
Department of the Treasury
Internal Revenue Service (99)

Net Profit From Business
(Sole Proprietorship)
▶ Partnerships, joint ventures, etc., generally must file Form 1065 or 1065-B.
▶ Attach to Form 1040, 1040NR, or 1041. ▶ See instructions on page 2.

OMB No. 1545-0074

2017

Attachment Sequence No. **09A**

Name of proprietor: Milton L. Brown
Social security number (SSN): 541-16-8194

Part I General Information

You May Use Schedule C-EZ Instead of Schedule C Only If You:
- Had business expenses of $5,000 or less,
- Use the cash method of accounting,
- Did not have an inventory at any time during the year,
- Did not have a net loss from your business,
- Had only one business as either a sole proprietor, qualified joint venture, or statutory employee,

And You:
- Had no employees during the year,
- Do not deduct expenses for business use of your home,
- Do not have prior year unallowed passive activity losses from this business, and
- Are not required to file Form 4562, Depreciation and Amortization, for this business. See the instructions for Schedule C, line 13, to find out if you must file.

A Principal business or profession, including product or service: **Minister**
B Enter business code (see page 2) ▶ **813000**
C Business name. If no separate business name, leave blank.
D Enter your EIN (see page 2)
E Business address (including suite or room no.). Address not required if same as on page 1 of your tax return.
   City, town or post office, state, and ZIP code
F Did you make any payments in 2017 that would require you to file Form(s) 1099? (see the Instructions for Schedule C) . . . . ☐ Yes ☒ No
G If "Yes," did you or will you file required Forms 1099? . . . . ☐ Yes ☐ No

Part II Figure Your Net Profit

1 Gross receipts. Caution: If this income was reported to you on Form W-2 and the "Statutory employee" box on that form was checked, see *Statutory employees* in the instructions for Schedule C, line 1, and check here . . . . ▶ ☐   **1** 1,650

2 Total expenses (see page 2). If more than $5,000, you **must** use Schedule C **2** 530

3 Net profit. Subtract line 2 from line 1. If less than zero, you **must** use Schedule C. Enter on both Form 1040, line 12, and **Schedule SE, line 2**, or on **Form 1040NR, line 13**, and **Schedule SE, line 2** (see page 2). (Statutory employees **do not** report this amount on Schedule SE, line 2.) Estates and trusts, enter on **Form 1041, line 3** **3** 1,120

Part III Information on Your Vehicle. Complete this part **only** if you are claiming car or truck expenses on line 2.

4 When did you place your vehicle in service for business purposes? (month, day, year) ▶ 1/1/08

5 Of the total number of miles you drove your vehicle during 2017, enter the number of miles you used your vehicle for:
   a Business 9,412   b Commuting (see page 2) 1,216   c Other 929 (Sch. C related)

6 Was your vehicle available for personal use during off-duty hours? . . . . ☒ Yes ☐ No
7 Do you (or your spouse) have another vehicle available for personal use? . . . . ☒ Yes ☐ No
8a Do you have evidence to support your deduction? . . . . ☒ Yes ☐ No
 b If "Yes," is the evidence written? . . . . ☒ Yes ☐ No

For Paperwork Reduction Act Notice, see the separate instructions for Schedule C (Form 1040). Cat. No. 14374D Schedule C-EZ (Form 1040) 2017

Gross receipts:
   Honoraria (weddings, etc.) $650
   Speaking honorarium   1,000
                                  $1,650

Expenses:
   See Attachment 1 on page 153.

Most ministers considered to be employees for income tax purposes (with that income reported on line 7, Form 1040, page 1) also have honoraria and fee income and related expenses that are reportable on Schedule C (C-EZ).

Schedule SE (Form 1040) 2016
Attachment Sequence No. **17** — Page **2**

Name of person with **self-employment** income (as shown on Form 1040 or Form 1040NR): Milton L. Brown
Social security number of person with **self-employment** income ▶ 541-16-8194

Section B—Long Schedule SE

Part I   Self-Employment Tax

Note. If your only income subject to self-employment tax is **church employee income,** see instructions. Also see instructions for the definition of church employee income.

A If you are a minister, member of a religious order, or Christian Science practitioner **and** you filed Form 4361, but you had $400 or more of **other** net earnings from self-employment, check here and continue with Part I . . . . . ▶ ☐

1a	Net farm profit or (loss) from Schedule F, line 34, and farm partnerships, Schedule K-1 (Form 1065), box 14, code A. **Note.** Skip lines 1a and 1b if you use the farm optional method (see instructions)	1a	
b	If you received social security retirement or disability benefits, enter the amount of Conservation Reserve Program payments included on Schedule F, line 4b, or listed on Schedule K-1 (Form 1065), box 20, code Z	1b (	)
2	Net profit or (loss) from Schedule C, line 31; Schedule C-EZ, line 3; Schedule K-1 (Form 1065), box 14, code A (other than farming); and Schedule K-1 (Form 1065-B), box 9, code J1. Ministers and members of religious orders, see instructions for types of income to report on this line. See instructions for other income to report. **Note.** Skip this line if you use the nonfarm optional method (see instructions)	2	84,753
3	Combine lines 1a, 1b, and 2	3	84,753
4a	If line 3 is more than zero, multiply line 3 by 92.35% (0.9235). Otherwise, enter amount from line 3	4a	78,269
	Note. If line 4a is less than $400 due to Conservation Reserve Program payments on line 1b, see instructions.		
b	If you elect one or both of the optional methods, enter the total of lines 15 and 17 here	4b	
c	Combine lines 4a and 4b. If less than $400, **stop;** you do not owe self-employment tax. **Exception.** If less than $400 and you had **church employee income,** enter -0- and continue ▶	4c	78,269
5a	Enter your **church employee income** from Form W-2. See instructions for definition of church employee income . . . 5a		
b	Multiply line 5a by 92.35% (0.9235). If less than $100, enter -0-	5b	
6	Add lines 4c and 5b	6	78,269
7	Maximum amount of combined wages and self-employment earnings subject to social security tax or the 6.2% portion of the 7.65% railroad retirement (tier 1) tax for 2016	7	118,500 00
8a	Total social security wages and tips (total of boxes 3 and 7 on Form(s) W-2) and railroad retirement (tier 1) compensation. If $118,500 or more, skip lines 8b through 10, and go to line 11 8a		
b	Unreported tips subject to social security tax (from Form 4137, line 10) 8b		
c	Wages subject to social security tax (from Form 8919, line 10) 8c		
d	Add lines 8a, 8b, and 8c	8d	
9	Subtract line 8d from line 7. If zero or less, enter -0- here and on line 10 and go to line 11 ▶	9	127,200
10	Multiply the **smaller** of line 6 or line 9 by 12.4% (0.124)	10	9,705
11	Multiply line 6 by 2.9% (0.029)	11	2,270
12	**Self-employment tax.** Add lines 10 and 11. Enter here and on **Form 1040, line 57,** or **Form 1040NR, line 55**	12	11,975
13	Deduction for one-half of self-employment tax. Multiply line 12 by 50% (0.50). Enter the result here and on **Form 1040, line 27,** or **Form 1040NR, line 27** 13 5,988		

Part II   Optional Methods To Figure Net Earnings (see instructions)

	Farm Optional Method. You may use this method **only** if **(a)** your gross farm income[1] was not more than $7,560, **or (b)** your net farm profits[2] were less than $5,457.		
14	Maximum income for optional methods	14	5,040 00
15	Enter the **smaller** of: two-thirds (2/3) of gross farm income[1] (not less than zero) **or** $5,040. Also include this amount on line 4b above	15	
	Nonfarm Optional Method. You may use this method **only** if **(a)** your net nonfarm profits[3] were less than $5,457 and also less than 72.189% of your gross nonfarm income,[4] **and (b)** you had net earnings from self-employment of at least $400 in 2 of the prior 3 years. **Caution.** You may use this method no more than five times.		
16	Subtract line 15 from line 14	16	
17	Enter the **smaller** of: two-thirds (2/3) of gross nonfarm income[4] (not less than zero) **or** the amount on line 16. Also include this amount on line 4b above	17	

[1] From Sch. F, line 9, and Sch. K-1 (Form 1065), box 14, code B.
[2] From Sch. F, line 34, and Sch. K-1 (Form 1065), box 14, code A—minus the amount you would have entered on line 1b had you not used the optional method.
[3] From Sch. C, line 31; Sch. C-EZ, line 3; Sch. K-1 (Form 1065), box 14, code A; and Sch. K-1 (Form 1065-B), box 9, code J1.
[4] From Sch. C, line 7; Sch. C-EZ, line 1; Sch. K-1 (Form 1065), box 14, code C; and Sch. K-1 (Form 1065-B), box 9, code J2.

Schedule SE (Form 1040) 2016

Line 2 – See Attachment 2 on page 153.

Line 13 – This line results in the deduction of a portion of the self-employment tax liability.

A minister must use Section B–Long Schedule if he or she received nonministerial wages (subject to FICA) and the total of these wages and net ministerial self-employment earnings (W-2 and Schedule C [C-EZ]-related) is more than $127,200. The Long Schedule is shown here for illustrative purposes.

SAMPLE RETURN NO. 1 ➤ MINISTER-EMPLOYEE FOR INCOME TAX PURPOSES (ACCOUNTABLE PLAN)

Attachment 1.
Computation of expenses, allocable to tax-free ministerial income, that are nondeductible.

		Taxable	Tax-Free	Total
Salary as a minister		$ 57,850		$ 57,850
Housing allowance:				
Amount designated and paid by church	$ 26,000			
Actual expenses	25,625			
Fair rental value of home (including furnishings and utilities)	25,000			
Taxable portion of allowance (excess of amount designated and paid over lesser of actual expenses or fair rental value)	$ 1,000	1,000		1,000
Tax-free portion of allowance (lesser of amount designated, actual expenses, or fair rental value)			25,000	25,000
Gross income from weddings, baptisms, and honoraria		1,650		1,650
Ministerial Income		$ 60,500	$ 25,000	$ 85,500

% of nondeductible expenses: $25,000/$85,500 = 29%

Schedule C-EZ Deduction Computation

Parking	$ 25
Meals & Entertainment ($50 x 50% deductible portion)	25
Other	200
Mileage (929 miles x 53.5 cents per mile)	497
Unadjusted Schedule C-EZ expenses	747
Minus:	
Nondeductible part of Schedule C-EZ expenses (29% x $747)	(217)
Schedule C-EZ deductions (line 2) (See page 148)	$ 530

Attachment 2.
Net earnings from self-employment (attachment to Schedule SE, Form 1040)

Church wages	$ 57,850
Housing allowance	26,000
Net profit from Schedule C-EZ	1,120
	84,970
Less:	
Schedule C-EZ expenses allocable to tax-free income	(217)
Net Self-Employed Income	
Schedule SE, Section A, line 2 (See page 149)	$ 84,753

2018 MINISTER'S TAX & FINANCIAL GUIDE

Housing Allowance Worksheet
Minister Living in Home
Minister Owns or Is Buying

Minister's name: _____Milton L. Brown_____

For the period _____January 1_____, 20 17 to _____December 31_____, 20 17

Date designation approved _____December 20_____, 20 16

Allowable Housing Expenses *(expenses paid by minister from current income)*

	Estimated Expenses	Actual
Down payment on purchase of housing	$	$
Housing loan principal and interest payments	18,117	18,875
Real estate commission, escrow fees		
Real property taxes	900	1,000
Personal property taxes on contents		
Homeowner's insurance	500	550
Personal property insurance on contents	150	200
Umbrella liability insurance	100	
Structural maintenance and repair		550
Landscaping, gardening, and pest control		200
Furnishings *(purchase, repair, replacement)*		400
Decoration and redecoration		
Utilities *(gas, electricity, water)* and trash collection	3,500	3,500
Local telephone expense *(base charge)*	150	150
Homeowner's association dues/condominium fees	219	200
Subtotal	23,636	
10% allowance for unexpected expenses	2,364	
TOTAL	$ 26,000	$ 25,625 (A)
Properly designated housing allowance		$ 26,000 (B)
Fair rental value of home, including furnishings, plus utilities		$ 25,000 (C)

Note: The amount excludable from income for federal income tax purposes is the lowest of A, B, or C.

The $1,000 difference between the designation ($26,000) and the fair rental value ($25,000) is reported as additional income on Form 1040, line 7.

SAMPLE RETURN NO. 1 ➤ MINISTER-EMPLOYEE FOR INCOME TAX PURPOSES (ACCOUNTABLE PLAN)

22222 Void ☐	**a** Employee's social security number: 541-16-8194 — For Official Use Only ▶ OMB No. 1545-0008
b Employer identification number (EIN): 38-9417217	**1** Wages, tips, other compensation: 57850.00 — **2** Federal income tax withheld: 12000.00
c Employer's name, address, and ZIP code: Magnolia Springs Church, 4805 Douglas Road, Springfield, OH 45504	**3** Social security wages — **4** Social security tax withheld — **5** Medicare wages and tips — **6** Medicare tax withheld — **7** Social security tips — **8** Allocated tips
d Control number	**9** Verification code — **10** Dependent care benefits
e Employee's first name and initial: Milton L. Last name: Brown Suff.	**11** Nonqualified plans — **12a** See instructions for box 12: E 500
418 Trenton Street, Springfield, OH 45504	**13** Statutory employee ☐ Retirement plan ☒ Third-party sick pay ☐ — **12b**
	14 Other: Housing Allowance 26,000 — **12c**, **12d**
f Employee's address and ZIP code	
15 State: OH Employer's state ID number: 677803 — **16** State wages, tips, etc.: 57850.00 — **17** State income tax: 1600.00 — **18** Local wages, tips, etc. — **19** Local income tax — **20** Locality name	

Form **W-2** Wage and Tax Statement **2017**
Copy A For Social Security Administration — Send this entire page with Form W-3 to the Social Security Administration; photocopies are **not** acceptable.
Do Not Cut, Fold, or Staple Forms on This Page

Department of the Treasury—Internal Revenue Service
For Privacy Act and Paperwork Reduction Act Notice, see the separate instructions.
Cat. No. 10134D

Explanation of compensation reported on Form W-2, Box 1:

Salary ($64,850 less $26,000 housing allowance and $500 403[b] contributions)	$38,350
Special occasion gifts	750
Reimbursement of self-employment tax	12,000
Moving expense reimbursement of nonqualified expenses	6,750
	$57,850

Pastor Brown received reimbursements of $7,593 under an accountable expense reimbursement plan. The reimbursements are not included on Form W-2 or deductible on Form 1040. There is no requirement to add the reimbursements to income taxable for social security purposes on Schedule SE.

Pastor Brown was also reimbursed for $6,750 of nonqualified moving expenses. He failed the distance test in that his new principal place of work was less than 50 miles farther from his old residence than the old residence was from his old place of work.

Sample Return No. 2

- Nonaccountable expense reimbursements
- Minister occupies a church-provided parsonage
- Pays federal taxes using Form 1040-ES
- Qualifies for the Earned Income Credit
- Church did not reimburse moving expenses
- Application of Deason Rule
- Tax Saver's Credit

Minister considered to be an employee for income tax purposes with a nonaccountable business expense plan.

The Halls live in church-provided housing.

Income, Benefits, and Reimbursements:

Church salary – Donald	$11,000
Salary – Julie (W-2 not shown)	
Federal withholding of $250	13,350
Christmas and other special occasion gifts paid by the church based on designated member-gifts to the church	500
Honoraria for performing weddings, funerals, baptisms, and outside speaking engagements	5,200
Interest income (taxable)	750
Reimbursement of self-employment tax	2,100
Business expense allowance (no accounting provided to church)	1,700

SAMPLE RETURN NO. 2 ➤ MINISTER-EMPLOYEE FOR INCOME TAX PURPOSES (NONACCOUNTABLE PLAN)

Business Expenses, Itemized Deductions, 403(b) Contributions, Housing Data, and Moving Expense Data:

Church-related expenses paid personally:

Business use of personally owned auto (W-2 related)	8,007 miles
Personal nondeductible commuting	2,432 miles
Seminar expenses:	
Airfare	$675
Meals	233
Lodging	167
Subscriptions	200
Books (less than one-year life)	100
Supplies	250
Entertainment expenses	1,207
Continuing education tuition (related to church employment)	500

Travel expense related to honoraria (Schedule C-EZ):

Airfare	2,042
Business use of personally owned auto 2,340 miles x 53.5¢ per mile	1,252
Lodging	400
Supplies	700

Potential itemized deductions:

Unreimbursed doctors, dentists, and drugs	3,050
State and local income taxes	460
Personal property taxes	300
Cash contributions	3,310

Housing data:

Designation	2,000
Actual expenses	1,000
Fair rental value, including furnishings and utilities	11,150

403(b) pre-tax contributions for Pastor Hall:

Voluntary employee contributions made under a salary reduction agreement	500
Moving expenses (deductible)	1,183

Estimated $24,500 in income for health insurance exchange subsidy at the beginning of year

Form 1095-A reports $12,153 on lines 33A and 33B, and $11,653 on line 33C

157

2018 MINISTER'S TAX & FINANCIAL GUIDE

Form **1040**	Department of the Treasury—Internal Revenue Service (99) **2017** U.S. Individual Income Tax Return	OMB No. 1545-0074	IRS Use Only—Do not write or staple in this space.

For the year Jan. 1–Dec. 31, 2017, or other tax year beginning , 2017, ending , 20 See separate instructions.

Your first name and initial: **Donald L.** Last name: **Hall** Your social security number: **482 | 11 | 6043**

If a joint return, spouse's first name and initial: **Julie M.** Last name: **Hall** Spouse's social security number: **720 | 92 | 1327**

Home address (number and street). If you have a P.O. box, see instructions. **804 Linden Avenue** Apt. no.

Make sure the SSN(s) above and on line 6c are correct.

City, town or post office, state, and ZIP code. If you have a foreign address, also complete spaces below (see instructions). **Pensacola, FL 32502**

Presidential Election Campaign Check here if you, or your spouse if filing jointly, want $3 to go to this fund. Checking a box below will not change your tax or refund. ☐ You ☐ Spouse

Foreign country name | Foreign province/state/county | Foreign postal code

Filing Status Check only one box.
1. ☐ Single
2. ☒ Married filing jointly (even if only one had income)
3. ☐ Married filing separately. Enter spouse's SSN above and full name here. ▶
4. ☐ Head of household (with qualifying person). (See instructions.) If the qualifying person is a child but not your dependent, enter this child's name here. ▶
5. ☐ Qualifying widow(er) (see instructions)

Exemptions
6a ☒ **Yourself.** If someone can claim you as a dependent, **do not** check box 6a.
b ☒ **Spouse**

Boxes checked on 6a and 6b: **2**

c Dependents:
(1) First name Last name	(2) Dependent's social security number	(3) Dependent's relationship to you	(4) ✓ if child under age 17 qualifying for child tax credit (see instructions)
David K. Hall	514 42 7465	Son	☒
Sarah E. Hall	416 49 9125	Daughter	☒

No. of children on 6c who:
• lived with you **2**
• did not live with you due to divorce or separation (see instructions)

Dependents on 6c not entered above

If more than four dependents, see instructions and check here ▶ ☐

d Total number of exemptions claimed . . . . Add numbers on lines above ▶ **4**

Income

Attach Form(s) W-2 here. Also attach Forms W-2G and 1099-R if tax was withheld.

If you did not get a W-2, see instructions.

7	Wages, salaries, tips, etc. Attach Form(s) W-2 _Incl. Excess Housing Allow, $1,000_	7	27,150
8a	Taxable interest. Attach Schedule B if required	8a	750
b	Tax-exempt interest. **Do not** include on line 8a . . .	8b	
9a	Ordinary dividends. Attach Schedule B if required	9a	
b	Qualified dividends	9b	
10	Taxable refunds, credits, or offsets of state and local income taxes	10	
11	Alimony received	11	
12	Business income or (loss). Attach Schedule C or C-EZ	12	2,520
13	Capital gain or (loss). Attach Schedule D if required. If not required, check here ▶ ☐	13	
14	Other gains or (losses). Attach Form 4797	14	
15a	IRA distributions . 15a	b Taxable amount . . .	15b	
16a	Pensions and annuities 16a	b Taxable amount . . .	16b	
17	Rental real estate, royalties, partnerships, S corporations, trusts, etc. Attach Schedule E	17	
18	Farm income or (loss). Attach Schedule F	18	
19	Unemployment compensation	19	
20a	Social security benefits 20a	b Taxable amount . . .	20b	
21	Other income. List type and amount	21	
22	Combine the amounts in the far right column for lines 7 through 21. This is your **total income** ▶	22	30,420

Adjusted Gross Income

23	Educator expenses	23	
24	Certain business expenses of reservists, performing artists, and fee-basis government officials. Attach Form 2106 or 2106-EZ	24	
25	Health savings account deduction. Attach Form 8889 . .	25	
26	Moving expenses. Attach Form 3903	26	1,183
27	Deductible part of self-employment tax. Attach Schedule SE .	27	1,403
28	Self-employed SEP, SIMPLE, and qualified plans . .	28	
29	Self-employed health insurance deduction	29	
30	Penalty on early withdrawal of savings	30	
31a	Alimony paid b Recipient's SSN ▶	31a	
32	IRA deduction	32	
33	Student loan interest deduction	33	
34	Reserved for future use	34	
35	Domestic production activities deduction. Attach Form 8903	35	
36	Add lines 23 through 35	36	2,586
37	Subtract line 36 from line 22. This is your **adjusted gross income** . . . . . ▶	37	27,834

For Disclosure, Privacy Act, and Paperwork Reduction Act Notice, see separate instructions. Cat. No. 11320B Form **1040** (2017)

Line 7 — Julie's W-2, $13,350; Donald's W-2, $12,800 (see page 171); plus $1,000 of excess housing allowance (see page 170).

Line 27 — See pages 125–26 for explanation of the self-employment tax deduction.

SAMPLE RETURN NO. 2 ➤ MINISTER-EMPLOYEE FOR INCOME TAX PURPOSES (NONACCOUNTABLE PLAN)

Form 1040 (2017) Page **2**

Tax and Credits	38	Amount from line 37 (adjusted gross income)	38	27,834
	39a	Check if: ☐ You were born before January 2, 1953, ☐ Blind. ☐ Spouse was born before January 2, 1953, ☐ Blind. Total boxes checked ▶ 39a		
	b	If your spouse itemizes on a separate return or you were a dual-status alien, check here▶ 39b☐		
Standard Deduction for—	40	Itemized deductions (from Schedule A) or your **standard deduction** (see left margin)	40	12,700
• People who check any box on line 39a or 39b **or** who can be claimed as a dependent, see instructions.	41	Subtract line 40 from line 38	41	15,134
	42	**Exemptions.** If line 38 is $156,900 or less, multiply $4,050 by the number on line 6d. Otherwise, see instructions	42	16,200
	43	**Taxable income.** Subtract line 42 from line 41. If line 42 is more than line 41, enter -0-	43	0
	44	**Tax** (see instructions). Check if any from: **a** ☐ Form(s) 8814 **b** ☐ Form 4972 **c** ☐	44	
	45	**Alternative minimum tax** (see instructions). Attach Form 6251	45	
• All others: Single or Married filing separately, $6,350	46	Excess advance premium tax credit repayment. Attach Form 8962	46	68
	47	Add lines 44, 45, and 46 ▶	47	68
	48	Foreign tax credit. Attach Form 1116 if required	48	
Married filing jointly or Qualifying widow(er), $12,700	49	Credit for child and dependent care expenses. Attach Form 2441	49	
	50	Education credits from Form 8863, line 19	50	
	51	Retirement savings contributions credit. Attach Form 8880	51	68
	52	Child tax credit. Attach Schedule 8812, if required	52	
Head of household, $9,350	53	Residential energy credit. Attach Form 5695	53	
	54	Other credits from Form: **a** ☐ 3800 **b** ☐ 8801 **c** ☐	54	
	55	Add lines 48 through 54. These are your **total credits**	55	68
	56	Subtract line 55 from line 47. If line 55 is more than line 47, enter -0- ▶	56	0
	57	Self-employment tax. Attach Schedule SE	57	2,806
Other Taxes	58	Unreported social security and Medicare tax from Form: **a** ☐ 4137 **b** ☐ 8919	58	
	59	Additional tax on IRAs, other qualified retirement plans, etc. Attach Form 5329 if required	59	
	60a	Household employment taxes from Schedule H	60a	
	b	First-time homebuyer credit repayment. Attach Form 5405 if required	60b	
	61	Health care: individual responsibility (see instructions) Full-year coverage ☒	61	
	62	Taxes from: **a** ☐ Form 8959 **b** ☐ Form 8960 **c** ☐ Instructions; enter code(s)	62	
	63	Add lines 56 through 62. This is your **total tax** ▶	63	2,806
Payments	64	Federal income tax withheld from Forms W-2 and 1099	64	250
	65	2017 estimated tax payments and amount applied from 2016 return	65	
If you have a qualifying child, attach Schedule EIC.	66a	**Earned income credit (EIC)**	66a	3,933
	b	Nontaxable combat pay election 66b		
	67	Additional child tax credit. Attach Schedule 8812	67	2,000
	68	American opportunity credit from Form 8863, line 8	68	
	69	Net premium tax credit. Attach Form 8962	69	
	70	Amount paid with request for extension to file	70	
	71	Excess social security and tier 1 RRTA tax withheld	71	
	72	Credit for federal tax on fuels. Attach Form 4136	72	
	73	Credits from Form: **a** ☐ 2439 **b** ☐ Reserved **c** ☐ 8885 **d** ☐	73	
	74	Add lines 64, 65, 66a, and 67 through 73. These are your **total payments** ▶	74	6,203
Refund	75	If line 74 is more than line 63, subtract line 63 from line 74. This is the amount you **overpaid**	75	3,397
	76a	Amount of line 75 you want **refunded to you.** If Form 8888 is attached, check here ▶ ☐	76a	3,397
Direct deposit? See instructions.	b	Routing number ▶ c Type: ☐ Checking ☐ Savings		
	d	Account number		
	77	Amount of line 75 you want **applied to your 2018 estimated tax** ▶ 77		
Amount You Owe	78	**Amount you owe.** Subtract line 74 from line 63. For details on how to pay, see instructions ▶	78	
	79	Estimated tax penalty (see instructions) 79		

Third Party Designee Do you want to allow another person to discuss this return with the IRS (see instructions)? ☐ Yes. Complete below. ☐ No
Designee's name ▶ Phone no. ▶ Personal identification number (PIN) ▶

Sign Here
Under penalties of perjury, I declare that I have examined this return and accompanying schedules and statements, and to the best of my knowledge and belief, they are true, correct, and accurately list all amounts and sources of income I received during the tax year. Declaration of preparer (other than taxpayer) is based on all information of which preparer has any knowledge.

Joint return? See instructions. Keep a copy for your records.
Your signature: *Donald L. Hall* Date: 4/15/18 Your occupation: Minister Daytime phone number:
Spouse's signature. If a joint return, **both** must sign.: *Julie M. Hall* Date: 4/15/18 Spouse's occupation: Secretary If the IRS sent you an Identity Protection PIN, enter it here (see inst.)

Paid Preparer Use Only
Print/Type preparer's name Preparer's signature Date Check ☐ if self-employed PTIN
Firm's name ▶ Firm's EIN ▶
Firm's address ▶ Phone no.

Go to www.irs.gov/Form1040 for instructions and the latest information. Form **1040** (2017)

Line 62 – The minister pays federal taxes (income and social security) by quarterly filing Form 1040-ES.

SCHEDULE C-EZ (Form 1040)

Department of the Treasury
Internal Revenue Service (99)

Net Profit From Business
(Sole Proprietorship)

▶ Partnerships, joint ventures, etc., generally must file Form 1065 or 1065-B.
▶ Attach to Form 1040, 1040NR, or 1041. ▶ See instructions on page 2.

OMB No. 1545-0074

2017

Attachment Sequence No. **09A**

Name of proprietor: Donald L. Hall

Social security number (SSN): 482-11-6043

Part I — General Information

You May Use Schedule C-EZ Instead of Schedule C Only If You:
- Had business expenses of $5,000 or less,
- Use the cash method of accounting,
- Did not have an inventory at any time during the year,
- Did not have a net loss from your business,
- Had only one business as either a sole proprietor, qualified joint venture, or statutory employee,

And You:
- Had no employees during the year,
- Do not deduct expenses for business use of your home,
- Do not have prior year unallowed passive activity losses from this business, and
- Are not required to file Form 4562, Depreciation and Amortization, for this business. See the instructions for Schedule C, line 13, to find out if you must file.

A Principal business or profession, including product or service: Minister

B Enter business code (see page 2) ▶ 8 1 3 0 0 0

C Business name. If no separate business name, leave blank.

D Enter your EIN (see page 2)

E Business address (including suite or room no.). Address not required if same as on page 1 of your tax return.
City, town or post office, state, and ZIP code

F Did you make any payments in 2017 that would require you to file Form(s) 1099? (see the Instructions for Schedule C) . . . . ☐ Yes ☒ No

G If "Yes," did you or will you file required Forms 1099? . . . . ☐ Yes ☒ No

Part II — Figure Your Net Profit

1 Gross receipts. Caution: If this income was reported to you on Form W-2 and the "Statutory employee" box on that form was checked, see *Statutory employees* in the instructions for Schedule C, line 1, and check here . . . . ▶ ☐ | **1** | 5,200 |

2 Total expenses (see page 2). If more than $5,000, you **must** use Schedule C . . . . | **2** | 2,680 | (1)

3 Net profit. Subtract line 2 from line 1. If less than zero, you **must** use Schedule C. Enter on both **Form 1040, line 12,** and **Schedule SE, line 2,** or on **Form 1040NR, line 13,** and **Schedule SE, line 2** (see page 2). (Statutory employees **do not** report this amount on Schedule SE, line 2.) Estates and trusts, enter on **Form 1041, line 3** . . . . | **3** | 2,520 |

Part III — Information on Your Vehicle. Complete this part **only** if you are claiming car or truck expenses on line 2.

4 When did you place your vehicle in service for business purposes? (month, day, year) ▶ 1/1/10

5 Of the total number of miles you drove your vehicle during 2017, enter the number of miles you used your vehicle for:

  a Business 2,340   **b** Commuting (see page 2) _____   **c** Other _____

6 Was your vehicle available for personal use during off-duty hours? . . . . ☒ Yes ☐ No

7 Do you (or your spouse) have another vehicle available for personal use? . . . . ☒ Yes ☐ No

8a Do you have evidence to support your deduction? . . . . ☒ Yes ☐ No

  b If "Yes," is the evidence written? . . . . ☒ Yes ☐ No

For Paperwork Reduction Act Notice, see the separate instructions for Schedule C (Form 1040). Cat. No. 14374D Schedule C-EZ (Form 1040) 2017

---

(1) Expenses have been reduced by 39% as allocable to tax-free income (see page 172 for percentage). Most ministers are employees for income tax purposes (with that income reported on line 7, Form 1040, page 1) and also have honoraria and fee income and related expenses that are reportable on Schedule C (C-EZ). For an explanation of expenses related to the honoraria in this sample return, see page 169.

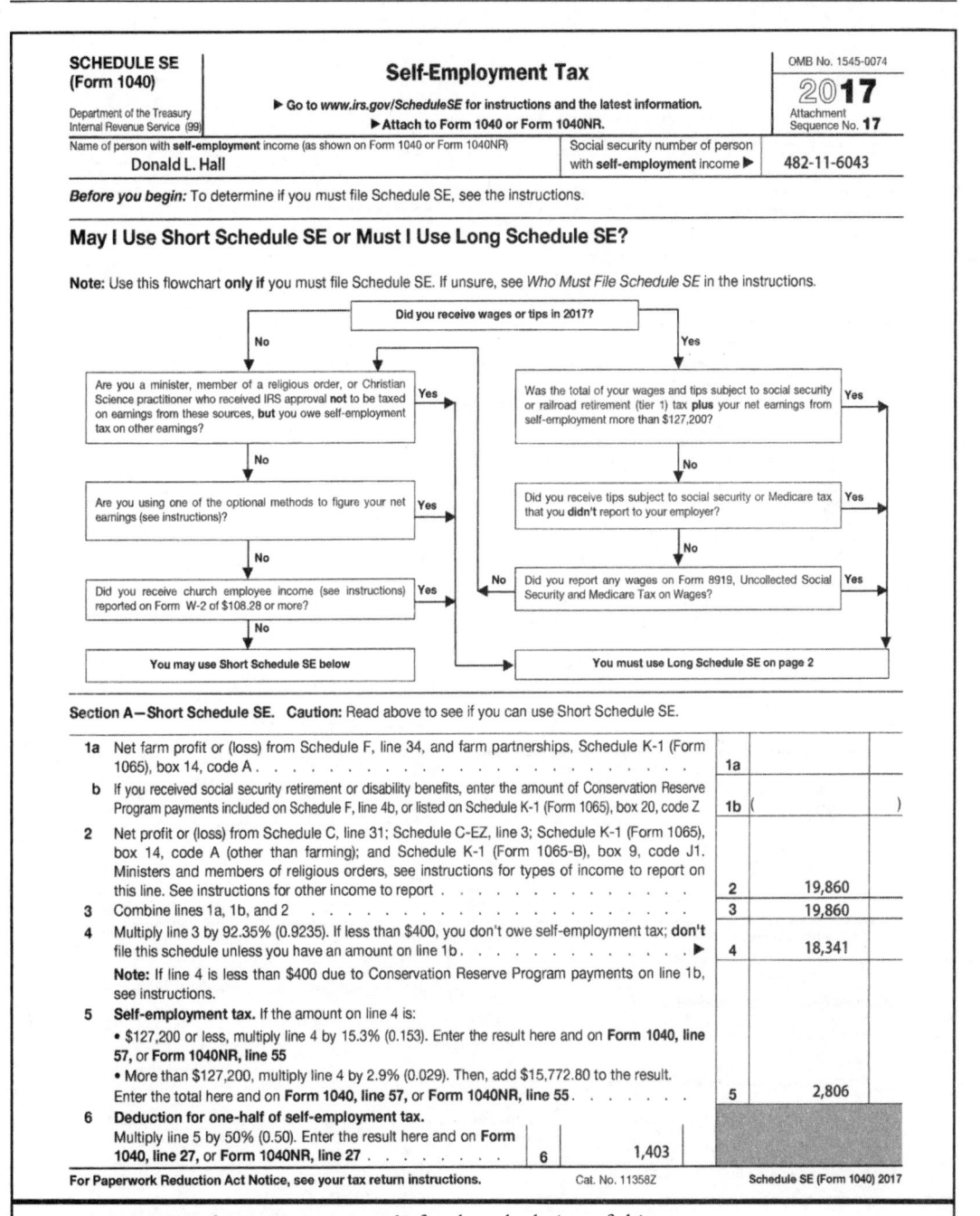

SAMPLE RETURN NO. 2 ➢ MINISTER-EMPLOYEE FOR INCOME TAX PURPOSES (NONACCOUNTABLE PLAN)

SCHEDULE SE (Form 1040)

Department of the Treasury
Internal Revenue Service (99)

Self-Employment Tax

▶ Go to *www.irs.gov/ScheduleSE* for instructions and the latest information.
▶ Attach to Form 1040 or Form 1040NR.

OMB No. 1545-0074

2017

Attachment Sequence No. **17**

Name of person with **self-employment** income (as shown on Form 1040 or Form 1040NR)	Social security number of person
Donald L. Hall	with **self-employment** income ▶ 482-11-6043

Before you begin: To determine if you must file Schedule SE, see the instructions.

May I Use Short Schedule SE or Must I Use Long Schedule SE?

Note: Use this flowchart **only if** you must file Schedule SE. If unsure, see *Who Must File Schedule SE* in the instructions.

[Flowchart leading to: "You may use Short Schedule SE below" or "You must use Long Schedule SE on page 2"]

Section A—Short Schedule SE. Caution: Read above to see if you can use Short Schedule SE.

1a	Net farm profit or (loss) from Schedule F, line 34, and farm partnerships, Schedule K-1 (Form 1065), box 14, code A	1a	
b	If you received social security retirement or disability benefits, enter the amount of Conservation Reserve Program payments included on Schedule F, line 4b, or listed on Schedule K-1 (Form 1065), box 20, code Z	1b	( )
2	Net profit or (loss) from Schedule C, line 31; Schedule C-EZ, line 3; Schedule K-1 (Form 1065), box 14, code A (other than farming); and Schedule K-1 (Form 1065-B), box 9, code J1. Ministers and members of religious orders, see instructions for types of income to report on this line. See instructions for other income to report	2	19,860
3	Combine lines 1a, 1b, and 2	3	19,860
4	Multiply line 3 by 92.35% (0.9235). If less than $400, you don't owe self-employment tax; **don't** file this schedule unless you have an amount on line 1b. . . . . ▶	4	18,341
	Note: If line 4 is less than $400 due to Conservation Reserve Program payments on line 1b, see instructions.		
5	**Self-employment tax.** If the amount on line 4 is:		
	• $127,200 or less, multiply line 4 by 15.3% (0.153). Enter the result here and on **Form 1040, line 57,** or **Form 1040NR, line 55**		
	• More than $127,200, multiply line 4 by 2.9% (0.029). Then, add $15,772.80 to the result. Enter the total here and on **Form 1040, line 57,** or **Form 1040NR, line 55**.	5	2,806
6	Deduction for one-half of self-employment tax. Multiply line 5 by 50% (0.50). Enter the result here and on **Form 1040, line 27,** or **Form 1040NR, line 27**	6	1,403

For Paperwork Reduction Act Notice, see your tax return instructions. Cat. No. 11358Z Schedule SE (Form 1040) 2017

Line 2 – See Attachment 2 on page 169 for the calculation of this amount.

Line 4 – This line results in the deduction of a portion of the self-employment tax liability. A minister may use Section A-Short Schedule unless he received nonministerial wages (subject to FICA) and the total of these wages and net ministerial self-employment earnings (W-2 and Schedule C-related) is more than $127,200.

161

2018 MINISTER'S TAX & FINANCIAL GUIDE

SCHEDULE EIC
(Form 1040A or 1040)

Department of the Treasury
Internal Revenue Service (99)

Earned Income Credit
Qualifying Child Information

▶ Complete and attach to Form 1040A or 1040 only if you have a qualifying child.
▶ Go to www.irs.gov/ScheduleEIC for the latest information.

OMB No. 1545-0074

2017

Attachment Sequence No. 43

Name(s) shown on return: Donald L. Hall
Your social security number: 482-11-6043

Before you begin:
- See the instructions for Form 1040A, lines 42a and 42b, or Form 1040, lines 66a and 66b, to make sure that (a) you can take the EIC, and (b) you have a qualifying child.
- Be sure the child's name on line 1 and social security number (SSN) on line 2 agree with the child's social security card. Otherwise, at the time we process your return, we may reduce or disallow your EIC. If the name or SSN on the child's social security card is not correct, call the Social Security Administration at 1-800-772-1213.

CAUTION
- You can't claim the EIC for a child who didn't live with you for more than half of the year.
- If you take the EIC even though you are not eligible, you may not be allowed to take the credit for up to 10 years. See the instructions for details.
- It will take us longer to process your return and issue your refund if you do not fill in all lines that apply for each qualifying child.

Qualifying Child Information	Child 1	Child 2	Child 3
1 Child's name If you have more than three qualifying children, you have to list only three to get the maximum credit.	David K. Hall	Sarah E. Hall	
2 Child's SSN The child must have an SSN as defined in the instructions for Form 1040A, lines 42a and 42b, or Form 1040, lines 66a and 66b, unless the child was born and died in 2017. If your child was born and died in 2017 and did not have an SSN, enter "Died" on this line and attach a copy of the child's birth certificate, death certificate, or hospital medical records showing a live birth.	514-42-7465	416-49-9125	
3 Child's year of birth	Year 2004 *If born after 1998 and the child is younger than you (or your spouse, if filing jointly), skip lines 4a and 4b; go to line 5.*	Year 2008 *If born after 1998 and the child is younger than you (or your spouse, if filing jointly), skip lines 4a and 4b; go to line 5.*	Year ____ *If born after 1998 and the child is younger than you (or your spouse, if filing jointly), skip lines 4a and 4b; go to line 5.*
4a Was the child under age 24 at the end of 2017, a student, and younger than you (or your spouse, if filing jointly)?	[X] Yes. Go to line 5. [ ] No. Go to line 4b.	[X] Yes. Go to line 5. [ ] No. Go to line 4b.	[ ] Yes. Go to line 5. [ ] No. Go to line 4b.
b Was the child permanently and totally disabled during any part of 2017?	[ ] Yes. Go to line 5. [ ] No. The child is not a qualifying child.	[ ] Yes. Go to line 5. [ ] No. The child is not a qualifying child.	[ ] Yes. Go to line 5. [ ] No. The child is not a qualifying child.
5 Child's relationship to you (for example, son, daughter, grandchild, niece, nephew, eligible foster child, etc.)	Son	Daughter	
6 Number of months child lived with you in the United States during 2017 • If the child lived with you for more than half of 2017 but less than 7 months, enter "7." • If the child was born or died in 2017 and your home was the child's home for more than half the time he or she was alive during 2017, enter "12."	12 months *Do not enter more than 12 months.*	12 months *Do not enter more than 12 months.*	____ months *Do not enter more than 12 months.*

For Paperwork Reduction Act Notice, see your tax return instructions.
Cat. No. 13339M
Schedule EIC (Form 1040A or 1040) 2017

If you are eligible for the Earned Income Credit, you must file page 1 of Schedule EIC if you have a qualifying child. Compute your credit on the worksheet in the IRS instruction booklet.

There could have been a much larger Earned Income Credit if Pastor Hall's business expenses had been reimbursed and a lower salary prospectively established. The expenses claimed on Form 2106-EZ do not offset earned income for the EIC calculation.

SAMPLE RETURN NO. 2 ➢ MINISTER-EMPLOYEE FOR INCOME TAX PURPOSES (NONACCOUNTABLE PLAN)

Worksheet B—2017 EIC—Lines 66a and 66b

Keep for Your Records

Use this worksheet if you answered "Yes" to Step 5, question 2.
- ✓ Complete the parts below (Parts 1 through 3) that apply to you. Then, continue to Part 4.
- ✓ If you are married filing a joint return, include your spouse's amounts, if any, with yours to figure the amounts to enter in Parts 1 through 3.

Part 1

Self-Employed, Members of the Clergy, and People With Church Employee Income Filing Schedule SE

1a. Enter the amount from Schedule SE, Section A, line 3, or Section B, line 3, whichever applies. — **1a 33,210**
 b. Enter any amount from Schedule SE, Section B, line 4b, and line 5a. — **+ 1b**
 c. Combine lines 1a and 1b. — **= 1c 33,210**
 d. Enter the amount from Schedule SE, Section A, line 6, or Section B, line 13, whichever applies. — **− 1d 1,403**
 e. Subtract line 1d from 1c. — **= 1e 31,807**

Part 2

Self-Employed NOT Required To File Schedule SE

For example, your net earnings from self-employment were less than $400.

2. Don't include on these lines any statutory employee income, any net profit from services performed as a notary public, any amount exempt from self-employment tax as the result of the filing and approval of Form 4029 or Form 4361, or any other amounts exempt from self-employment tax.

 a. Enter any net farm profit or (loss) from Schedule F, line 34, and from farm partnerships, Schedule K-1 (Form 1065), box 14, code A*. — **2a**
 b. Enter any net profit or (loss) from Schedule C, line 31; Schedule C-EZ, line 3; Schedule K-1 (Form 1065), box 14, code A (other than farming); and Schedule K-1 (Form 1065-B), box 9, code J1*. — **+ 2b**
 c. Combine lines 2a and 2b. — **= 2c**

*If you have any Schedule K-1 amounts, complete the appropriate line(s) of Schedule SE, Section A. Reduce the Schedule K-1 amounts as described in the Partner's Instructions for Schedule K-1. Enter your name and social security number on Schedule SE and attach it to your return.

Part 3

Statutory Employees Filing Schedule C or C-EZ

3. Enter the amount from Schedule C, line 1, or Schedule C-EZ, line 1, that you are filing as a statutory employee. — **3**

Part 4

All Filers Using Worksheet B

Note. If line 4b includes income on which you should have paid self-employment tax but didn't, we may reduce your credit by the amount of self-employment tax not paid.

4a. Enter your earned income from Step 5. — **4a**
 b. Combine lines 1e, 2c, 3, and 4a. **This is your total earned income.** — **4b 31,807**

If line 4b is zero or less, **STOP** You can't take the credit. Enter "No" on the dotted line next to line 66a.

5. If you have:
 - 3 or more qualifying children, is line 4b less than $48,340 ($53,930 if married filing jointly)?
 - 2 qualifying children, is line 4b less than $45,007 ($50,597 if married filing jointly)?
 - 1 qualifying child, is line 4b less than $39,617 ($45,207 if married filing jointly)?
 - No qualifying children, is line 4b less than $15,010 ($20,600 if married filing jointly)?

 [X] **Yes.** If you want the IRS to figure your credit, see *Credit figured by the IRS*, earlier. If you want to figure the credit yourself, enter the amount from line 4b on line 6 of this worksheet.

 [ ] **No.** **STOP** You can't take the credit. Enter "No" on the dotted line next to line 66a.

Need more information or forms? Visit IRS.gov.

Included on Line 1a:	
Julie Hall's salary	$ 13,350
Schedule SE income	19,860
	$33,210

-60-

Worksheet B is found in the IRS instruction booklet. Complete this worksheet whether or not you have a qualifying child.

163

Worksheet B — 2017 EIC — Lines 66a and 66b — *Continued*　　　　　*Keep for Your Records*

Part 5
All Filers Using Worksheet B

6. Enter your total earned income from Part 4, line 4b. .... **6** | 31,807

7. Look up the amount on line 6 above in the EIC Table to find the credit. Be sure you use the correct column for your filing status and the number of children you have. Enter the credit here. .... **7** | 3,953

   If line 7 is zero, (STOP) You can't take the credit.
   Enter "No" on the dotted line next to line 66a.

8. Enter the amount from Form 1040, line 38. .... **8** | 27,834

9. Are the amounts on lines 8 and 6 the same?
   ☐ **Yes.** Skip line 10; enter the amount from line 7 on line 11.
   ☒ **No.** Go to line 10.

Part 6
Filers Who Answered "No" on Line 9

10. If you have:
    - No qualifying children, is the amount on line 8 less than $8,350 ($13,950 if married filing jointly)?
    - 1 or more qualifying children, is the amount on line 8 less than $18,350 ($23,950 if married filing jointly)?

    ☐ **Yes.** Leave line 10 blank; enter the amount from line 7 on line 11.

    ☒ **No.** Look up the amount on line 8 in the EIC Table to find the credit. Be sure you use the correct column for your filing status and the number of children you have. Enter the credit here. .... **10** | 4,796
    Look at the amounts on lines 10 and 7.
    Then, enter the **smaller** amount on line 11.

Part 7
Your Earned Income Credit

11. **This is your earned income credit.** .... **11** | 3,953

    Enter this amount on Form 1040, line 66a.

    Reminder—
    ✓ If you have a qualifying child, complete and attach Schedule EIC.

    ⚠ **CAUTION** *If your EIC for a year after 1996 was reduced or disallowed, see Form 8862, who must file, earlier, to find out if you must file Form 8862 to take the credit for 2017.*

SAMPLE RETURN NO. 2 ➤ **MINISTER-EMPLOYEE FOR INCOME TAX PURPOSES (NONACCOUNTABLE PLAN)**

SCHEDULE 8812
(Form 1040A or 1040)

Department of the Treasury
Internal Revenue Service (99)

Child Tax Credit

➤ Attach to Form 1040, Form 1040A, or Form 1040NR.
➤ Go to *www.irs.gov/Schedule8812* for instructions and the latest information.

OMB No. 1545-0074

2017

Attachment Sequence No. **47**

Name(s) shown on return: **Donald L. and Julie M. Hall**

Your social security number: **482-11-6043**

Part I — Filers Who Have Certain Child Dependent(s) with an Individual Taxpayer Identification Number (ITIN)

⚠ **CAUTION**: Complete this part only for each dependent who has an ITIN and for whom you are claiming the child tax credit.
If your dependent is **not** a qualifying child for the credit, you cannot include that dependent in the calculation of this credit.

Answer the following questions for each dependent listed on Form 1040, line 6c; Form 1040A, line 6c; or Form 1040NR, line 7c, who has an Individual Taxpayer Identification Number (ITIN) and that you indicated is a qualifying child for the child tax credit by checking column (4) for that dependent.

A For the first dependent identified with an ITIN and listed as a qualifying child for the child tax credit, did this child meet the substantial presence test? See separate instructions.
    [X] Yes   [ ] No

B For the second dependent identified with an ITIN and listed as a qualifying child for the child tax credit, did this child meet the substantial presence test? See separate instructions.
    [X] Yes   [ ] No

C For the third dependent identified with an ITIN and listed as a qualifying child for the child tax credit, did this child meet the substantial presence test? See separate instructions.
    [ ] Yes   [ ] No

D For the fourth dependent identified with an ITIN and listed as a qualifying child for the child tax credit, did this child meet the substantial presence test? See separate instructions.
    [ ] Yes   [ ] No

Note: If you have more than four dependents identified with an ITIN and listed as a qualifying child for the child tax credit, see separate instructions and check here ➤ [ ]

Part II — Additional Child Tax Credit Filers

1 If you file Form 2555 or 2555-EZ, **stop** here; you cannot claim the additional child tax credit.

If you are required to use the worksheet in **Pub. 972**, enter the amount from line 8 of the Child Tax Credit Worksheet in the publication. Otherwise:

  1040 filers: Enter the amount from line 6 of your Child Tax Credit Worksheet (see the instructions for Form 1040, line 52).

  1040A filers: Enter the amount from line 6 of your Child Tax Credit Worksheet (see the instructions for Form 1040A, line 35).

  1040NR filers: Enter the amount from line 6 of your Child Tax Credit Worksheet (see the instructions for Form 1040NR, line 49).

  1   2,000

2 Enter the amount from Form 1040, line 52; Form 1040A, line 35; or Form 1040NR, line 49   **2**

3 Subtract line 2 from line 1. If zero, **stop** here; you cannot claim this credit   **3**   2,000

4a Earned income (see separate instructions)   31,807 - 11,150 - 1,000   **4a**   19,657

  b Nontaxable combat pay (see separate instructions)   **4b**

5 Is the amount on line 4a more than $3,000?
  [ ] **No.** Leave line 5 blank and enter -0- on line 6.
  [X] **Yes.** Subtract $3,000 from the amount on line 4a. Enter the result   **5**   16,657

6 Multiply the amount on line 5 by 15% (0.15) and enter the result   **6**   2,499

Next. Do you have three or more qualifying children?
  [X] **No.** If line 6 is zero, **stop** here; you cannot claim this credit. Otherwise, skip Part III and enter the **smaller** of line 3 or line 6 on line 13.
  [ ] **Yes.** If line 6 is equal to or more than line 3, skip Part III and enter the amount from line 3 on line 13. Otherwise, go to line 7.

For Paperwork Reduction Act Notice, see your tax return instructions.   Cat. No. 59761M   Schedule 8812 (Form 1040A or 1040) 2017

Line 4 – Earned income from EIC Worksheet B, line 4b (plus nontaxable combat pay), less the rental value of a home or the nontaxable portion of an allowance for a furnished home (per Form 8812 instructions)

165

Schedule 8812 (Form 1040A or 1040) 2017 Page **2**

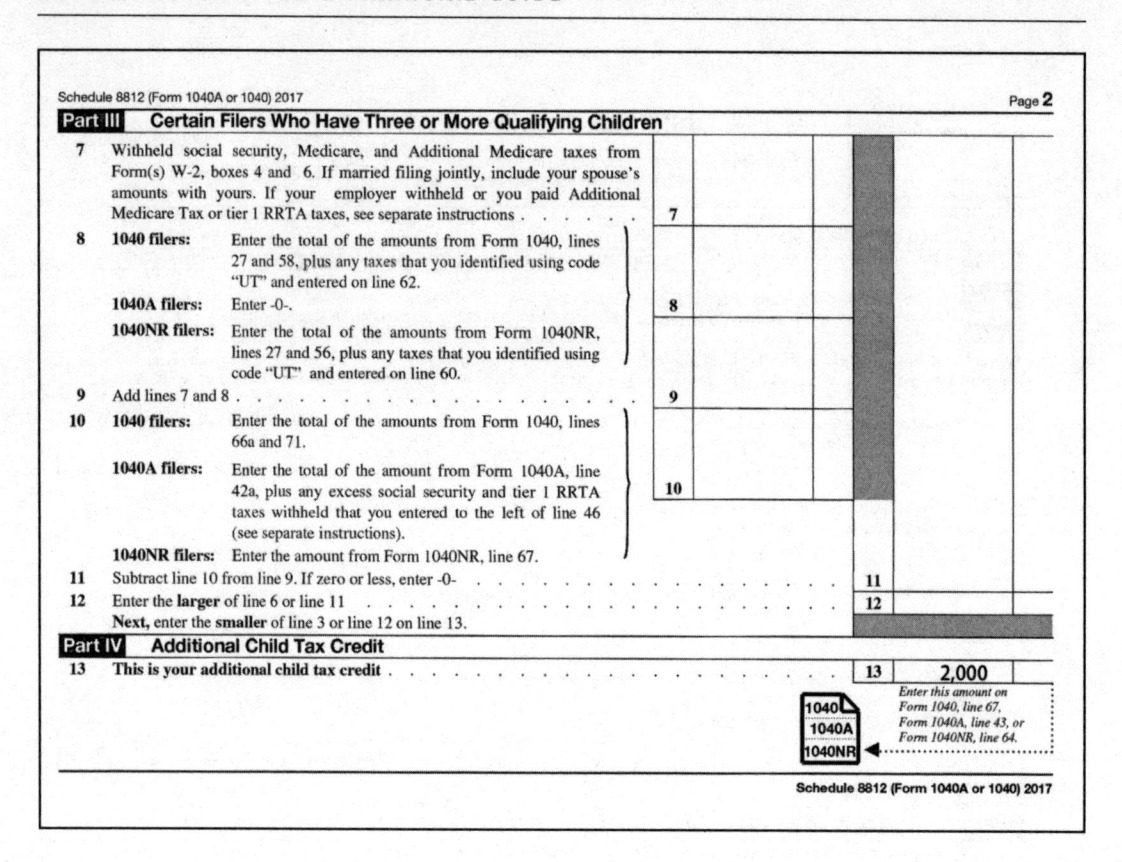

Part III Certain Filers Who Have Three or More Qualifying Children

7	Withheld social security, Medicare, and Additional Medicare taxes from Form(s) W-2, boxes 4 and 6. If married filing jointly, include your spouse's amounts with yours. If your employer withheld or you paid Additional Medicare Tax or tier 1 RRTA taxes, see separate instructions	7
8	**1040 filers:** Enter the total of the amounts from Form 1040, lines 27 and 58, plus any taxes that you identified using code "UT" and entered on line 62. **1040A filers:** Enter -0-. **1040NR filers:** Enter the total of the amounts from Form 1040NR, lines 27 and 56, plus any taxes that you identified using code "UT" and entered on line 60.	8
9	Add lines 7 and 8	9
10	**1040 filers:** Enter the total of the amounts from Form 1040, lines 66a and 71. **1040A filers:** Enter the total of the amount from Form 1040A, line 42a, plus any excess social security and tier 1 RRTA taxes withheld that you entered to the left of line 46 (see separate instructions). **1040NR filers:** Enter the amount from Form 1040NR, line 67.	10
11	Subtract line 10 from line 9. If zero or less, enter -0-	11
12	Enter the **larger** of line 6 or line 11	12
	Next, enter the **smaller** of line 3 or line 12 on line 13.	

Part IV Additional Child Tax Credit

13	This is your additional child tax credit	13	2,000
		1040 1040A 1040NR	Enter this amount on Form 1040, line 67, Form 1040A, line 43, or Form 1040NR, line 64.

Schedule 8812 (Form 1040A or 1040) 2017

SAMPLE RETURN NO. 2 ➣ MINISTER-EMPLOYEE FOR INCOME TAX PURPOSES (NONACCOUNTABLE PLAN)

2017 Form 1040—Line 52

2017 Child Tax Credit Worksheet—Continued

Keep for Your Records

Before you begin Part 2: ✓ Figure the amount of any credits you are claiming on Form 5695, Part II*; Form 8910; Form 8936; or Schedule R.

Part 2

7. Enter the amount from Form 1040, line 47.   **7**   68

8. Add any amounts from:

    Form 1040, line 48   _____

    Form 1040, line 49 + _____

    Form 1040, line 50 + _____

    Form 1040, line 51 +   68

    Form 5695, line 30*+ _____

    Form 8910, line 15 + _____

    Form 8936, line 23 + _____

    Schedule R, line 22 + _____

    Enter the total.   **8**   68

9. Are the amounts on lines 7 and 8 the same?

    [X] **Yes.** (STOP)
    You can't take this credit because there is no tax to reduce. However, you may be able to take the **additional child tax credit.** See the **TIP** below.

    [ ] **No.** Subtract line 8 from line 7.

    9

10. Is the amount on line 6 more than the amount on line 9?

    [ ] **Yes.** Enter the amount from line 9. Also, you may be able to take the **additional child tax credit.** See the **TIP** below.

    [ ] **No.** Enter the amount from line 6.

    } **This is your child tax credit.**

    10

    Enter this amount on Form 1040, line 52.

TIP

You may be able to take the **additional child tax credit** on Form 1040, line 67, if you answered "Yes" on line 9 **or** line 10 above.

- First, complete your Form 1040 through lines 66a and 66b.
- Then, use Schedule 8812 to figure any additional child tax credit.

* If applicable.

167

2018 MINISTER'S TAX & FINANCIAL GUIDE

Form **2106-EZ**	**Unreimbursed Employee Business Expenses**	OMB No. 1545-0074
Department of the Treasury Internal Revenue Service (99)	▶ Attach to Form 1040 or Form 1040NR. ▶ Go to *www.irs.gov/Form2106EZ* for the latest information.	**2017** Attachment Sequence No. **129A**

Your name	Occupation in which you incurred expenses	Social security number
Donald L. Hall	Minister	482 : 11 : 6043

You Can Use This Form Only if All of the Following Apply.

• You are an employee deducting ordinary and necessary expenses attributable to your job. An ordinary expense is one that is common and accepted in your field of trade, business, or profession. A necessary expense is one that is helpful and appropriate for your business. An expense doesn't have to be required to be considered necessary.

• You **don't** get reimbursed by your employer for any expenses (amounts your employer included in box 1 of your Form W-2 aren't considered reimbursements for this purpose).

• If you are claiming vehicle expense, you are using the standard mileage rate for 2017.

Caution: You can use the standard mileage rate for 2017 **only if: (a)** you owned the vehicle and used the standard mileage rate for the first year you placed the vehicle in service, **or (b)** you leased the vehicle and used the standard mileage rate for the portion of the lease period after 1997.

Part I   **Figure Your Expenses**

1	Complete Part II. Multiply line 8a by 53.5¢ (0.535). Enter the result here	1	2,613
2	Parking fees, tolls, and transportation, including train, bus, etc., that **didn't** involve overnight travel or commuting to and from work	2	
3	Travel expense while away from home overnight, including lodging, airplane, car rental, etc. **Don't** include meals and entertainment	3	514
4	Business expenses not included on lines 1 through 3. **Don't** include meals and entertainment .	4	640
5	Meals and entertainment expenses: $ __878__ × 50% (0.50). (Employees subject to Department of Transportation (DOT) hours of service limits: Multiply meal expenses incurred while away from home on business by 80% (0.80) instead of 50%. For details, see instructions.)	5	439
6	**Total expenses.** Add lines 1 through 5. Enter here and on **Schedule A (Form 1040), line 21** (or on **Schedule A (Form 1040NR), line 7**). (Armed Forces reservists, fee-basis state or local government officials, qualified performing artists, and individuals with disabilities: See the instructions for special rules on where to enter this amount.)	6	4,206

Part II   **Information on Your Vehicle.** Complete this part **only** if you are claiming vehicle expense on line 1.

7   When did you place your vehicle in service for business use? (month, day, year) ▶   01 / 01 / 08

8   Of the total number of miles you drove your vehicle during 2017, enter the number of miles you used your vehicle for:

    a Business __8,007__   **b** Commuting (see instructions) __2,432__   **c** Other __2,340 (Sch. C Related)__

9   Was your vehicle available for personal use during off-duty hours? . . . . ☒ Yes ☐ No

10   Do you (or your spouse) have another vehicle available for personal use? . . . . ☒ Yes ☐ No

11a   Do you have evidence to support your deduction? . . . . ☒ Yes ☐ No

   b If "Yes," is the evidence written? . . . . ☒ Yes ☐ No

For Paperwork Reduction Act Notice, see your tax return instructions.   Cat. No. 20604Q   Form **2106-EZ** (2017)

Lines 1, 3, 4, 5 – See allocations on page 169.

Line 6 – The total expenses on this line are carried forward to Form 1040, Schedule A, line 21.

SAMPLE RETURN NO. 2 ➢ MINISTER-EMPLOYEE FOR INCOME TAX PURPOSES (NONACCOUNTABLE PLAN)

Form **3903**
Department of the Treasury
Internal Revenue Service (99)

Moving Expenses

▶ Information about Form 3903 and its instructions is available at www.irs.gov/form3903.
▶ Attach to Form 1040 or Form 1040NR.

OMB No. 1545-0074
2017
Attachment Sequence No. **170**

Name(s) shown on return: Donald L. Hall
Your social security number: 482-11-6043

Before you begin:
✓ See the **Distance Test** and **Time Test** in the instructions to find out if you can deduct your moving expenses.
✓ See **Members of the Armed Forces** in the instructions, if applicable.

1	Transportation and storage of household goods and personal effects (see instructions)	1	1,183
2	Travel (including lodging) from your old home to your new home (see instructions). **Do not** include the cost of meals	2	
3	Add lines 1 and 2	3	1,183
4	Enter the total amount your employer paid you for the expenses listed on lines 1 and 2 that is **not** included in box 1 of your Form W-2 (wages). This amount should be shown in box 12 of your Form W-2 with code P	4	
5	Is line 3 **more than** line 4? ☐ **No.** You **cannot** deduct your moving expenses. If line 3 is less than line 4, subtract line 3 from line 4 and include the result on Form 1040, line 7, or Form 1040NR, line 8. ☒ **Yes.** Subtract line 4 from line 3. Enter the result here and on Form 1040, line 26, or Form 1040NR, line 26. This is your **moving expense deduction**	5	1,183

For Paperwork Reduction Act Notice, see your tax return instructions. Cat. No. 12490K Form **3903**

Computation of expenses related to honoraria on Sample Return No. 2/page 159

			Deductible	Nondeductible
Airfare	$2,042 x 61% =		1,246	796
Auto	2,340 x .535 x 61% =		764	488
Lodging	400 x 61% =		244	156
Supplies	700 x 61% =		427	273
	4,394 x 61% =		2,680	1,714

Form 8880 — Credit for Qualified Retirement Savings Contributions
OMB No. 1545-0074
2017
Department of the Treasury / Internal Revenue Service
▶ Attach to Form 1040, Form 1040A, or Form 1040NR.
▶ Go to www.irs.gov/Form8880 for instructions and the latest information.
Attachment Sequence No. 54

Name(s) shown on return: **Donald L. Hall**
Your social security number: 482-11-6043

⚠ **CAUTION**
You **cannot** take this credit if **either** of the following applies.
- The amount on Form 1040, line 38; Form 1040A, line 22; or Form 1040NR, line 37 is more than $31,000 ($46,500 if head of household; $62,000 if married filing jointly).
- The person(s) who made the qualified contribution or elective deferral **(a)** was born after January 1, 2000, **(b)** is claimed as a dependent on someone else's 2017 tax return, or **(c)** was a **student** (see instructions).

		(a) You	(b) Your spouse
1	Traditional and Roth IRA (including myRA) contributions for 2017. **Do not** include rollover contributions		
2	Elective deferrals to a 401(k) or other qualified employer plan, voluntary employee contributions, and 501(c)(18)(D) plan contributions for 2017 (see instructions)	500	
3	Add lines 1 and 2	500	
4	Certain distributions received **after** 2014 and **before** the due date (including extensions) of your 2017 tax return (see instructions). If married filing jointly, include **both** spouses' amounts in **both** columns. See instructions for an exception		
5	Subtract line 4 from line 3. If zero or less, enter -0-	500	
6	In each column, enter the **smaller** of line 5 or $2,000	500	
7	Add the amounts on line 6. If zero, **stop**; you cannot take this credit		500
8	Enter the amount from Form 1040, line 38*; Form 1040A, line 22; or Form 1040NR, line 37	27,834	
9	Enter the applicable decimal amount shown below.		

If line 8 is—		And your filing status is—		
Over—	But not over—	Married filing jointly	Head of household	Single, Married filing separately, or Qualifying widow(er)
		Enter on line 9—		
---	$18,500	.5	.5	.5
$18,500	$20,000	.5	.5	.2
$20,000	$27,750	.5	.5	.1
$27,750	$30,000	.5	.2	.1
$30,000	$31,000	.5	.1	.1
$31,000	$37,000	.5	.1	.0
$37,000	$40,000	.2	.1	.0
$40,000	$46,500	.1	.1	.0
$46,500	$62,000	.1	.0	.0
$62,000	---	.0	.0	.0

9 .... X .5

Note: If line 9 is zero, **stop**; you cannot take this credit.

10	Multiply line 7 by line 9	250
11	Limitation based on tax liability. Enter the amount from the Credit Limit Worksheet in the instructions	68
12	**Credit for qualified retirement savings contributions.** Enter the **smaller** of line 10 or line 11 here and on Form 1040, line 51; Form 1040A, line 34; or Form 1040NR, line 48	68

*See Pub. 590-A for the amount to enter if you are filing Form 2555, 2555-EZ, or 4563 or you are excluding income from Puerto Rico.

For Paperwork Reduction Act Notice, see your tax return instructions.
Cat. No. 33394D
Form **8880** (2017)

SAMPLE RETURN NO. 2 ➤ MINISTER-EMPLOYEE FOR INCOME TAX PURPOSES (NONACCOUNTABLE PLAN)

Form **8962**
Department of the Treasury
Internal Revenue Service

Premium Tax Credit (PTC)
➤ Attach to Form 1040, 1040A, or 1040NR.
➤ Go to www.irs.gov/Form8962 for instructions and the latest information.

OMB No. 1545-0074
2017
Attachment Sequence No. 73

Name shown on your return: Donald L. Hall
Your social security number: 482-11-6043

You cannot take the PTC if your filing status is married filing separately unless you qualify for an exception (see instructions). If you qualify, check the box ➤ ☐

Part I — Annual and Monthly Contribution Amount

1	Tax family size. Enter the number of exemptions from Form 1040 or Form 1040A, line 6d, or Form 1040NR, line 7d	1	4
2a	Modified AGI. Enter your modified AGI (see instructions)	2a	27,834
2b	Enter the total of your dependents' modified AGI (see instructions)	2b	0
3	Household income. Add the amounts on lines 2a and 2b (see instructions)	3	27,834
4	Federal poverty line. Enter the federal poverty line amount from Table 1-1, 1-2, or 1-3 (see instructions). Check the appropriate box for the federal poverty table used. a ☐ Alaska b ☐ Hawaii c ☒ Other 48 states and DC	4	23,000
5	Household income as a percentage of federal poverty line (see instructions)	5	114 %
6	Did you enter 401% on line 5? (See instructions if you entered less than 100%.) ☒ No. Continue to line 7. ☐ Yes. You are not eligible to take the PTC. If advance payment of the PTC was made, see the instructions for how to report your excess advance PTC repayment amount.		
7	Applicable Figure. Using your line 5 percentage, locate your "applicable figure" on the table in the instructions	7	0.0204
8a	Annual contribution amount. Multiply line 3 by line 7. Round to nearest whole dollar amount	8a	568
8b	Monthly contribution amount. Divide line 8a by 12. Round to nearest whole dollar amount	8b	47

Part II — Premium Tax Credit Claim and Reconciliation of Advance Payment of Premium Tax Credit

9. Are you allocating policy amounts with another taxpayer or do you want to use the alternative calculation for year of marriage (see instructions)?
   ☐ Yes. Skip to Part IV, Allocation of Policy Amounts, or Part V, Alternative Calculation for Year of Marriage. ☒ No. Continue to line 10.

10. See the instructions to determine if you can use line 11 or must complete lines 12 through 23.
    ☒ Yes. Continue to line 11. Compute your annual PTC. Then skip lines 12–23 and continue to line 24.
    ☐ No. Continue to lines 12–23. Compute your monthly PTC and continue to line 24.

	(a) Annual enrollment premiums (Form(s) 1095-A, line 33A)	(b) Annual applicable SLCSP premium (Form(s) 1095-A, line 33B)	(c) Annual contribution amount (line 8a)	(d) Annual maximum premium assistance (subtract (c) from (b), if zero or less, enter -0-)	(e) Annual premium tax credit allowed (smaller of (a) or (d))	(f) Annual advance payment of PTC (Form(s) 1095-A, line 33C)
Annual Calculation						
11 Annual Totals	12,153	12,153	568	11,585	11,585	11,653

	(a) Monthly enrollment premiums (Form(s) 1095-A, lines 21–32, column A)	(b) Monthly applicable SLCSP premium (Form(s) 1095-A, lines 21–32, column B)	(c) Monthly contribution amount (amount from line 8b or alternative marriage monthly calculation)	(d) Monthly maximum premium assistance (subtract (c) from (b), if zero or less, enter -0-)	(e) Monthly premium tax credit allowed (smaller of (a) or (d))	(f) Monthly advance payment of PTC (Form(s) 1095-A, lines 21–32, column C)
Monthly Calculation						
12 January						
13 February						
14 March						
15 April						
16 May						
17 June						
18 July						
19 August						
20 September						
21 October						
22 November						
23 December						

24. Total premium tax credit. Enter the amount from line 11(e) or add lines 12(e) through 23(e) and enter the total here **24** 11,585
25. Advance payment of PTC. Enter the amount from line 11(f) or add lines 12(f) through 23(f) and enter the total here **25** 11,653
26. Net premium tax credit. If line 24 is greater than line 25, subtract line 25 from line 24. Enter the difference here and on Form 1040, line 69; Form 1040A, line 45; or Form 1040NR, line 65. If line 24 equals line 25, enter -0-. Stop here. If line 25 is greater than line 24, leave this line blank and continue to line 27 . . . . **26**

Part III — Repayment of Excess Advance Payment of the Premium Tax Credit

27. Excess advance payment of PTC. If line 25 is greater than line 24, subtract line 24 from line 25. Enter the difference here . . **27** 68
28. Repayment limitation (see instructions) **28** 600
29. Excess advance premium tax credit repayment. Enter the smaller of line 27 or line 28 here and on Form 1040, line 46; Form 1040A, line 29; or Form 1040NR, line 44 . . . . **29** 68

For Paperwork Reduction Act Notice, see your tax return instructions.   Cat. No. 37784Z   Form **8962** (2017)

Attachment 1.
Computation of expenses, allocatable to tax-free ministerial income, that are nondeductible

	Taxable	Tax-Free	Total
Salary as a minister (less housing allowance designation and 403(b) contributions)	$ 8,500		$ 8,500
Special occasion gifts	500		500
Reimbursement of self-employment tax	2,100		2,100
Expense allowance under nonaccountable plan	1,700		1,700

Housing allowance:
    Amount designated and paid by church $ 2,000
    Actual expenses   1,000
    Taxable portion of allowance $ 1,000   1,000 $ 1,000   2,000

Fair rental value of home (including furnishings and utilities)		11,150	11,150
Schedule C gross income from ministry	5,200		5,200
Ministerial income	$ 19,000	$ 12,150	$ 31,150

% of nondeductible expenses: $12,150/$31,150 = 39%

Unreimbursed Employee Business Expenses

	61% Deductible	39% Not Deductible
Business mileage:		
8,007 x 53.5¢ per mile	$ 2,613	$ 1,671
Travel expense:		
Airfare	412	263
Lodging	102	65
Business expenses:		
Subscriptions	122	78
Books and supplies	213	137
Continuing education tuition	305	195

Meals and entertainment expenses:
  Meals $ 233
  Entertainment   1,207
       $ 1,440 x 50% = $720   439   281

Form 2106-EZ $ 4,206 $2,690

Attachment 2.
Net earnings from self-employment (attachment to Schedule SE, Form 1040)

Salary paid by church as reflected on Form W-2, Box 1	$ 12,800
Net profit or loss as reflected on Schedule C or C-EZ (includes speaking honoraria, offerings you receive for weddings, baptisms, funerals, and other fees)	2,520
Housing allowance excluded from salary on Form W-2	2,000
Fair rental value of church-provided housing (including paid utilities)	11,150
	28,470

Less:
  Unreimbursed ministerial business and professional expenses or reimbursed expenses paid under a nonaccountable plan
    A. Deductible on Schedule A before the 2% of AGI limitation   4,206
    B. Not deductible on Form 2106/2106 EZ ($2,690) or Schedule C/C-EZ ($1,714) because expenses were allocated to taxable/nontaxable income   4,404

Total deductions   8,610

Net earnings from self-employment (to Schedule SE) (See page 158) $ 19,860

SAMPLE RETURN NO. 2 ➤ MINISTER-EMPLOYEE FOR INCOME TAX PURPOSES (NONACCOUNTABLE PLAN)

Housing Allowance Worksheet
Minister Living in a Parsonage
Owned by or Rented by the Church

Minister's name: __Donald L. Hall__

For the period __January 1__, 20_17_ to __December 31__, 20_17_

Date designation approved __December 20__, 20_16_

Allowable Housing Expenses *(expenses paid by minister from current income)*

	Estimated Expenses	Actual
Utilities *(gas, electricity, water)* and trash collection	$	$
Local telephone expense *(base charge)*	250	275
Decoration and redecoration		
Structural maintenance and repair		
Landscaping, gardening, and pest control		
Furnishings *(purchase, repair, replacement)*	1,218	460
Personal property insurance on minister-owned contents	200	190
Personal property taxes on contents	150	75
Umbrella liability insurance		
Subtotal	1,818	
10% allowance for unexpected expenses	182	
TOTAL	$ 2,000	$ 1,000 (A)
Properly designated housing allowance		$ 2,000 (B)

The amount excludable from income for federal income tax purposes is the lower of A or B.

Because actual housing expenses are less than the designated allowance, the housing exclusion is limited to $1,000. The $1,000 difference between the designation ($2,000) and the exclusion ($1,000) is reported as excess housing allowance on Form 1040, line 7 (see page 155).

173

2018 MINISTER'S TAX & FINANCIAL GUIDE

22222 Void ☐	**a** Employee's social security number 482-11-6043	For Official Use Only ▶ OMB No. 1545-0008

b Employer identification number (EIN) 25-7921873	**1** Wages, tips, other compensation 12800.00	**2** Federal income tax withheld
c Employer's name, address, and ZIP code Lancaster Community Church 1425 Spencer Avenue Wabash, IN 46992	**3** Social security wages	**4** Social security tax withheld
	5 Medicare wages and tips	**6** Medicare tax withheld
	7 Social security tips	**8** Allocated tips
d Control number	**9** Verification code	**10** Dependent care benefits
e Employee's first name and initial Last name Suff. Donald L. Hall 804 Linden Avenue Pensacola, FL 32502	**11** Nonqualified plans	**12a** See instructions for box 12
	13 Statutory employee ☐ Retirement plan ☒ Third-party sick pay ☐	**12b** E 500
	14 Other Parsonage Allowance 11150 Housing Allowance 2000	**12c**
		12d
f Employee's address and ZIP code		

| **15** State Employer's state ID number
FL | **16** State wages, tips, etc.
12800.00 | **17** State income tax | **18** Local wages, tips, etc. | **19** Local income tax | **20** Locality name |

Form **W-2** Wage and Tax Statement   **2017**   Department of the Treasury—Internal Revenue Service
Copy A For Social Security Administration — Send this entire page with Form W-3 to the Social Security Administration; photocopies are **not** acceptable.
For Privacy Act and Paperwork Reduction Act Notice, see the separate instructions.
Cat. No. 10134D
Do Not Cut, Fold, or Staple Forms on This Page

Explanation of compensation reported on Form W-2, Box 1:

Salary ($11,000 less $2,000 housing allowance and $500 403[b] contributions)	$ 8,500
Special occasion gifts	500
Reimbursement of self-employment tax	2,100
Expense allowance under nonaccountable plan	1,700
	$12,800

Citations

Chapter 1, Taxes for Ministers

- **Administrative and teaching positions**

Treas. Reg. 31.3401(a)(9)-1(b)(3)-(5)

Treas. Reg. 31.3121(b)(8)-1(c)(2)-(3)

Treas. Reg. 1.1402(c)-5(b)(2)

Ltr. Rul. 200318002

Haimowitz v. Commissioner, T.C.M. 40 (1997)

Ltr. Rul. 9126048

T.A.M. 9033002

Ltr. Rul. 9608027

Ltr. Rul. 9144047

Ltr. Rul. 8922077

Ltr. Rul. 8930038

Ltr. Rul. 8826043

Ltr. Rul. 8646018

Ltr. Rul. 8520043

Flowers v. Commissioner, 82-1 USTC para. 9114 (N.D. Tex. 1981)

Ltr. Rul. 8142076

Ltr. Rul. 80929145

Ltr. Rul. 8004087

Ltr. Rul. 7907160

Ltr. Rul. 7833017

Boyer v. Commissioner, 69 T.C. 521 (1977)

Rev. Rul. 70-549

Rev. Rul. 63-90

Rev. Rul. 57-129

- **Commissioned ministers**

Ltr. Rul. 9221025

- **Counseling and chaplaincy positions**

Ltr. Rul. 200002040

Ltr. Rul. 9743037

Ltr. Rul. 9231053

Ltr. Rul. 9124059

Ltr. Rul. 8825025

Ltr. Rul. 8519004

Ltr. Rul. 8138184

Ltr. Rul. 8004046

Ltr. Rul. 7809092

Ltr. Rul. 7727019

Rev. Rul. 71-258

- **Employees v. self-employed for income tax purposes**

Treas. Reg. 31.3401(c)-1(b)-(c)

Alford v. U.S., 116 F.3d 334, 8th Cir. (1997)

Radde v. Commissioner, T.C.M. 490 (1997)

Greene v. Commissioner, T.C.M. 531 (1996)

Weber v. Commissioner, 103 T.C. 378 (1994), Affirmed, 60 F.3d 1104, 4th Cir. (1995)

Shelley v. Commissioner, T.C.M. 432 (1994)

Ltr. Rul. 9825002

Ltr. Rul. 9414022

Ltr. Rul. 8333107

Cosby v. Commissioner, T.C.M. Sum. Op. 141 (1987)

Rev. Rul. 87-41

Rev. Proc. 85-18

Rev. Rul. 80-110

- **Exempt from FICA**

Code Sec. 3121(b)(8)(A)

- **Exempt from income tax withholding**

Code Sec. 3121(b)(8)

Code Sec. 3401(a)(9)

Treas. Reg. 31.3401(a)(8)-1

- **Qualifying tests for ministerial status**

Treas. Reg. 1.1402(c)-5

Ltr. Rul. 199910055

Haimowitz v. Commissioner, T.C.M. 40 (1997)

Mosley v. Commissioner, T.C.M. 457 (1994)

Reeder v. Commissioner, T.C.M. 287 (1993)

Ltr. Rul. 9221025

Eade v. U.S., Dist. Court, Western Dist., VA, Roanoke Division (1991)

Knight v. Commissioner, 92 T.C.M. 12 (1989)

T.A.M. 8915001

Wingo v. Commissioner, 89 T.C.M. 922 (1987)

Ballinger v. Commissioner, 728 F.2d 1287, 10th Cir. (1984)

Rev. Rul. 78-301

Rev. Rul. 68-68

Lawrence v. Commissioner, 50 T.C. 494 (1968)

Kirk v. Commissioner, 51 T.C. 66 (1968)

Salkov v. Commissioner, 46 T.C. 190 (1966)

Rev. Rul. 59-270

- **Religious orders**

Ltr. Rul. 199938013

Ltr. Rul. 199937013

Ltr. Rul. 9630011

Ltr. Rul. 9418012

Ltr. Rul. 9219012

Rev. Proc. 91-20

- **Subject to income tax**

Murdock v. Pennsylvania, 319 U.S. 105 (1943)

- **Voluntary withholding of income tax for ministers**

Treas. Reg. 31.3402(p)-1

Treas. Reg. 31.4302(i)-1(a)

Rev. Rul. 68-507

- **Withholding of income tax for nonministerial employees**

Bethel Baptist Church v. U.S., 822 F.2d 1334 (3rd Cir. 1987)

Eighth Street Baptist Church, Inc. v. U. S., 295 F. Supp. 1400 (D. Kan. 1969)

Chapter 2, Compensation Planning

- **Avoiding recharacterization of income**

Ltr. Rul. 9325023

Chapter 3, The Pay Package

- **Deferred compensation**

Code Sec. 409A

Code Sec. 457

Rev. Proc. 92-64

- ***De Minimis* fringes**

Code Sec. 132(e)(1)

- **Dependent care**

Code Sec. 129

- **Disability payments**

Code Sec. 104(a)(3)

Reg. 1.104-1(d)

Ltr. Rul. 9103014

Ltr. Rul. 9103043

Ltr. Rul. 9105032

- **Educational assistance**

Code Sec. 127

- **Employer-paid vehicle fuel**

Notice 91-41

- **403(b) plans (tax-sheltered annuities)**

Code Sec. 403(b)

Code Sec. 415

Code Sec. 1402(a)

Code Sec. 3121(a)(5)(D)

Rev. Rul. 78-6

Rev. Rul. 68-395

Azad v. Commissioner, 388 F.2d 74 (8th Cir. 1968)

Rev. Rul. 66-274

- **Frequent flyer awards**

IRS Announcement 2002-18

- **Group-term life insurance**

Code Sec. 3401(a)(14)

- **Health care flexible spending account**

Code Sec. 105(b), (e)

IRS Notice 2004-42

- **Health care reform**

Patient Protection and Affordable Care Act (P.L. 111-148)

Health Care and Education Reconciliation Act of 2010 (P.L. 111-152)

- **Health reimbursement arrangements**

Code Sec. 105(b)

Rev. Rul. 2002-41

IRS Notice 2002-45

IRP 80,600

- **Health savings accounts**

Code Sec. 233

IRS Notice 2004-2

Rev. Proc. 2004-22

IRS Notice 2004-23

Rev. Rul. 2004-38

Rev. Rul. 2004-45

IRS Notice 2004-50

- **Highly compensated employees**

Code Sec. 414(q)

Treas. Reg. 1.132-8(f)(1)

- **Key employees**

Code Sec. 416(i)(1)

CITATIONS

- **Loans to employees**

  Code Sec. 7872(c)(1)(B)

  Code Sec. 7872(c)(3)(A)

  Code Sec. 7872(f)(10)

- **Meals and lodging**

  Code Sec. 119(a)

  Kalms v. Commissioner, T.C.M. 394 (1992)

  Ltr. Rul. 9129037

  Goldsboro Christian School, Inc. v. Commissioner, 436 F. Supp. 1314 (D.D.C. 1978), Affirmed 103 S. Ct. 2017 (1983)

  Ltr. Rul. 8213005

  Bob Jones University v. Commissioner, 670 F.2d 167 Ct. Cl. (1982)

  Rev. Rul. 77-80

- **Medical insurance premiums paid by employee/ reimbursed by church**

  Ltr. Rul. 9022060

  Rev. Rul. 85-44

  Rev. Rul. 75-241

  Rev. Rul. 61-146

- **Medical insurance premiums paid by the employer**

  Code Sec. 106(a)

  Code Sec. 4980B

  Treas. Reg. 1.106-1

  Rev. Rul. 70-179

  Rev. Rul. 58-90

- **Moving expenses**

  Code Sec. 132(g)

  Code Sec. 217

- **Nontaxable fringe benefits**

  Code Sec. 132

- **Payment of personal payments**

  Whittington v. Commissioner, T.C.M. 296 (2000)

  Thompson v. Commissioner, T.C.M. 2 (2004)

- **Pension plans**

  Code Sec. 83

  Code Sec. 401(a)

  Code Sec. 414(e)

- **Property transfers**

  Treas. Reg. 1.61-2(d)(2)

  Potito v. Commissioner, 534 F.2d 49 (5th Cir. 1976)

- **Reasonable compensation**

  Truth Tabernacle, Inc. v. Commissioner, T.C.M. (1989)-451

- **Reimbursement payments excludable from recipient's income**

  Ltr. Rul. 9112022

- **Retirement gifts**

  Code Sec. 102(c)

  Joyce v. Commissioner, 25 T.C.M. 914 (1966)

  Commissioner v. Duberstein, 363 U.S. 278 (1960)

  Perkins v. Commissioner, 34 T.C. 117 (1960)

  Stanton v. U.S., 163 F.2d 727 (2nd Cir. 1959)

  Rev. Rul. 55-422

  Abernathy v. Commissioner, 211 F.2d 651 (D.C. Cir. 1954)

  Kavanagh v. Hershman, 210 F.2d 654 (6th Cir. 1954)

  Mutch v. Commissioner, 209 F.2d 390 (3rd Cir. 1954)

  Schall v. Commissioner, 174 F.2d 893 (5th Cir. 1949)

  Rev. Rul. 55-422

- **Sabbatical pay**

  Kant v. Commissioner, T.C.M. 217 (1997)

- **Social security reimbursements**

  Rev. Rul. 68-507

- **Special occasion gifts**

  Goodwin v. U.S., 67 F.3d 149, 8th Cir. (1995)

  Banks v. Commissioner, 62 T.C.M. 1611 (1991)

- **Tuition and fee reductions**

  Code Sec. 117(d)

  Ltr. Rul. 200149030

  Rasmussen v. Commissioner, T.C. 7264-92 (1994)

Chapter 4, Housing Exclusion

- **Allowed without documentation**

  Kizer v. Commissioner, T.C.M. 582 (1992)

- **Designation of housing allowance**

  Treas. Reg. 1.107-1(b)

177

Whittington v. Commissioner, T.C.M. 296 (2000)

Logie v. Commissioner, T.C.M. 387 (1998)

Mosley v. Commissioner, T.C.M. 457 (1994)

Ltr. Rul. 9052001

Kizer v. Commissioner, T.C.M. 584 (1992)

Ltr. Rul. 8511075

Holland v. Commissioner, 47 T.C.M. 494 (1983)

Libman v. Commissioner, 44 T.C.M. 370 (1982)

Hoelz v. Commissioner, 42 T.C.M. 1037 (1981)

Boyd v. Commissioner, 42 T.C.M. 1136 (1981)

T.A.M. 8120007

Rev. Rul. 75-22

Rev. Rul. 62-117

Ling v. Commissioner, 200 F. Supp. 282 D.D.C. (1962)

Eden v. Commissioner, 41 T.C. 605 (1961)

- **Determination of housing exclusion amount**

  Clergy Housing Allowance Clarification Act of 2002, Public Law 107-181

  Warren v. Commissioner, 114 T.C. No. 23 (1998) Appealed by IRS to 9th Cir. Court of Appeals (2000) Case dismissed by 9th Cir. Court of Appeals (2002)

Radde v. Commissioner, T.C.M. 490 (1997)

Rasmussen v. Commissioner, T.C.M. 311 (1994)

Ltr. Rul. 8937025

Swaggart v. Commissioner, 48 T.C.M. 759 (1984)

Ltr. Rul. 8350005

Hoelz v. Commissioner, 42 T.C.M. 1037 (1981)

Rev. Rul. 78-448

Rev. Rul. 59-350

- **Double deduction of interest and taxes**

  Code Sec. 265(6)

  Rev. Rul. 87-32

- **Exclusion of the housing allowance**

  Code Sec. 107

- **Fair rental value test**

  Warren v. Commissioner, 114 T.C. No. 23 (2000)

  Rucker v. David, 203 F.3d 627, 638 9th Cir. (2000)

  Ltr. Rul. 200435022

  Ltr. Rul. 200435021

  Ltr. Rul. 200435020

  Ltr. Rul. 200435019

  Ltr. Rul. 8825025

  Reed v. Commissioner, 82 T.C. 208, 214 (1984)

  Rev. Rul. 71-280

  Rev. Rul. 63-156

- **Housing expenses only applicable to years in which paid**

  Ltr. Rul. 8348018

  T.A.M. 8039007

- **Including interest on home equity loan**

  Ltr. Rul. 9115051

- **Minister performing routine services**

  Rev. Rul. 57-129

- **Minister who owns home outright cannot exclude parsonage allowance**

  Ltr. Rul. 9115051

Chapter 5, Business Expenses

- **Accountable expense reimbursement plans**

  Treas. Reg. 1.62-2

  Treas. Reg. 1.274-5T(f)

  Ltr. Rul. 9317003

  Ltr. Rul. 9325023

- **Accounting for business and professional expenses by independent contractors**

  Treas. Reg. 1.274-5(g)

- **Allocation of unreimbursed business expenses**

  Young v. Commissioner, T.C.M. 440 (1992)

  McFarland v. Commissioner, T.C.M. 440 (1992)

  Dalan v. Commissioner, T.C.M. 106 (1988)

Deason v. Commissioner,
41 T.C.M. 465 (1964)

- **Auto depreciation**

  Rev. Proc. 2003-75

  Rev. Proc. 2004-20

- **Auto expense substantiation**

  Parker v. Commissioner,
  T.C.M. 15 (1993)

- **Cellular phones**

  INFO 2007-0025

  Ltr. Rul. 200435022

  Ltr. Rul. 200435020

- **Club dues**

  T.D. 8601

- **Computer expenses**

  Bryant v. Commissioner,
  T.C.M. 597 (1993)

- **Contributions treated as business expenses**

  Forbes v. Commissioner,
  T.C. Sum. Op. 167 (1992)

- **Deductibility of spouse's travel**

  Code Sec. 1.162-2(c)

  Stockton v. Commissioner,
  36 T.C.M. 114 (1977)

  U.S. v. Disney, 413 F.2d 783
  9th Cir. (1969)

- **Educational expenses**

  Ltr. Rul. 9431024

  Burt v. Commissioner,
  40 T.C.M. 1164 (1980)

Glasgow v. Commissioner,
31 T.C.M. 310 (1972)

- **Holy Land trips**

  Rev. Rul. 64-154

- **Home-office expenses**

  Code Sec. 280A

  Rev. Rul. 94-24

  Rev. Rul. 94-47

- **Other business and professional expense deductions**

  Treas. Reg. 1.1402(a)-11(a)

  T.A.M. 200435018-22

  Bass v. Commissioner,
  T.C.M. 536 (1983)

  Rev. Rul. 80-110

  Rev. Rul. 79-78

- **Per diem allowance**

  IRS Publication 1542

- **Personal computer expenses**

  Code Sec. 280F

  Rev. Rul. 86-129

- **Substantiation of business expenses**

  Temp. Rev. 1.274-5T

  Code Sec. 274(d)

  Rev. Proc. 92-71

- **Temporary workplace**

  Rev. Rul. 99-7

- **Travel/away from home**

  Rev. Rul. 83-82

  Rev. Rul. 75-432

- **Travel/commuting**

  Treas. Reg. 1.262-1(b)(5)

  Rev. Rul. 94-47

  Rev. Rul. 90-23

  Walker v. Commissioner,
  101 T.C.M. 537 (1993)

  Soliman v. Commissioner,
  94 T.C.M. 20 (1990),
  Supreme Court (1993)

  Hamblen v. Commissioner,
  78 T.C.M. 53 (1981)

- **Travel/mileage rates**

  Rev. Proc. 2003-76

- **Unreimbursed business expenses**

  Gravett v. Commissioner,
  T.C.M. 156 (1994)

Chapter 6, Retirement and Social Security

- **General**

  IRS Publication 517

  IRS Publication 1828

  Social Security Protection Act of 2004

- **Age not a limitation**

  Levine v. Commissioner,
  T.C.M. 469 (1992)

- **Exemption for certain religious faiths**

  U.S. v. Lee,
  455 U.S. 252 (1982)

  Varga v. U.S.,
  467 F. Supp. 1113 (D. Md. 1979)

- **Nullifying the exemption**

  Rev. Rul. 70-197

- **Opting out of social security**

  Code Sec. 1402(e)

  Treas. Reg. 1.1402(e)-3A

  Brannon v. Commissioner, T.C.M. 370 (1999)

  McGaffin v. Commissioner, T.C.M. 290 (1996)

  Hairston v. Commissioner, T.C.M. (1995)

  Hall v. Commissioner, (10th Cir. 1994)

  Ltr. Rul. 9431024

  Reeder v. Commissioner, T.C.M. 287 (1993)

  Keaton v. Commissioner, T.C.M. 365 (1993)

  Ltr. Rul. 9221025

  Eade v. U.S., Dist. Court, Western Dist. VA, Roanoke Div. (1991)

  T.A.M. 8741002

  Balinger v. Commissioner, 728 F.2d 1287 10th Cir. (1984)

  Treadway v. Commissioner, 47 T.C.M. 1375 (1984)

  Olsen v. Commissioner, 709 F.2d 278 (4th Cir. 1983)

  Holland v. Commissioner, 47 T.C.M. 494 (1983)

  Paschall v. Commissioner, 46 T.C.M. 1197 (1983)

  Hess v. Commissioner, 40 T.C.M. 415 (1980)

  Rev. Rul. 80-59

  Rev. Rul. 82-185

  Rev. Rul. 75-189

- **Private insurance program participation**

  T.A.M. 8741002

  Rev. Rul. 77-78

- **Second ordination/social security exemption**

  Hall v. Commissioner, T.C.M. 360 (1993), 10th Cir. (1994)

- **Social security coverage for ministers**

  Code Sec. 1402(c)(2) and (4)

  Code Sec. 3121(b)(8)(A)

  Code Sec. 3401(a)(9)

  Rev. Rul. 80-110

  Rev. Rul. 79-78

  Silvey v. Commissioner, 35 T.C.M. 1812 (1976)

- **Social security deductions for unreimbursed business expenses**

  Young v. Commissioner, T.C. Summary Opinion 76 (2005)

- **Social security recipients must still pay social security taxes**

  Foster v. Commissioner, T.C.M. 552 (1996)

- **Taxability of fair rental value of church-owned parsonage for social security purposes**

  Treas. Reg. 1.1402(a)-11(a)

  Flowers v. Commissioner, T.C.M. 542 (1991)

  Bass v. Commissioner, T.C.M. 536 (1983)

Federal Tax Regulation (Reg.)

Treasury Decision (T.D.)

Private Letter Ruling (Ltr. Rul.)

Field Service Advice (F.S.A.)

Revenue Ruling (Rev. Rul.)

Revenue Procedure (Rev. Proc.)

Tax Court Memorandum (T.C.M.)

Technical Advice Memorandum (T.A.M.)

Index

A

Accountable plan, *16, 24-26, 30-31, 69-72, 76-77, 79-81, 146-55*
Administrative positions, *7, 64*
Agency of a religious organization, *7*
Allocation of business expenses, *91-93, 172*
Allowances, *31, 156-74*
Amended returns, *124-25*
American Opportunity Credit, *135*
Annuities, tax-sheltered, *23, 30, 44-45, 63-64*
Assignment by a church, *6-8*
Automobiles
    Actual expense method, *79, 81, 85*
    Allowances, *31 156-74*
    Commuting, *82, 83-85, 87*
    Deductions, *79-81*
    Depreciation, *81*
    Documenting expenses, *73, 85*
    Employer-provided, *48-49, 81-82*
    Interest expense, *90*
    Leasing, *83*
    Luxury, *83*
    Mileage rate method, *79-80*
    Nonpersonal use, *49*
    Personal use, *48-49, 81-82*
    Reporting auto expenses, *85, 133-34, 168*
Awards, *30*

B

Birthday gifts, *37-38*
Bonuses, *30, 72*
Books, *30, 91*
Business and professional expenses
    Accounting for, *70-74*
    Allocation of, *91-93, 153*
    Allowances, *31, 156-74*
    Automobile, *79-85*
    Books, *30, 91*
    Cellular phones, *47, 88-89*
    Clothing, *31, 89*
    Club dues and memberships, *31*
    Computers, *31-32, 90-91*
    Conventions, *32*
    Depreciation, *81*
    Dues, *34-35*
    Educational expenses, *35, 89*
    Entertainment expenses, *36, 89-90*
    Gifts, *87-88*
    Home office, *40, 85-87*
    Interest expense, auto, *90*
    Memberships, *31*
    Ministerial dues, *34*
    Moving expenses, *42, 90*
    Per diem, *77*
    Personal computers, *31-32, 90-91*
    Recordkeeping requirements, *73, 85*
    Reimbursements, *16, 24-26, 30-31, 69-72, 76-77, 79-81, 146-55*
    Section 179 deduction, *88*
    Subscriptions, *47, 91*
    Telephone expenses, *47, 88-89*
    Travel expenses, *47-48, 74-75*

C

Cafeteria plans, *36-37*
Canada Pension Plan, *111*
Cellular telephones, *47, 88-89*
Chaplain, *129*
Child care, *33, 37*
Child tax credit, *165-67*
Christmas gifts, *37-38*
Clothing, *31, 89*
Club dues and memberships, *31*
Commissioned ministers, *4-5*
Common law rules, *10-11*
Commuting expenses, *82, 83-85, 87*
Compensation
    Deferred compensation, *33*
    Packages, *18-22*
    Recharacterization, *24, 26, 72*
    Reporting to the church, *17*
    Worksheet, *18*
Computers, *31-32, 90-91*
Continuing education, *35, 89*
Conventions, *32*

D

Deason rule, *91-93, 153*
Deferred compensation, *33*
Denominational pension plans, *45*
Denominational service, *7*
Dependent care, *33, 37*
Dependent educational benefits, *33*
Depreciation, *81*
Disability
    Insurance, *34*
    Pay, *46*
Discretionary fund, *34*
Discrimination of benefits, *29-30*
Documenting expenses, *73, 85*
Double benefit of interest and taxes, *2, 63*
Dues, ministerial, *34*

E

Earned income tax credit, *118-119, 162-64*
Educational assistance benefit plans, *35*
Educational credits, *135*
Educational expenses, *35, 89*
Educational reimbursement plans, *35*
Employee vs. self-employed, *11-13*
Entertainment expenses, *36, 89-90*
Equipment write-off, *88*
Equity allowance, *36*
Estimated taxes, *114-18*
Evangelists
    Housing allowance, *6, 64*
    Qualifications, *6*
Exemption from social security tax, *106-10*
Expense allowances, *31, 156-74*
Expense reimbursement, *16, 24-26, 30-31, 69-72, 76-77, 79-81, 146-55*
Extension of time to file, *119-21*
Extension of time to pay, *121-22, 123*

F

Fair rental value of parsonage, *54-57, 61*
Federal Insurance Contributions Act (FICA), *101-2, 115, 116*
First-year write-off of business expense, *88, 91*
Flexible spending accounts
    Dependent care, *37*
    Medical, *36-37*
Foreign earned income exclusion, *6*
Forgiveness of debt, *41*
Form W-2, *25, 116, 155, 174*
Form 656, *124*
Form 941, *116*
Form 1040, *127-31, 136-37, 148-49, 158-59*
Form 1040-ES, *115, 116-18*
Form 1040X, *124-25*
Form 1127, *122-24*
Form 2106, *74, 75, 80, 85*

181

Form 2106-EZ, *74, 75, 80, 85, 133-34, 142, 168*
Form 2210, *120*
Form 2441, *134, 143*
Form 3903, *169*
Form 4361, *109*
Form 4868, *119-20, 122*
Form 8829, *86*
Form 8863, *135, 144*
Form 8880, *145, 170*
Form 8889, *135*
Form 8962, *134-35*
Form 9465, *121-22*
401(k) plans, *44, 63*
403(b) plans, *30, 44-45, 63-64, 129*
Frequent flyer awards, *37*
Fringe benefits
    Minimal, *42*
    Other, *22-24, 29-30, 50-51*
Furlough travel, *76*

G

Gifts
    Business and professional, *87-88*
    Personal, *37*
    Special occasion, *37-38*
Group-term life insurance, *11-12, 40-41*

H

Health care sharing ministries, *38*
Health club memberships, *31*
Health insurance, *11-12, 38, 99*
Health reimbursement arrangement, *12, 38-39*
Health Savings Account, *12, 39-40, 135*
Highly compensated employees, *30*
Holy Land trips, *75-76*
Home equity loans, *62*
Home office, *40, 85-87*
Housing exclusion
    Accounting for the exclusion, *61-62*
    Allowable expenses, *66-68*
    Amending the designation, *60*
    Cost to the church, *63*
    Denominational, *60*
    Designating the allowance, *57-60*
    Eligibility, *3-5*
    Evangelists, *6, 64*
    Excess, *61*

Fair rental value, *54-57, 61*
General, *40*
Limits on the designation, *59-60*
Limits on the exclusion, *61-62*
Multiple homes, *60*
Ordained, commissioned, or licensed ministers, *3-5*
Parsonage owned or rented by church, *56, 66*
Parsonage owned or rented by minister, *56-57, 67-68*
Payment of, *62-63*
Reporting, *58, 60-61*
Retired ministers, *63-64*
Second mortgages, *62*
Worksheets, *66-68, 154, 173*

I

Income, reporting, *11-13, 50-51*
Income tax status of ministers, *9-11*
Individual mandate, *38*
Individual Retirement Accounts (IRA), *45-46*
Installment payments, *121-22*
Insurance
    Disability, *34*
    Health, *11-12, 38, 99*
    Life, *12, 40-41, 97*
    Long-term care, *41, 99*
Integral agencies of a church, *6-9*
Interest
    Auto, *90*
    Federal tax return, *120*
    Mortgage, *2, 62, 131-32*
Interim appointments, *77-79*
International travel, *75*
IRA, *45-46*
Itemized deductions
    Mortgage interest, *2, 62, 131-32*
    Real estate taxes, *2, 63, 131-32*

K

Keogh plans, *46*

L

Leased car, *83*
Licensed ministers, *3-5*
Life insurance, *12, 40-41, 97*
Lifetime learning credit, *135*
Loan-grants, *41*
Loans to clergy, *41*
Long-term care insurance, *41, 99*
Luxury auto, *83*

M

Meals and entertainment, *36, 89-90, 134*
Meals, employer-provided, *41-42*
Medical
    Flexible spending accounts, *36-37*
    Health reimbursement arrangement, *12, 38-39*
    Insurance, *11-12, 38, 99*
Memberships, *31*
Mileage rates, *79-80*
Minister
    Administrative and teaching positions, *7, 64*
    Assignment, *6-8*
    Commissioned, *3-5*
    Denominational service, *6-7*
    Eligibility for treatment as, *1-9*
    Employee, *11-12*
    Income tax status, *9-13*
    Licensed, *3-5*
    Nonqualifying, *9*
    Ordained, *3-4*
    Other service, *8-9*
    Self-employed, *11-13*
    Serving local churches, *5-6*
    Social security tax status, *13*
Missionary
    Furlough travel, *76*
    Qualifications, *6*
    Social security tax, *46-47*
Mortgage interest, *2, 62, 131-32*
Moving expenses, *42, 90*

N

Nonaccountable plan, *9-10, 11, 16, 31, 72, 156-74*
Nondiscrimination rules, *29-30*
Nonqualified deferred compensation plans, *33*
Nonqualifying clergy, *9*

O

Offers in compromise, *122, 124*
Office-in-home, *40, 85-87*
Opting into social security, *110*
Opting out of social security, *106-10*
Ordination by local church, *3-4*

INDEX

P

Parking, *42*
Parsonage allowance (See Housing exclusion)
Payroll deductions, *49*
Penalties, failure to pay, *120*
Pension plans
    Denominational, *45*
Per diem, *77*
Permanent work location, *83-85*
Personal computers, *31-32, 90-91*
Personal gifts, *37*
Pre-employment expense reimbursements, *42-43*
Property
    Purchased from church, *43*
    Transferred to minister, *43*

R

Rabbi Trust, *43-44*
Rates, social security tax, *103*
Real estate taxes, *2, 63, 131-32*
Recharacterization of income, *24, 26, 72*
Recordkeeping requirements, *73, 85*
Recreational expenses, *44*
Reimbursements
    Expenses, *16, 24-26, 30-31, 69-72, 76-77, 79-81, 146-55*
    Social security, *46-47, 102*
Renting home, *56-57, 68*
Retired ministers
    Housing allowance, *63-64*
    Working after retirement, *100, 110-11*
Retirement gifts, *44*
Retirement planning, *95-101*
Retirement plans
    Deferred compensation plans, *33*
    Denominational plans, *45*
    401(k) plans, *44, 63*
    Housing allowances, *63-64*
    IRAs, *45-46*
    Keogh plans, *46*
    Rabbi Trust, *43-44*
    Roth IRA, *46*
    SEPs, *46*
    Tax-sheltered annuities, Section 403(b) plans, *23, 30, 44-45, 63-64*
Roth IRAs, *46*

S

Sabbatical pay, *23-24, 46*
Salary, *46*
Saver's credit, *145, 170*
Schedule 8812, *165-66*
Schedule A, *131-32, 150*
Schedule C, *132*
Schedule C-EZ, *74, 75, 132-33, 139, 151, 160*
Schedule EIC, *118-19, 165-67*
Schedule SE, *133, 140-41, 152, 161*
Second mortgages, *62*
Section 179 deductions, *88, 91*
Self-employed vs. employee, *11-13*
Self-Employment Contributions Act (SECA) social security, *102-110*
Self-employment earnings, *102-4*
Self-employment tax deductions, *105-6*
SEPs, *46*
Severance pay, *46*
Sick pay, *46*
Six-month extension of time to file, *122*
Simplified Employee Pension (SEP) plans, *46*
Social security
    Both spouses are ministers, *105*
    Canada Pension Plan, *111*
    Computation of tax, *102-4*
    Deductions, *105-6*
    Exemption of ministers, *106-10*
    Form 4361, *109*
    Full retirement age, *100, 110-11*
    General, *101-12*
    Opting into, *110*
    Opting out of, *106-10*
    Reimbursement, *46-47, 102*
    Services in which exemption applies, *1-9*
    Tax rates, *103*
    Tax status of ministers, *13*
    Voluntary withholding agreement, *106*
    Working after retirement, *100, 110-11*
Special occasion gifts, *37-38*
Spousal or children travel, *76-77*
Spouse, minister, *105*
Standard mileage rate, *79-80*
State extensions, *121*
Subscriptions, *47, 91*

T

Tax rates, social security tax, *103*
Tax withholding, *1, 12, 49, 106, 113-14*
Taxes, real estate, *2, 63, 131-32*
Tax-sheltered annuities, *25, 30, 44-45, 63-64*
Teaching positions, *64*
Telephone, *47, 88-89*
Temporary work location, *77-79, 83-85*
Travel expenses
    Furlough, *76*
    General, *47-48, 74-75*
    Holy Land, *75-76*
    International, *75*
    Per diem allowance, *77*
    Spousal or children, *76-77*
Trust, Rabbi, *43-44*
Tuition reductions, *48*

U

Underpayment penalty, *120*
Unreimbursed business and professional expenses, *70-71*

V

Vacation pay, *48*
Vehicle
    Nonpersonal, *49*
    Personal use of employer-provided, *48-49, 81-82*
Vestments, *31, 89*
Voluntary withholding, *12, 49, 106, 113-14*

W

Withholding
    Exemption of ministers, *113-14*
    In general, *49*
    Voluntary, *12, 49, 106, 113-14*
Workers' Compensation, *49*

Projected 2018 Filing Dates

January

16 Quarterly Estimated Taxes (last payment for prior tax period)

February

15 W-4 (if claimed an exemption, to continue same exemption in current year)

April

16 Personal tax returns due (unless automatic extension, see October 15)

16 Quarterly Estimated Taxes, if not paid with return (first payment for current tax year)

June

15 Quarterly Estimated Taxes (2nd payment for current tax year)

September

17 Quarterly Estimated Taxes (3rd payment for current tax year)

October

15 Personal tax returns due (if automatic extension)

10 Biggest Tax Mistakes Made by Ministers

1. Filing as self-employed for income tax purposes on the church salary, using tax benefits only available to employees, and becoming vulnerable to reclassification by the IRS to employee status. (Chapter 1)

2. Failure to have unreimbursed medical expenses covered under a properly documented plan. (Chapter 3)

3. Failing to have at least a modest housing allowance designated when living in a church-provided parsonage. (Chapter 4)

4. Failure to understand the implications of the fair rental test associated with the housing exclusion. (Chapter 4)

5. Claiming office-in-the-home treatment—rarely justified under present law. (Chapter 5)

6. Failure of minister-employees to use an accountable reimbursement plan. (Chapter 5)

7. Not documenting business expenses to reflect business purpose, business relationship, cost, time, and place. (Chapter 5)

8. Failing to keep a log of miles driven using personal vehicles vs. church purposes. (Chapter 5)

9. Insisting that the church deduct FICA-type social security from ministerial compensation. (Chapter 6)

10. Improperly opting out of social security because of the belief that it is not a good investment. (Chapter 6)

10 Tax and Finance Questions Most Frequently Asked by Ministers

1. **Social security filing status.** Should I have FICA-type social security tax withheld from my pay or pay self-employment social security tax calculated on Schedule SE and pay it with my income tax return? (Chapter 1)

2. **Income tax filing status.** Should I file as an employee (receiving a Form W-2 from my employer) or as an independent contractor (receiving a Form 1099-MISC) for income tax purposes? (Chapter 1)

3. **Unreimbursed medical expenses.** Which of the three approved plans should I use to get tax-free treatment for my unreimbursed medical expenses: health savings account (HSA), health reimbursement arrangement (HRA), or health care flexible spending account (FSA)? (Chapter 3)

4. **Structuring the pay package.** How should my pay package be structured to achieve the best tax benefit for me? (Chapter 3)

5. **Fringe benefit planning.** How do I determine which fringe benefits I receive are tax-free, tax-deferred, or taxable? (Chapter 3)

6. **Housing allowance exclusion.** How much can I exclude as a housing allowance for income tax purposes? (Chapter 4)

7. **Accountable expense reimbursements.** Do the payments I am receiving from the church or parachurch ministry for expenses qualify as tax-free reimbursements? (Chapter 5)

8. **Cell phone expense.** How do ministers cope with the tough IRS regulations on the documentation of the business use of cell phones? (Chapter 5)

9. **Opting out of social security.** Under what conditions is it appropriate for me to opt out of social security? (Chapter 6)

10. **Paying income and social security taxes.** Should I have enough income tax withheld from my salary to cover my income and social security tax obligation or should I pay quarterly estimated taxes? (Chapter 6)